His Hand is Stretched Out Still

365 Days of Encouragement Through Life's Storms

JOSEPH NATHAN GRIFFIN

Dedication

To my Linda, the best friend I've ever had! I dedicate this to you, for all the endless hours you spent on your own, on the phone with me, on the phone with your son, Mark for technical support, for the endless hours editing and typing, searching scriptures with me and for working right by my side to help me put this book together; I couldn't have done it without you. With *His Hand Is Stretched Out Still,* you gave me the inspirations through the conversations we had, there would just be one word or sentence that you'd say that would stand out to me and Jesus gave me the words to write with each and every post.

The four years that I've talked with you; although there was a slight detour of time, you've cried with me, you've encouraged me, you've laughed with me, you've walked with me through sickness and hardships in my life, I couldn't have asked for anyone any more Christ-like and loving

in my eyes to spend my life with. I thought it would be unique to ask you to marry me in this dedication, but not knowing how long it would take to publish, I couldn't wait and I'm glad I blurted it out on the phone and you said you'd love to marry me. I'm so happy I can tell everyone, I've got my Linda now and I'll make it official next time we're together, I love you.

I also want to thank each person that encouraged me to put my posts into a book. My desire is that the proceeds of this Devotional book be donated to the Building Fund for my home church, Bethel Baptist Church of Richmond Hill, GA.

— Joseph Griffin

ISBN: 978-1-962402-85-9

Published by

Fideli Publishing, Inc.
119 W. Morgan St.
Martinsville, IN 46151
www.FideliPublishing.com

Day 1

Through Trying, Anxious Times, We Can Find A Peaceful Heart

Key Scripture: **Philippians 4**

In the midst of hard circumstances or anxiety, it is difficult to see past the problems we're facing, much less present our requests rationally, clearly or with thankfulness. What is there to be thankful for when you're facing circumstances like bankruptcy? Shouldn't you be anxious when the relationship you thought would last forever suddenly falls apart? What is there to rejoice about when you keep falling into that sin over and over and can't get victory over it?

In Philippians 4:4-6, Paul isn't telling us to ignore what circumstances we have. He's directing us to get perspective on those circumstances. He writes in Philippians 4:8,

"Finally, brethren, whatsoever things are true, whatsoever things are honest, whatsoever things are just, whatsoever things are pure, whatsoever things are lovely, whatsoever things are of good report; if there be any virtue, and if there be any praise, think on these things."

Paul is not saying difficulties don't matter, but they are part of a larger picture, a whole world filled with blessings, also. If you are in the midst of difficult circumstances, two things are true: those circumstances are threatening to consume your every thought and waking moment. Maybe they already have. Next, in addition to your problems, your life is filled with wonderful blessings you can't see because your focus is elsewhere. When you're tempted to worry, thank God for something different. Maybe you're facing bankruptcy, but you're alive and healthy; Maybe the relationship did fall apart, but there is a God who loves you more than that person ever could; Maybe you're in a pattern of sin, but there is a Savior who can help you through it.

Trouble and anxiety are real, but when we pause to recognize and thank God for His blessings in the midst of them, He gives us peace. Whatever good thing you think about may seem irrelevant, but if it is only for a moment, it is a moment of peace.

Problems do exist. Are you searching for a solution; are you letting your problems overwhelm you? Turn them over to God, He'll give you peace.

"Thou wilt keep him in perfect peace, whose mind is stayed on thee: because he trusteth in thee."
— Isaiah 26:3

Day 2

❧❧❦❧❧

Feeling Forgotten?

Key Scripture: **Psalm 77:7-9**

In the past few years it has felt as if I were drowning in one circumstance after another. Through this time, God felt farther and farther away. I prayed about matters and it was as if He was silent. Emotions at this time were a bit crazy. What I felt was not God's kindness and love, but abandonment. I knew that was not true at all, but in these times, it's where my emotions brought me.

To me, the writer of Psalm 77 went through these same feelings of doubt. Pleading for God's deliverance from these circumstances, he asked why God rejected him and also, did He even care?

I'm sure most of us have experienced these feelings and wondered "why" and questioned if God had forgotten us. There are many reasons why we can feel rejected in this broken world, but feeling forgotten by God really hurts.

When we find ourselves feeling forgotten, we have two choices… either turn away from God in anger, or allow the words of Psalm 77: 11-14 to speak to us, recognizing the sovereignty of God and continue to trust and praise Him while going through the difficult time. These verses show us that this writer remembered that God was truly his only help. The psalmist changed his attitude completely by remembering what God had done for him through the years. Instead of dwelling on his own troubles, he meditated on God's ability to overcome anything he would face.

If we feel rejected, we must remember to keep our focus on Christ and not ourselves, rather than sulking in our despair, thankfully praise Him for all He has brought us through. God is waiting with open heart, ears and outstretched arms, because we, my friends, are too loved to be forgotten.

"And ye shall seek me, and find me, when you search for me with all your heart. And I will be found of you, saith the LORD: and I will turn away your captivity, and I will gather you from all the nations, and from all the places whither I have driven you, saith the LORD; and I will bring you again into the place whence I caused you to be carried away captive."

—Jeremiah 29:13-14

Day 3

Pushing Through

Key Scripture: **Psalm 71:20**

"Push. Until. Something. Happens." I recently heard this from a pastor that has really spoken to me and I pray it always will. There are many different directions I could write about concerning this subject and I have chosen this, and pray it speaks to your heart as it does mine.

Remember the story in Luke 2 as Mary and Joseph were in route to Bethlehem to be counted in a census and she was nine months pregnant. Imagine the discomfort she was encountering but she pushed through; a destination was in mind. As Joseph searched for a place for them to stay, she pushed on, only to find a lowly stable with no place for a child to lay, yet she still pushed on, because she knew her purpose… bringing into this world the only Son of God. It really does not matter about the location of our birth or even the surroundings we live in that determines our gift, because we too are destined for greatness. (Jeremiah 1:5) says:

> *"Before I formed thee in the belly I knew thee; and before thou camest forth out of the womb I sanctified thee, and I ordained thee a prophet unto the nations."*

No matter what your past has dealt you, nor the circumstances you're in now, just please remember this one thing: "God doesn't call the qualified, but He qualifies the called." Like our key passage says, He can take you, no matter what sin you've committed, put you through the fire and erase everything you have done, and bring you through, causing you to shine like pure gold.

God is not worried about what or where you've come from as long as you "push through" allowing Him to lead you where you ought to be. Trust Him, He's not worried about your past and He wants you to stay focused on your journey. Just a reminder, this journey may not always be easy, and sometimes you may want to give up and take an easier route, but the right thing to do is to "push through" the pain and keep your eyes on Christ. Remember you're a new creation in Christ and old things are passed away. (2 Corinthians 5:17). God does not count those who start the journey and give up, He wants us all to push through the pain, and along with His unlimited help, we can be a strong finisher. Remember that the last shall be first because our God is in control, and as long as we determine in our hearts that we will "Push Through" the pain, our reward is we will get God's blessings, and abundant life with Him on earth and life everlasting with our Savior. As Mary had her destination, we too have one that is important; to remain faithful and serve the Lord, becoming a vibrant witness in all we say or do.

Pray Until Something Happens!

"Faithful is he that calleth you, who also will do it."
— 1 Thessalonians 5:24

Day 4

What Matters to You, Matters to God

Key Scripture: **Lamentations 3:25, John 10:11, John 3:16**

Have you ever asked yourself "If what concerns me, does it also concern God?" Many times, throughout my life I have started different journals, some for my own thoughts, some for prayer and needs for others, and some reminding me of blessings given to me from God.

It is refreshing to revisit these from time to time and to add new things as needed. I wished I used them more, because it is a great concept. Some may think it's silly but for myself I think it's a reminder that no matter how big or how small my problem is, knowing God cares builds within me a sense of belonging and closeness. Most things others may never see, only God knows my innermost thoughts and feelings. Nothing is more special than pouring your heart out to God and He gives you an answer. This brings you closer to Him.

Many times, I know I miss out on an opportunity of blessing when I feel that something is not important to bother God with. I might think it's silly spending time praying for something so trivial. I am so thankful that I serve a God that does not categorize my needs and desires, whether big or small, they matter to Him the same. In 1 Peter 5:7; God says to: "Cast all your cares upon Him, for He careth for you." This scripture does not say to cast the big things on Him; it says to cast "ALL" things on Him, because He cares. Just who are we to decide what God cares about? We would all be a lot better off if we would wrap our head around the truth and believe that God cares, and whatever matters to us, matters to the Master. I love this thought, and my prayer is that I live it.

Check out the lyrics to the chorus of: "It Matters to the Master" — you'll enjoy it.

"Cast thy burden upon the LORD,
and he shall sustain thee: he shall never suffer the righteous to be moved."

— Psalm 55:22

Day 5

Mulligans (Do-Overs)

Key Scripture: **Colossians 2:13-14**

I am so glad that people we come in contact with do not have the final words about our destination in life. God is the One that has full control in that part of life.

A quote I heard recently says: "Life is a very special occasion, don't miss it."

The game of golf has something in place called a "Mulligan" which means to get a "do over" for a shot made that was probably not a good shot. In life, we take bad directions and because we have a gracious and forgiving God, we can get a "do over."

We no longer have to miss special occasions; our God wants us to get it right, even if we have

to do it over; a loving realization that God has initiated since the days of Adam, in the garden.

Though others fall short of the same forgiving spirit, we all need to ask God to give us His heart, that we too could be able to forgive others their shortcomings in life. Life would be much easier with the one needing forgiveness and also free the bitter spirit for the one who needs to initiate forgiveness. By not doing so, we will miss this part of life that shows the love of Christ placed in our hearts at the time we receive Christ as our Savior. Can we pray with a sincere heart, asking God to place within us the ability to freely forgive others as Christ has forgiven us?

"And be ye kind one to another,
tenderhearted, forgiving one another,
even as God for Christ's sake hath forgiven you."
— Ephesians 4:32

We Are All Made Differently, But Should Have One Mind

Key Scripture: **Ephesians 4:1-13**

Having the same mind does not always mean we see things the same way. In life, others see things in a much different perspective but it would be nice if we all understood each other's point of view on certain matters. Seeing things differently can cause conflict. What if God made everyone the same? That could get quite boring. God blesses us by creating us as unique individuals and not robots, with preference and a free will. We are made in His image precisely as He planned. (Ephesians 4:1).

James 1: 17 says:

"Every good gift and every perfect gift is from above."

We're all designed with His tender love and care. We are meant to be different, but are called to be unified. This is what Paul meant as he said, "We are to walk worthy of the vocation wherewith ye are called."

God wants us to be aware of what makes us special and not try to be like someone else. In Ephesians 4:2-3; God said, we should be "forbearing one another in love; endeavoring to keep the unity of the Spirit in the bond of peace." What unites us as believers is the shared belief and attachment with the Father, Son, and the Spirit. (Ephesians 4:4-5). We may dress a little differently, sing differently, and have different political views. In the long run, our relationship with Christ is what matters. These things will not matter in eternity. Our eternal relationship with Christ is the one thing that will last forever.

Being unified in the Spirit requires us to stay focused on the main thing: Jesus saves, sets us free from sin, and gives us an eternal hope in Heaven. Unity can be difficult, but is worth the effort. When Christians work together, the message God wants us to spread unfolds as He desires. His grace is declared freely and people grow in the knowledge and understanding what Christianity should represent. (Ephesians 4:12-13).

Pray that God gives us a desire to be unified in His Spirit for our own growth and His glory.

"Fulfill ye my joy, that ye be likeminded,
having the same love, being of one accord, of one mind."

— Philippians 2:2

Day 7

Fearful of the Unknown?

Key Scripture: **James 4:13-17**

I am drawn to watching certain things on television that deal with adventure and seeking the mysterious truths about the unknown places around the world. Watching these can sometimes bring fearful thoughts as I watch people exploring unknown caves and tunnels through ancient ruins. I'd have to say that I would l rather watch others doing these things than me being the one doing the exploring.

James tells us in our key passage that I don't know what will happen tomorrow, and I know this is true. I can plan and think that I know what I'll do in the future, but in the end, with all the planning and hoping that I know about tomorrow, the future does not promise me any-thing. I simply don't know what the future will hold, and for me not knowing, this can be a bit frightening. Things are out of my control.

What isn't frightening is knowing that God is in control. When Jesus was teaching the disciples how to pray, He said; "God's will be done." For me knowing and having the faith in Him, I believe that God's will, will be done. So whatever fear I might have about the future, I can be assured that God not only knows what will happen, but also has all things in His control. He has me in the palm of His hand and I can rest in the fact that He is in control of my future. My trust is in Him.

"For I know the thoughts that I think toward you, saith the LORD,
thoughts of peace, and not of evil, to give you an expected end."
—Jeremiah 29:11

"And they that know thy name will put their trust in thee: for thou, LORD,
hast not forsaken them that seek thee."
— Psalm 9:10

Day 8

Can I Really Make a Difference?

Key Scripture: **Luke 10:1-20, Focus on Verse 19**

Satan tries every way possible to keep us from sharing our faith with others to make an impact on the world for Christ. (Luke 10:19.) Our society is morally and spiritually in a state of apathy today and this causes us to look at our own selves and say "What can I really do about it?"

I heard a story that may give us a little insight on how to answer this question.

One morning after a heavy storm and the seas were tossed to and fro, a man was walking along the beach. The tide was low and he noticed lots of starfish and trash washed up on the beach. He also noticed a boy in the distance tirelessly bending over picking things up and throwing what he picked up back into the sea.

As he approached the boy, the man asked him what he was doing. The boy replied, "I'm saving the starfish."

The man looked along the beach and said "Don't you see that there are miles of beach, and starfish everywhere along every mile. Do you really think you can make a difference?"

The boy picked up another starfish and threw it into the ocean. "It makes a difference to that one," the boy said.

I know that I may not reach the world for Christ, but I can reach some. There are so many lost people seeking spiritual direction, so many hungering and thirsting people seeking spiritual nourishment, and so many lonely people seeking spiritual companionship. By God's power and authority, I need to do all I can to make a difference, and so do you.

> 'Lord, lay some soul upon my heart
> And love that soul through me;
> And may I ever do my part
> To win that soul for Thee.'

"And of some have compassion, making a difference:
And others save with fear, pulling them out of the fire;
hating even the garment spotted by the flesh."

—Jude 1:22-23

Day 9

Learn By Taking Responsibility for Your Actions

Key Scripture: **Proverbs 19**

I have worked with kids for a number of years and first hand, I've seen how children very seldom accept the fact that they've done something wrong. It's always them pointing the finger to someone else. They make excuses, blaming or placing the fault on others rather than themselves.

Children seem to act impulsively and are very quick to pass blame on others, and often can't control their temper. They have not developed self-discipline and aren't mature enough to see or understand this is a result of their behavior.

Age is not always an indicator of maturity; adults often have the same issues as children. Being older does not stop adults from making irrational impulsive decisions or saying things they don't really mean. The Bible teaches us that when we fall short, we are to take responsibility for our actions.

God has given us the ability to: control our temper, to show maturity and understanding by making wise choices and avoid the consequences of living foolishly. (Proverbs 19:11-29). For us to choose wisdom, it takes practice and self-discipline and most importantly, adhering to the Bible's instructions.

Through the Word, God gives us a guide to avoid foolish choices and to live pleasing to Him each day. Proverbs 19:27 says;

> *"Cease, my son, to hear the instruction that causeth to err from the words of knowledge."*

Our best defense to avoid the sinful lifestyle is to always be sensitive to the leading of the Spirit and never stop listening to God's instructions from His Word.

"My sheep hear my voice, and I know them, and they follow me."

— John 10:27

Day 10

The Direction We're Headed is Determined by Our Focus

Key Scripture: **Hebrews 12:2**

I believe the word "focus" is a powerful word and it is what makes change possible.

I have read and heard many sermons preached on the story of Peter walking on water in Matthew 14:29. Peter literally climbed out of the boat and walked on water. Peter learned a valuable lesson that day; as he stayed focused on Jesus, he was able to walk toward the Lord. Only when he looked down at the waves tossing under his feet, is when he went down.

If we could take time to find one word to help us keep our focus on what is needed to continue looking unto Jesus and not our surroundings, memorize scripture that word would represent, it would transform our lives and we would never be swallowed up by the waves.

Reading our key verse reminds me to take my eyes off myself and the difficult circumstances, off the waves beneath my feet, and focus squarely on Jesus Christ. What I put my focus on determines the direction I'm headed.

What treacherous waves are beneath you, trying to cause you to take your eyes off Jesus?

"Seek the LORD, and His strength:
seek His face evermore."

— Psalm 105:4

"For they that are after the flesh
do mind the things of the flesh;
but they that are after the Spirit
the things of the Spirit."

— Romans 8:5

Day 11

What Right Do We Have to Complain?

Key Scripture: **Numbers 11:1-9**

For a lot of people walking on this great earth, complaining must be their favorite pastime. They complain about any and everything. The food, the weather, the traffic, the country, not having anything to do; they simply complain because they like to complain.

This was certainly second nature to the nation of Israel during the wilderness years. Only three days after leaving Egypt they started complaining. They complained about how hard things were and the manna they ate day after day; like what they ate in Egypt was any better.

Life can be hard, but when we complain we fall into Satan's trap. Sin!!! When we complain we seem to glamorize what we don't have. Did the Israelites really have it good in Egypt? Somehow, they forgot the hardships they went through while in slavery. When we complain we view life in some distorted way. Complaining comes from people who somehow think they deserve something better.

In Philippians 2:14, Paul calls us to do everything without murmuring and disputing. This is possible only when we learn to concentrate on God's grace in Christ. How can we complain so often when we know how much we are loved by God? His grace can move us from complaining to gratitude.

After all, what right do we have to complain and grumble? We as God's children are to be as much like Christ as possible and follow His example. We complain over the smallest things, yet Jesus went all the way to Calvary without one complaint. Our hearts should stay overwhelmed with love and gratitude. Would, or could any of us do what Christ did for us?

There is a song titled: "Jesus Went All the Way to Calvary" by May M. Brewster that goes:

Jesus went all the way to Calvary,
All the way for me;
There, 'midst sorrow and shame, at last, He came,
To the cross, to the cross for me.

Refrain:
Jesus went all the way to Calvary,
'Twas a dreary and blood-stain'd way,
That His grace I might know, who lov'd me so,
Jesus went all the way for me.

"In every thing give thanks:
for this is the will of God in Christ Jesus concerning you."

— 1 Thessalonians 5:18

Day 12

We All Have Choices to Make, This Includes Me

Key Scripture: Isaiah 30:21

We as Christians make thousands of decisions each and every day. If we would just pause and think about all the decisions we have made already in our present day, it would amaze us all. From getting out of bed, choosing what to wear, or not to wear, what to eat, or not to eat, our minds are constantly making decisions.

Some of our everyday decisions are random, and others are decisions that mean a lot and are weighty. Some of these weighty decisions seem insignificant, yet they lead us into a certain direction like; I choose to react in anger or respond in an understanding way with friends or family members. When someone hurts our feelings, we may choose to cause drama or not to. Spiritually we choose to spend time with the Lord, reading His Word, praying, and listening to the Holy Spirit as He gives us direction.

How would we react if we were traveling and missed an important leg of our trip due to a missed bus, train, or flight connection after a long exhausting day? Times like this show us exactly where the rubber meets the road; what we are made of. We could show our frustration through anger or we could choose to have an understanding wisdom about things that happen beyond our control and show a gracious attitude.

Remember our key verse? God speaks through a still small voice and if we could grasp these words spoken by Isaiah we would have a better control of our choices. He said, *"This is the way, walk in it."* We need to understand that in all situations we are faced with, it is a privilege to be in God's perfect will.

Because of our delays or how our plans change, God is in control; we were put here for a purpose, and could be used mightily for God's glory in our present situation. God gives us opportunities to share His plan of salvation, or pray with a hurting brother or sister in Christ, God will make ways beyond our thinking to use a willing vessel.

I wish we could handle each of our choices this way, but we sometimes fail. It's my prayer that we do a better job in handling the choices that matter, because our choices affect those around us and not just ourselves. So, let's take a moment among the many thousands of decisions we make each day and ask the Holy Spirit for His guidance and counsel and choose to follow as He leads us in His way.

"A man's heart deviseth his way:
But the LORD directeth his steps."

— Proverbs 16:9

Day 13

How Do You React on Days Where Nothing Goes Right?

Key Scripture: **Romans 8:28**

I personally have had a Christian life of ups and downs. I know that some of the down times are no one's fault but my own. But looking on the up side of things, I can honestly say as a testimony of the unmerited grace of God, that in the last few years, I have experienced a renewed close fellowship with Jesus Christ.

I still have circumstances that arise and I believe I'll always have them, but having a spirit of trust and faith that God will bring me out of difficult times comes with a peaceful rest from my Lord's guiding hand. Some days when I place my eyes on myself rather than the Lord, I simply don't know whether to laugh or cry.

What I really think is when everything is going great and no worries and really getting close to God, this is when I seem to get a new devil, trying to disrupt my flourishing relationship with Christ. I am not sure if this theology is correct but I do know that Satan does not like it when I am obedient to Christ. Saying yes to God brings abundant blessings, but it is not always easy.

God wants me to be obedient, but not out of a sense of duty. The shallowness of this would result in me easily giving up when things go haywire; however, if my desire comes from delight and from a love relationship with Christ, Satan has a hard time extinguishing this fire.

When I fall hopelessly in love with someone, I'll do anything for that person, and do it with pure joy. That's how I want to feel about Jesus, because of my in-depth love for Him, I'd serve and do anything I could for Him. A real sign of spiritual maturity is looking to God for purpose and perspective and not just for comfort and convenience. It would do each of us good to review the story of Jacob and Rachel in Genesis 29, a great love story.

Our key verse does not mean everything that happens in our Christian life will be good, but it does mean that God will work in and through every situation for His glory and our good. The last four words "according to His purpose," means He has a purpose for me and you, and His plans to accomplish that purpose are perfect. Trust Him!

I can know that in the midst of all the days when nothing seems to go right, something good will come from those tough days.

"And he said,
The things which are impossible with men are possible with God."

— Luke 18:27

Day 14

Is Accountability Necessary?

Key Scripture: **Romans 14:12**

What is your idea of what accountability means? In simple terms it is answering hard questions which include opening your life to a few selected, trusted individuals who speak and stand for truth; who have the right to examine, to question, to appraise, and to give council. These individuals usually have these qualities:

- Vulnerability — capable of being wounded, shown to be wrong, and able to admit it before being confronted.

- Teachability — willingness to learn, being quick to hear and respond to correction; being open to council.

- Availability — accessible, touchable, able to be interrupted.

- Honesty — committed to the truth regardless of how it hurts; willing to admit to truth no matter the cost; despising anything that is false or phony.

These are tough qualities, and this is why accountability is resisted by most people. Their egos just can't handle it. Their greatest desire is to look good and make huge impressions more than anything else. No one is allowed to probe into their life.

Remember what accountability means; opening up to a few trusted, loyal individuals. They have earned the right to stand beside and when it becomes necessary, ask the difficult questions, serving in an advisory capacity, causing our eyes to be opened, and giving wise council as needed.

In our society today, a lack of accountability is considered the norm. Despite the belief of most, we need others to hold us accountable. An objective opinion can reveal a blind spot, and sometimes we may simply need a sounding board to help keep us focused on what is truthful and right.

None of us is an island; we need one another and we need to be held accountable if we waver beyond God's purpose. Others see and hear things that we can't. I pray that each of us will seek Godly council when needed, and accept it.

"Iron sharpeneth iron;
so a man sharpeneth the countenance of his friend."

— Proverbs 27:17

Day 15

God Uses Brokenness for Blessings

Key Scripture: John 12:24

I am a living example that through brokenness, God has brought blessings into my life; the kind of brokenness that causes my eyes to sting from the many tears and the deep hurt that is not easily healed. No one enjoys the suffering pain of brokenness, for with me, I had to give up something near and dear to me, and through this I learned brokenness brings unexpected blessings from God. This is why God broke me, not that I go through undue suffering and pain, nor because He doesn't love me. Instead, God used my brokenness to bless me.

God used the brokenness of me losing an important person in my life, along with an unhealthy relationship to change areas of my life that I was not willingly submitting to Him. God removed my counterfeit self-sufficient tendencies I wanted to hold to because He alone knew the truth and that what I wanted was not His plans for me. God chose what was needed for me to focus on His plan and purpose.

Our key verse says if a corn of wheat falls to the ground and dies, it will abide alone, but if it dies, it will bring forth much fruit. Let's look at the life of Jesus on earth. He was like a single stalk of corn; yet through His death, burial, and resurrection, His life continued to produce a harvest of souls.

Now looking at my life, if I seek only my desires, I produce little. But, if I die to self and live as God plans, I will live a fruitful life for God's glory and for others. The more I become like Him, I'm living according to His plan. Think of it this way: Matthew 16:25 says:

"If I want to save my life for me, I'll lose it, but if I save my life for His sake, I'll find it."

Sometimes God has to break me to bless me, for this I now can say, "Thank you Lord," because I want to live my life as God desires instead of living a counterfeit life for myself. God has richly blessed me with a new outlook on life, and given me dear, thoughtful friends that really care. Most of all He has given me a peace of heart and mind; brokenness has brought blessings beyond measure.

"He that loveth his life shall lose it,
and he that hateth his life in this world shall keep it
unto life eternal."

— John 12:25

Day 16

A Convicting Spirit is Not a Condemning Spirit

Key Scripture: **John 3:17**

I'm sure that many would agree with me and say that they, like myself, have lost their temper or out of frustration said things they regretted. After doing so I immediately felt guilty for my words and actions. I really believe that is exactly the way God wanted me to feel at that moment.

Satan wants to destroy our joy any way he can and by feeling condemned either through guilt or shame, he can make our lives miserable. When condemnation sweeps through our minds we may make degrading statements such as: "I'm such a failure; I'm a big hypocrite; I can never be counted on." This is Satan himself belittling us, causing us to feel condemned, questioning and confused by his accusations, leaving us with guilt and shame.

In contrast, the conviction by the Holy Spirit will be specific, meaning He will reveal a sinful action or attitude and leave us with a solution to right the wrong, like restoring a broken relationship or making amends for words spoken uncharacteristically. When we've said something critical or hurtful, we must apologize and ask forgiveness; then say something to build that person up, instead of tearing them down.

Satan condemns us accusingly to make us feel guilty. God, on the other hand, lovingly leads our hearts to repentance. Conviction leads us from a behavior of destruction that affects our relationship with God and others. Let's guard our hearts from Satan's lies of condemnation and listen and follow the loving conviction of the Holy Spirit of God, rescuing us with His redeeming grace.

"And the Word was made flesh,
and dwelt among us, and we beheld his glory,
the glory as of the only begotten of the Father,
full of grace and truth."

— John 1:14

Day 17

Are We Silencing the Holy Spirit?

Key Scripture; **1 Thessalonians 5:19**

A question often asked by many is: "Why am I not hearing from the Holy Spirit?" By answering this we need to look in several directions. It could be we don't understand "how God speaks to us." It could be we are not "spending time in His Word." It could also be because of our busy lives, we have trouble discerning the voice of God from all other noises.

There could be many reasons why we're not hearing God speak to us; the main reason being: we stopped listening to Him. True, we're not experiencing God's fullness because we've pushed Him away. Please understand, God always loves His children and will always be here for us. The Holy Spirit is the third person of the Godhead, and not some faraway being. He directs our ways and how we respond to Him affects our relationship with Him.

In our key passage, Paul tells the church not "To quench the Spirit." This happens when we don't listen to the Spirit; when we do what we know is wrong, following our own worldly desires. It's like throwing water on a fire, dampening it instead of fanning it, causing it to be stronger.

As a Christian, we feel conviction when we sin. This is how the Holy Spirit guides us. But, when we ignore the conviction and continue in our sin, it's harder to hear the voice of the Holy Spirit. Our hearing, along with our heart, is now hardened. This grieves the Spirit. Our quenching and grieving the Spirit comes from us desiring our own self-centered ways over love, faith, and intimacy with God.

The Holy Spirit helps us (John 14:26); the same Spirit that convicts also loves us with a perfect love. The same Spirit that causes us to feel guilt gives us grace and helps us grow.

God knows we're not perfect, we will make mistakes. Like any parent, He wants us to listen when He corrects us. Let's not ignore His correction. God wants each of us to live a life of intimacy in His fullness.

"And grieve not the Holy Spirit of God, whereby ye are sealed unto the day of redemption.
Let all bitterness, and wrath, and anger, and clamour,
and evil speaking, be put away from you, with all malice:
And be ye kind one to another, tenderhearted, forgiving one another,
even as God for Christ's sake hath forgiven you."

— Ephesians 4:30-32

Day 18

Jesus said, "Take Ye Away the Stone"

Key Scripture: John 11:39

I heard a great message last evening from our Assistant Pastor, Tim Patterson. This was a powerful thought he brought out about the stone and it was well worth writing about.

Jesus said these words from our key passage to Martha and Mary after their brother Lazarus had been laid in a tomb behind the stone for four days. Martha cautioned Jesus saying that her brother was sure to stink by now after four days since he had died. She could not conceive what Jesus was about to do. However, there was one thing that stood between her seeing the greatest miracle she would ever witness. It was a stone, but Jesus told her to take away the stone.

It's sad to think there are stones blocking us from seeing God's glory manifested in our lives. For Martha it was a stone of unbelief, and this same stone still blocks us from seeing breakthroughs in many areas of our lives. Sure, it is difficult to understand that there are many believers screaming for God to rescue them, yet they never hear Him shouting to them to "Take away the stone."

Jesus wants to help, but we have some stones that need to be taken out. We cannot sow a seed or buy our way to remove the stone of sin in our lives. Neither can we pray to bypass a stone of anger that might be ruining our relationship and testimony with Christ. It's left up to every child of God to recognize the stones and "take them away" so our lives are free to see a faithful, loving God working His purpose and will in our lives.

I pray that God will help each of us identify stones in our life and honestly take the needed action to remove any obstructive stone that hinders our relationship with Jesus Christ.

"…let us lay aside every weight,
and the sin which doth so easily beset us,
and let us run with patience the race that is set before us."

— Hebrews 12:1

Day 19

We Can Learn the Great Power in Vulnerability

Key Scriptures: **Matthew 26:39; Psalm 73:26**

I met a friend online several years ago who is an accomplished writer. I enjoyed reading her eloquent words that flowed off the pages she printed and though we never communicate anymore, I'll never forget her encouraging words. She saw through me like an open book and expressed words of wisdom from what she saw that would possibly help me in my days ahead. She told me that I carried my heart on my sleeve, exposed to any and all elements and was extremely vulnerable to experience deep hurt and heartache.

Boy was she ever so right. Thanks, Kim, you warned me and I'll never forget those words.

Now back to a spiritual matter of vulnerability. It gets sometimes a bad rap and is often perceived as weakness. However, when God is involved, what we might consider as weakness is precisely what gives us strength. Being vulnerable with God draws us closer to Him, and we're strengthened by His mighty power. In our scripture passages, Jesus Himself expressed utter vulnerability, fully aware of His impending gruesome death on the cross, and more excruciating, total separation from the Father.

Although He was fully God, and also fully man, no human could face what He did without crying out for relief. We could never fully grasp what Jesus experienced, but we can follow His example and pour out our anguished hearts to God in prayer. God knows what we've done and what we are struggling with, and what lies ahead.

Yet still, He wants to listen, to share such intimate moments with His children. As we cling to His strength and comply with His will, He ushers in healing, comfort, and guidance that only He can bring into our lives. When we are weak, He is our strength. Talk to Him, He's just a prayer away. So, be vulnerable, pour out your heart in His presence, and listen to His voice; He always has the right words for each of us.

Tell God what's on your heart today, rest your mind on His promises, and be still, and listen to His voice.

"And he said unto me, My grace is sufficient for thee:
for my strength is made perfect in weakness.
Most gladly therefore will I rather glory in my infirmities,
that the power of Christ may rest upon me."

— 2 Corinthians 12:9

Day 20

What Happens When We Question God and Tell Him We're Just Not Ready for This

Key Scripture: **Psalm 23:4a**

We all have dark moments and probably some can testify of a similar situation as mine. I remember so vividly the last days my late wife was with me. She was hospitalized and slowly I saw the life leave her body and throughout those days I told the Lord "I am not ready for this."

When your life has been through many ups and downs, and now facing a much different reality than ever before, the moment the last breath left her body, I told the Lord, "I'm not ready for this valley." We're never ready for any kind of heartbreak, we're unprepared, unsteady and uncertain of God's will as we enter into our valleys.

Life isn't just a walk in the park; it's more like a journey through the mountains; on top of the world one minute and the next in the valley. But, remember this, the same God that gives us the mountaintop experience is the same God that doesn't let us walk alone in the valley.

In Psalm 23 where our key passage is taken from, David paints a picture of those valleys and how to endure them. When we walk through the darkest valley, we'll not be afraid, because God is walking with us. He is always present, and always close. God has never promised that we will avoid the valleys, but He did promise that we'll never have to walk through them alone.

The very dreadful moments that we go through, like losing a loved one, are the ones that make us aware that God is with us the Psalm 23 way. The valley we dread is the exact place where we come to experience God's presence.

Even though we say we're not ready for heartbreaks, we can know through our distress that "God is with us." He enters our pain and pledges His faithful presence every step we take, through the mountaintops and through the valleys, until we reach our Heavenly home, He's always close beside.

"….I am with you alway, even unto the end of the world."
— Matthew 28:20b

Day 21

Do You Have a Song in Your Heart? What Does it Say?

Key Scripture: **Psalm 30:1-5, 11-12**

The transformation that God performs in the hearts of people is nothing short of amazing. Psalm 30 really celebrates the saving power of the Lord. When the first humans chose to disobey God in the garden, God could have let them suffer the penalty of sin forever. But instead, God promised redemption and salvation. When the Israelites rebelled against God in the wilderness, He could have let them wander in their sin forever. Instead, God kept His promise to His people.

In this Psalm, David praises God at the dedication of the temple. It was a glorious event for the nation of Israel, and David led the people in remembering God's faithfulness. Here we are thousands of years later, and we can celebrate the same steadfast unconditional love of God.

We also can remember the events in our own lives where God has lifted us up, shown us His hand of protection, and restored us by giving us His eternal grace. Personally, He has saved me from the bondage of sin, and set my feet on the path of righteousness, and His joy is always present when I'm experiencing those dark hours. God has chosen to remain faithful despite my unfaithfulness. His grace turns my mourning into joy.

Ultimately, when I look back on my life and journey with Jesus Christ, I too join David in saying, *"… O Lord my God, I will give thanks unto thee forever."* (Psalm 30:12). God has definitely opened my eyes of faith, and as a testament to His powerful love, I can say He has been good to me. Life has not always been easy, simple or happy, but God has remained faithful to me through His Almighty grace. I will forever give glory and thanks to my Lord and Savior.

My song right now is "The Goodness of God" by Bethel Music and Jenn Johnson.

Lord, help me to stop focusing on my self-perceived insecurities and inadequacies, and focus on Your power and sufficient abilities to finish the work in me You have started.

"O taste and see that the LORD is good:
blessed is the man that trusteth in him."

— Psalm 34:8

Day 22

Who Cares?

Key Scriptures: **Matthew 6:31-33; Luke 12:6-7**

Who's taking care of you? How committed are they to you?

Everyone needs care, and care requires commitment. Caring can't happen without a conscious concern for the well-being of someone, a consistent awareness of their condition and needs, a willingness to adequately and abundantly meet those needs, and an ability or capacity to do so. At the core of caring for someone is a bedrock, unchanging commitment to them. This is real love.

The Bible teaches us that God is love. It describes God's love as personal and individual. God just doesn't love "people" as broad faceless, and generic. No, God actually cares for individuals. He knows the names, addresses, needs, pains, problems, hopes and dreams of individual people, including Me and You.

I can't wrap my head around this reality. My head hurts just thinking about how God could individually know and truly care for every single person. But facing facts, it is true.

In the verses in Matthew, God tells us we shouldn't be concerned about our needs, and if we seek Him above everything else, He'll supply all our needs. The verses in Luke tell us that God cares for the sparrow and we're much more important than many sparrows. We need to learn to put our full-time trust in Him.

Most of us have a problem believing that God has adequate and abundant resources. He is God. The Bible teaches us that He is the Resource. The Fountainhead, the Spring, the Supplier of everything we could ever need. To have a relationship with God is to have a relationship with the One who is all we'll ever need.

God wants our faith to increase to another level, by resting in the fact that He will provide any resource we need. It's not just believing that God *can* provide for us, it's also believing that He will; confidently believing that He will CARE for us adequately and abundantly. So, "Who Cares?" God does.

Remember the old hymn: "He hideth my soul in the cleft of the Rock, and covers me there with His hand."

"...and when My glory passes by, I will put you in a cleft in the rock."
— Exodus 33:22

Day 23

Simply Sick and Tired of Being Good

Key Scripture: **Philippians 3**

As we grow older the need to be good is continually reinforced. We justify ourselves with how good we are, whether it's as an employee, spouse or person. The way we describe each other confirms it, for example, "He's such a good person" or "She has a good heart."

In the beginning of Philippians 3, Paul points out the flaws in this kind of thinking. If we're chasing goodness, we're chasing a moving target.

If anyone reading Paul's letter thought he or she was a good person, Paul was better. He was raised in the right family, went to the right schools and followed the right path, but he said all these things are garbage compared to knowing Jesus. (Philippians 3:8). That's because knowing Jesus isn't about meeting a standard but following a person.

The relationship Paul had with Jesus was more fulfilling than all the religious accomplish-ments of his past. Paul still did good things but not because he was trying to be good. Instead, Paul's good deeds were an overflow of the love he experienced from Jesus. The same is true for us; when we put Jesus above everything else in our lives, we end up doing good things, not because we have to, but because we want to.

After writing that everything in his life is worthless, compared to knowing Jesus, Paul goes on to say he hasn't lived up to Jesus' exam-ple yet. Paul wasn't perfect, but *"forgetting those things which are behind, and reaching forth unto those things which are before..."* he continued his whole-hearted pursuit of Jesus. (Philippians 3:12-13). Like Paul, many of us need to give up trying to be good enough and run to the One who is enough.

What do you value above Jesus right now in your life?

"I can do all things through Christ which strengtheneth me."
— Philippians 4:13

Day 24

Refine Me, Oh Lord; I Want Your Blessings

Key Scripture: **Malachi 3:3**

Are any who read this at all like me, really tired of the constant battles in your life? I do understand and feel your pain. There are times when I feel that just as I get one thing resolved, another difficult time begins. Problems just seem to find me.

The sooner we all learn and accept the fact they're coming, we can view them as "growth opportunities." They give us a chance to recognize that God is shaping and molding our lives to fit His calling for each of us. God is interested in our character, not our comfort.

In our key passage, (Malachi 3:1-3) God wants His people to know they have some character issues that need addressing. In verse 3, it reveals that the Lord comes both "like a refiner's fire and like fuller soap." The fuller soap (alkali) was a strong soap used to whiten clothing. The refiner's fire is a method used to purify precious metals with intense heat. As the intense heat purifies the metal, the impurities rise to the top and are then skimmed off. The refiner knows the process is complete when he can look into the open furnace and see his reflection, because the dross has been removed.

In Genesis 1:27, God tells us we are created in His likeness and image, but when sin entered the world, we became "marred" by sin. We were left defiled. When the purification process begins, our spiritual defilement is removed, restoring our ability to reflect the goodness of God.

Another word for the refining work is "sanctification."

It's the Lord's continual process of making us holy and wholly set apart for Him. As our key passage reminds us, sometimes the sanctification process involves suffering.

If you ever have an opportunity to watch a silversmith in action, I would encourage you to do so. As he takes a piece of raw metal and begins forming it into a work of art, that metal has to go through a rigorous process of pounding, turning, heating, and more of the same until it's ready for polishing. Every bit of this process has a purpose and the final results are amazing.

I pray that God will stir our hearts to trust Him in the midst of our troubles. Our God is not a cruel God; He allows all the shaping of our lives for a reason. They are purifying and smoothing us so we'll reflect Him. It's not always an easy task. I believe that reflecting our Creator and having lives that point the hearts of others toward Him is worth every discomfort. Nothing God allows us to go through is pointless. Even through our hurt, He will work things for our good and His glory.

"For Thou, O God, hast proved us: Thou hast tried us, as silver is tried."

— Psalm 66:10

Day 25

The One Who Keeps Bottled Tears; Keeps Bottled Prayers

Key Scripture: **Psalm 56:8**

Our scripture passage is one of the most beautiful powerful images found in God's Word. It is a precious promise that should be marked or highlighted in every believer's Bible. God Himself has collected all our tears.

There are many different kinds of tears: those of a mother for their beloved child, stricken with a disease. There are tears of the father of the bride on her wedding day as he walks her down the aisle. There are tears of a broken relationship that has been torn apart because of sin that has not been dealt with.

There are tears of joy from a group of men that have just won a championship. There are also tears shed in prayer. Each and every teardrop is precious to God. They are eternal keepsakes. The day will come when He wipes away every tear in Heaven. Until then, God will move Heaven and earth to honor every tear that has been shed. Not a single tear will be lost. He remembers each one, He honors each one, and He collects each one.

In much the same way that God bottles our accumulated tears, God also collects our prayers. Each one is precious to Him, and sealed by God. We never know when He is going to reveal His answers.

We all at times struggle with fear, and for me I fear that my children, who are so far from God, will not surrender to God's will. I have learned to rebuke myself, because fear is not of God and I remind myself of another verse that tells me I must give my children to the Lord. We all should mark in our Bibles and visit this verse often; Luke 2:52. Those prayers are bottled by God, and the Holy Spirit will unseal them in the lives of our children long after we are gone.

Sometimes I struggle with doubt. I'm afraid that I will someday mishandle the blessings of God, and I remember Psalm 84:11.

Sometimes we struggle with faith. Then I remind myself of another verse: Deuteronomy 33:16. I have no idea what the future holds, but I know who holds the future. Our lives are in His hands, and our prayers are in His bottle. He hears the prayers of a righteous man and He answers those prayers in His Sovereign will. Those bottled prayers will be unsealed in God's time and in God's way.

God will answer somewhere, sometime, somehow. All we need to do is faithfully stay in His Word, highlighting those scriptures, visiting them often, and let His Word guide us by the Holy Spirit.

"The effectual fervent prayer of a righteous man availeth much."
— James 5:16

Day 26

Are You Looking for Approval in the Wrong Places?

Key Scripture: **2 Chronicles 1**

Each of us have wants and desires. Maybe you're searching for more money, popularity, more authority in your job, less stress, or a better relationship. We pray for the results we want to see, read guides on how to do this or that and put our time, energy, and effort into achieving our goals. But how often do we actually stop and ask what God wants for us?

In our passage, Solomon had an opportunity to ask God for everything he wanted. While he could have asked for wealth, fame, authority, or even an easier task from God, he asked for God's wisdom. His sole request was to have the knowledge to lead God's people. Because of his selflessness, God recognized him and gave him so much more. Not only did God give him wisdom, He also gave him wealth, riches, and honor.

In Matthew 6:33, Jesus promises that when we seek God first, everything we truly need will be given to us.

Jesus does not promise that we'll end up rich, famous, and powerful as Solomon, but He does promise that we'll be rewarded for our obedience when we follow after His wisdom. When we put God and the needs of others before our own, we can know that God is faithful and will take care of our needs as well.

Our prayers should be selfless and we must rely on God's wisdom and not our own.

"But my God shall supply all your need according to His riches in glory by Christ Jesus."
— Philippians 4:19

Day 27

Is it Difficult for You to Ask for Help?

Key Scripture; **2 Chronicles 2**

For some, one of the hardest things for them to do is ask for help. This may be a pride issue. For others, it might be they feel if they ask for help they are admitting defeat. Even when others volunteer to help, their help is refused.

In our scripture passage, Solomon writes to Hiram, a neighboring king who knew Solomon's father, to ask for help building the temple. In the letter Solomon was very clear about everything he needed, including manpower and supplies. Hiram is not put out or bothered by the request. In fact he praises Solomon's wisdom in asking for help. (2 Chronicles 2:12).

Solomon was building a temple, but we have challenges also that to us can seem just as big. Our jobs may be wearing on us and we may need help praying through our day. For others it may be a family issue that feels too difficult to share outside our walls.

In order to receive help, we must simply ask for help; and in order to ask for help, we have to admit we need help. Like Solomon, we are not meant to do life alone.

Jesus promises to provide what we need to accomplish our God-sized dreams. In John 14:13-14, God explains this,

"Jesus said, whatsoever you shall ask in my name, that will I do, that the Father may be glorified in the Son. If you shall ask any thing in my name, I will do it."

He gives us strength and power, but He also works through the friends He's already put in our lives. In the church, we find friends and fellow believers who want to lend a helping hand. We just have to be willing to ask.

Pride is an awful thing that is often difficult to overcome. At least ask for prayer if something is going on in your life. So many are willing and ready to lift you up to God in prayer.

"Pride goeth before destruction, and an haughty spirit before a fall."

— Proverbs 16:18

Day 28

Grace Does Not Give Us Liberty to Sin

Key Scripture: **Romans 6:1-2**

God's grace sets us free from sin, not free to sin. The grace of God is not a blank check to live in constant and willful rebellion. Like the legalistic views of those who disagree with the aforementioned statement, they fail to understand that Jesus' death for sin and God's saving grace enable our death to sin. They see God's grace as having no affect until after they have sinned, meaning grace merely forgives the evil we do without transforming us.

Paul argued this point as our key passage states;

> *"What shall we say then?*
> *Shall we continue in sin,*
> *that grace may abound?*
> *God forbid. How shall we,*
> *that are dead to sin,*
> *live any longer therein?"*

Paul is not saying that we'll achieve sinless perfection in this life. Rather, he is saying that whoever has experienced the saving grace of God knows that Jesus can and will forgive sin, and transform with new hearts, empowered by the Holy Spirit to pursue new desires for holiness and service for the glory of God and the good of others by the grace of God.

So, those who want to continue in sin and simply expect Jesus' forgiveness without experiencing any real repentance or life change may not have a true saving relationship with God and are abusing His grace.

Some who claim they are Christians believe they are free to do whatever they want and Jesus is obligated to forgive them and give them grace. God is not obligated to give anything, because grace is a gift to the ill-deserving. God's grace not only forgives our sin but also transforms our lives so that we put sin to death because Jesus died for sin.

Another argument they have is because of eternal security, they aren't worried, because they say they have liberty. I too believe in eternal security but by what I can see, those who believe this way are trying to justify their summation of grace and they are not a Christian at all. You can't lose something you never had; saving faith. Grace gets us away from sin, not into sin.

> *"Examine yourselves, whether ye be in the faith;*
> *prove your own selves. Know ye not your own selves,*
> *how that Jesus Christ is in you,*
> *except ye be reprobates?"*
>
> —2 Corinthians 13:5

Day 29

How Close to Jesus Do We Really Want to Be?

Key Scripture: **Revelation 3:14-20**

How would we react or what would we do if Jesus Christ knocked on our door today? Would you swing the door open wide and invite Him in, messy house and all? Or, would you hide behind the blinds and hope He'd just go away like any other salesman?

How and where we interact with someone says a lot about the intimacy we share, or want, with that person. For example, we can talk with co-workers all day about everything, yet never be fully known because we've never invited them into our life at home.

The great invitation of Revelation 3:20 is part of a letter Jesus writes to the church at Laodicea.

Laodicea wants to keep Jesus at a respectful, safe distance. In fact, the church of Laodicea thinks they have enough Jesus. They don't want a relationship that will inevitably make demands on them. They'd rather text or Face-Time every now and again. Jesus describes that church as "pitiable" and rebukes them for being "lukewarm."

They know Jesus but only as a passing acquaintance. But who will treat Jesus as a true friend? Who will walk with Jesus knowing that His passions and burdens must inevitably end up becoming our own?

Jesus is not calling for a lukewarm commitment. He invites us into an intimate, family relationship. Only those who risk a genuine relationship with Jesus will experience the delight of true fellowship with Him.

How is your relationship with Christ? Are you just a 'sometime acquaintance' that feels you have enough of Jesus and think you're good enough? He invites you to accept Him into your heart and genuinely have a relationship with Him. Let's get serious!!!

"And ye shall seek me, and find me, when ye shall search for me with all your heart."
— Jeremiah 29:13

Day 30

Is Grumbling All Right?

Key Scripture: **Philippians 2**

We can never wrap our heads around why it seems life never goes the way we imagine it should go. No matter the effort we put into preparing our day-to-day lives, unforeseen circumstances can really leave us frustrated. Don't believe the lie that Christians never have troubles. Jesus plainly tells us in John 16:33, that in this world we will always have trouble; but take heart, He has overcome the world.

We will have problems, but the question is, what will we do when we face obstacles?

In Philippians 2, Paul writes that we are to have the same mindset as Jesus. His life was full of difficulties and He had every reason to complain, but never did. Even though Jesus was divine in nature, He never used His equality with God to His advantage. He humbled Himself and took the position as Servant.

We complain about most anything like: the traffic is too slow and messed "My" schedule up; restaurants never get "My" order straight, or, why did I not get "My" promotion? Could pride be at the root of most of our complaints?

Jesus never deserved the pain and suffering He endured, yet He never once protested. That kind of behavior certainly gets others' attention. Can you imagine if we all did the same? We would stand out among our peers as "stars in the sky" (Philippians 2:15).

Jesus came to bring people to His Father. When He left, He challenged us to do the same. As we choose to humble ourselves, taking on an attitude of gratitude instead of grumbling, we point people toward our Father.

We have an example to follow. We are without excuse.

"For even hereunto were ye called;
because Christ also suffered for us,
leaving us an example,
that ye should follow his steps."

— 1 Peter 2:21

Day 31

Ever Feel You've Let God Down?

Key Scripture: **Ephesians 1**

Have you ever felt that you're trapped in a deep depression? Have you ever felt the weight of past mistakes or the effects of a failed relationship?

When everything seems to be falling apart, and we are certain we have let God down, grace intervenes and reminds us the story's not over yet.

Paul's life was certainly not going the way he had planned when he found himself alone in a prison cell. In Philippians 1:4-6 he wrote,

"Always in every prayer of mine for you all making request with joy, For your fellow-ship in the gospel from the first day until now; Being confident of this very thing, that he which hath begun a good work in you will perform it until the day of Jesus Christ."

Your circumstances may not look good today. Paul's didn't, yet we can have joy and confidence knowing if it's not good, God's not done. Not only is He not done, He wants to use the very circumstances you are struggling through today. In Philippians 1: 12-14, we are reminded that God can use even the difficult things that happen to us to draw us closer to Him and also bring others to a saving knowledge of Christ.

Our mistakes, our failures, and our heart-aches are all part of our story. When we fear we have let God down, grace trades our shame for courage, knowing our pain is not wasted and God is bigger than the circumstances we feel "chained" to right now.

"God's not done" should change our outlook of our future, giving confidence that we are usable to Him in bringing others to Christ.

"Let no man despise thy youth;
but be thou an example of the believers,
in word, in conversation, in charity,
in spirit, in faith, in purity."
— 1 Timothy 4:12

Day 32

Knowledge of Good and Evil

Key Scripture: **Genesis 3:7-13**

Can you even imagine not knowing "Evil?" Adam's instructions were simple; he was to maintain the garden, rule the animals, and enjoy God's creation. He had only one restriction: to not eat of the tree of the knowledge of good and evil. God told him that if he did, he would surely die.

This seemed like an easy charge from God, yet Adam failed. He didn't rule the animals nor protect his wife. She was deceived by the serpent and ate from the forbidden tree. Adam did also.

Immediately, things changed for them. God told the truth, and they didn't believe Him. Instead they disobeyed, and their eyes were open to something called "Evil." Before this time, they had no sense of evil, they were pure and innocent. Things were now different; so "they sewed fig leaves together and made themselves clothes." Genesis 3:7. Now they were ashamed.

Later when God went through the garden to visit them, they hid from Him. "Where are you?" God asked. Adam replied, "I was afraid, because I was naked, and I hid myself." Genesis 3:10.

God already knew what had happened, and there was no reason to hide from God. Sin had come between them, and God questioned Adam about the forbidden tree. As people do today, Adam blamed Eve and Eve blamed the serpent. No one was taking responsibility for their own actions. This is the way of evil. Once Adam and Eve only knew good; but now they knew the way of evil as well. This put an awkward strain on them because now all creation began to die.

So many stories in the Bible reflect reality and as Christians, it is our responsibility to learn from the mistakes made by others. It's really sad that people today seem to never learn that we all sin, but the way to deal with sin is to admit our shortcomings and ask a Holy God for the needed forgiveness. Accept your responsibility and understand that not seeking forgiveness means living separated from God. It's not worth trying to hide who you are and what you've done. God knows and sees all and no one can seek forgiveness for your sins but you. We are responsible for our own actions.

"He that covereth his sins shall not prosper:
but whoso confesseth and forsaketh them shall have mercy."

— Proverbs 28:13

Day 33

Do You Know Who Knows and Holds the Future?

Key Scripture: **Exodus 16:4**

Whenever we face circumstances one after another, the one thing that stands out more than any other is the fact that we all seem to fear the lack of provisions. As our lives change because of circumstances, we can't really see our future or the security we once had. These feelings are real and though we as Christians know we are supposed to stop fearing the unknown and start trusting God with our unknown, we often fall short.

As we look in the Scriptures, we see over and over God provided for His chosen people and throughout the New Testament He provided for so many men and women of faith, as He does for each of us today. We can easily see Him say; "He alone is our Provider." Whenever we realize this truth, God will open our eyes and heart as we read His Word, listening to our pastors, or read our daily devotion. We continually see that God speaks through each one showing us His provisions through every circumstance we face. All we have to do is, as the Scripture says, "Look unto Jesus..."

For most of us when we look for provision, the last place we look is "up." I pray for myself and others that we learn to look to Him first, eliminating the days of insecure thoughts. Remember, He was the One who always provided for you in the past and He'll continue to do so in the future. Cast your care on Him, He'll not fail.

I still may not know what the future holds, but I know Who holds my future. He also has your future in His hands as well.

"But my God shall supply all your need according to His riches in glory by Christ Jesus."
— Philippians 4:19

Day 34

Staying Faithful Through the Sifting of the Chaff

Key Scripture: Luke 22:31

Have you ever gone through a time in your life that made you fear that your faith was non-existent? Any insecurities you had now looked bigger than ever. Your tears, fears and endless struggles with God multiplied as you always came up short. Maybe you have experienced things which caused you to just wither away into a feeling of dark faithlessness. Where is God in this darkness?

Like me, you may be going through a "Sifting" season; a period of deep pain with a divine purpose of purifying your faith. Sifting in the scriptures usually refers to the process of separating the wheat from the inedible chaff. Same with us, the sifting season has an important role in separating and purifying our hearts.

Centuries ago, Simon Peter went through a similar experience. Jesus told him it was coming as our key scripture says. Satan told him he wanted to sift him like wheat, and Jesus said,

"He prayed for him that his faith might not fail." Peter shrugged off the thought that his faith would fail, but just hours after Jesus spoke these words, he denied that he ever knew his condemned Savior.

It was indeed a low moment in Peter's life, yet the results of fear, doubt, and cowardice was sifted away. While Satan hoped to sift Peter right out of history, God strengthened, purified, and empowered Peter to become the "rock" Christ would use to build His church. (Matthew 16:18).

God desires the same for us. Like Peter, we can learn to survive and even thrive because of the seasons of "sifting the chaff." As we fight to stay faithful, remember as we go through these times of sifting, God is moving us to a closer relationship with Him. I am eternally grateful for all the "chaff" He has removed from my heart. He'll faithfully do the same for you, if you will let Him carry you through your "seasons of sifting."

"But He knoweth the way that I take:
when He hath tried me, I shall come forth as gold."

— Job 23:10

Day 35

Doubting That You're Accepted?

Key Scripture: **Ephesians 1:6**

"To the praise of the glory of His grace, wherein He hath made us accepted in the beloved."

Many Christians find it hard to believe they are an accepted individual, but as our scripture states; *"He hath made us accepted in the beloved."* The reality of this is that we think that God accepts everyone but us. This is so far from the truth. Christians wrongfully believe that: If I am good then I am accepted. If I am a help to others and being a blessing and not a burden, then I am accepted; but if I fail and really make a mess of things, I feel like a reject because I don't feel accepted by me, others and certainly not by God.

We are Christians, and should know that we are accepted and loved by God unconditionally. The belief that we are only accepted when everything is going right and living in God's will is a gross misconception. This shows we have not truly embraced our identity in Christ, because acceptance is what we already have.

Many of us struggle with trusting the truth that we're accepted by God. We are accepted not because of what we do or don't do; we are accepted not because of how we succeed or if we're good. We are accepted not because of who we are, but because of who God is.

"God loves us with an everlasting love"

— Jeremiah 31:3

and

"as many as receive Him, to them gave He power to become sons and daughters of God."

—John 1:12

How can we not be accepted?

When we accepted Jesus Christ as Savior, He accepted us. We may sometimes feel rejected, but how we feel is not who we are. We are acceptable, and accepted; With No Exceptions!

We are indeed accepted in the beloved and by "The Beloved."

"For we are His workmanship, created in Christ Jesus unto good works, which God hath before ordained that we should walk in them."

— Ephesians 2:10

Day 36

Emptiness in Our Lives, Only God Can Fill

Key Scripture: **Psalm 63:1**

Remember the story of the woman at the well? The well was a place she depended on to get her needs met; even having to come back every day, it was never enough. While filling her pot with water, she heard the Savior ask for a drink. He offered her "living water," much different than what she came for that day; this water would satisfy her so deeply, she'd never again thirst.

Not believing His promise she said, "You have nothing to draw with and the well is deep. Where can you get this living water?" (John 4:11). Not realizing He only needed His Spirit to draw with and this would satisfy the longing He'd created in her heart. Jesus was not worried at all about the depth of the well, it was her heart He was looking into. She was the only one able to stop Him from reaching the empty places in her heart.

We are fully aware of the emptiness in our hearts and that Christ is the only One able to fill those needs. Like the woman at the well, we depend on other means to get our needs met, yet when we do, we find that our ways, instead of Jesus' are not enough.

We are human and it comes natural for us to be this way, but if we could learn that no matter how much we do or get for ourselves, it's never enough. Why is that? Because the empty spaces in our hearts are designed to be filled by Christ alone. The deepest thirst of our souls can only be quenched by Him.

As David said in our key scripture, he searched for God with his whole being and thirsted for Him. If you'd read now the next three verses in Psalm 63, you would see David's satisfaction from having his empty spaces filled by God only.

The same thing happened to this woman at the well whom Jesus met. She drank deeply of His love and was filled to overflowing. We too can have this filling. Until God's love and acceptance is enough to fill our emptiness, nothing else will.

"Cause me to hear thy lovingkindness in the morning;
for in thee do I trust: cause me to know the way wherein I should walk;
for I lift up my soul unto thee."

— Psalm 143:8

Day 37

God Will Make A Way

Key Scripture: **Isaiah 43:19**

Sometimes we find ourselves in circumstances and situations that seem impossible. We see no way out. Never could we imagine how we will ever get through this problem; because all we see is a massive obstacle looming before our eyes.

"God will make a way,
where there is no way."

— Isaiah 43:19

In our key passage, God tells us that He will make a way and He sees everything; things we are not aware of. He already has a solution. If by faith we put our trust in Him instead of our problems, He will faithfully lead us through every situation.

God is omnipotent, omniscient, and omnipresent. Nothing surprises Him, and so much we can't see or understand ourselves, we just have to place our faith in Him, and then God, in all His power, *"is able to do more than we could ask or think."* (Ephesians 3:20).

Remember the Hebrew children, they went through the fire and Daniel in the den of lions; however, they kept their eyes on God, knowing He was faithful.

We ourselves can only see the moment we're in and often we see no way out of our present circumstances. By placing our focus on God who knows and sees all things, we can rest in the fact that He has a way out of the circumstances that we are not aware of. (1 Corinthians 13:12).

With the pressure placed on us by others, along with what we place on ourselves, it's so easy to lose our focus on God because of our problems. God has promised never to leave or forsake us if we trust in His wisdom and not our own. When you accept Jesus Christ as your Savior you have the Holy Spirit, God Almighty living within. He wants to work wonders in your life; let Him lead you in His plans.

When things get hard, remember God loves each of us, and He will make a way, no matter how impossible it may seem. I have several small children that I'm praying for who are facing life-threatening issues with "cancer." There is a song with this title: "God will make a way, where there seems to be no way."

"The righteous cry, and the LORD heareth,
and delivereth them out of all their troubles."

— Psalm 34:17

Day 38

Expect Great Things from God

Key Scripture: **Mark 6:48-50**

As in our key passage, we find the disciples in the middle of a storm, unable to gain ground, they were probably exhausted from rowing; and found themselves standing in the need of Jesus. How many times in our own life have we, ourselves been in the same predicament, needing help from our Lord Jesus Christ?

He had told them that He would be following them and even when He showed up, they hardly recognized Him. Strangely, we work the same way; we become overwhelmed or sidetracked with our own thoughts and seek our own abilities to work out our problems. We cannot see Jesus, standing in our midst ready to help in our despair. Will we ever learn?

The disciples had just witnessed the miracle of the feeding of the 5,000 with the few loaves and fishes. They were then as we are now, without the needed faith to accept who and what Jesus Christ is capable of accomplishing. Our faith is weakened because our hearts are somewhat hardened to the fact that our minds can't accept who Christ really is or what He should be.

Understanding that Christ is Lord of our every situation and not just One available when we get into trouble. We have not come into full resolution and belief that He is the true, faithful, Christ, the Son of God. He was placed here for the disciples and also for each of us.

We believe and confess that He is the Christ of the Living God, but as our human instinct kicks in and we want to place limitations of just where and when we want to be controlled by Jesus Christ. When we find ourselves in some dilemma, what do we do? We may panic, become despondent, or even get angry or fearful.

When this happens, we are forgetting the power of Jesus Christ. We are underestimating His love, and forgetting about the promises of God and His ability and determination to fulfill them. So, we must remove our eyes from ourselves and "expect great things from God" by placing our faith and trust in Jesus Christ.

"For I know the thoughts that I think towards you, saith the LORD;
thoughts of peace, and not of evil, to give you an expected end."

— Jeremiah 29:11

Day 39

Consequences Always Follow Disobedience

Key Scripture: **Luke 6:46**

There are consequences when we get caught doing something wrong like stealing candy from a store, hiding the mess in your room under your bed, cheating on an exam, or padding an expense account. We might be reprimanded, lose privileges, receive a zero, or get fired. The results of disobedience can range from just an inconvenience to a life-altering situation.

For Saul, disobedience of not following God's instructions had severe consequences. As seen in our passage, many fell dead, all the Israelites were forced to flee, and Saul's army, along with his sons, were killed. Because of his disobedience, he no longer had the Lord's protection and the Philistine's arrows found him.

Fearing what would happen when the enemy found him wounded, Saul asked his armor bearer to kill him. The armor bearer refused out of fear, so Saul took his own life. We can learn some valuable lessons from the downfall of Saul:

- Obedience brings God's presence and favor; disobedience leaves us on our own to suffer the consequences of our actions.

- Even one bad choice can bring lasting consequences. Successive bad choices can bring catastrophic results. Our disobedience does not just affect us, but also affects everyone around us.

- Sometimes we can fix disobedience without a lot of pain, and sometimes we can't fix it at all.

Saul was the Lord's chosen king for the Israelites, but rather than trusting that God knew best, Saul's ego took precedence in his heart. When it did, disobedience, doing things his own way, became his undoing. Saul lost everything by losing sight of the only thing that mattered: his relationship with the One true King.

Have you learned through your own disobedience that it brings consequences? How can we keep ourselves obedient to God's will?

"…Behold, to obey is better than sacrifice, and to hearken than the fat of rams."
— 1 Samuel 15:22

Day 40

A Question We Should Ask
When We're Up Against What Seems Like a Losing Battle

Key Scripture: **1 Samuel 4:1-11**

Nothing seems more demoralizing than fighting a losing battle. Emotionally, it's exhausting, and for a Christian, it's confusing. Romans 8:37 assures us *"we are more than conquerors through Him that loved us,"* yet there are enemies we can't seem to conquer, so then we ask ourselves if God is for us. But there is another question that's more likely to turn a defeat into victory.

The Israelites had a reputation as conquerors. Their past victories created fear among their enemies. Unfortunately, this led to an apathetic spirit in their relationship with God. In the past they sought God for a plan and He always gave them a specific strategy for victory.

Now, they didn't acknowledge Him at all. They just assumed they could do as they once did and victory would follow. They found out that past conquests don't produce present conquerors.

To be conquerors, we need to ask "Lord, what do I need to do to win this battle?" Proverbs 3:5-6 says:

> *"Trust in the LORD with all thine heart, and lean not unto thine own understanding; In all thy ways acknowledge Him, and He shall direct thy paths."*

God desires to give us a strategy to win every battle. Our acknowledgement that we need His guidance in all we do keeps our relationship with Him fresh, as well as effective.

Battles cause emotions and confusion. Are you facing one that you feel you're losing? Acknowledge the Lord and ask Him for a strategy…the first step to victory.

"A man's heart deviseth his way: but the LORD directeth his steps."

— Proverbs 16:9

Day 41

I Am the Blame

Key Scripture: **Deuteronomy 5:3-4**

Not accepting the blame for our own short comings is and always has been a major problem for us and our ancestors. The blame game, as old as Adam and Eve, enlists new players with every child born into this world. I was told long ago that the definition of an excuse is: The skin of a reason wrapped in a lie. Strong words, but so true.

"It's not my fault! I grew up in the wrong neighborhood. My teacher taught the wrong thing. The government didn't help out." These are just a few examples of passing the blame from ourselves.

"No excuses," Moses said to Israel. "God spoke to you; you've heard His words. You have your marching orders. When the moment comes to enter and live in the land, you know what to do." "When in Canaan," Moses said to God's people, "do not do as the Canaanites do!"

Knowing God's Word brings awareness that we cannot blame others for our failure to do what is right. Blaming others for doing wrong is a cop-out and a waste of time. We all know what matters most: Now that we have heard God's voice, what is our response?

Sins of our ancestors do powerfully ring out in our lives. Generations of abuse and addicted persons know this. But God's people are no longer looked at as victims of a sinful past. Be responsible and accept the blame for your own sins by confessing them to yourself first and then to God.

Place your sins on the only innocent victim who carried the blame of the world's misery, Jesus Christ. Be responsible by admitting the truth; we are without blame. We all have heard and know the Word of Truth.

We cannot accept nor be responsible for someone else's sin. We must individually look at our own hearts and listen to the Spirit of God instead of pointing fingers when the problem rests within us and not others.

"He that covereth his sins shall not prosper:
but whoso confesseth and forsaketh them shall have mercy."

— Proverbs 28:13

Day 42

Lord, Give Unto Me "Your Heart"

Key Scripture: **Luke 19:41-42**

Have you ever been in a prayer meeting and prayer requests were being offered up? Many would lift their hands saying they had a special unspoken request. Most times we as participants never know anything about the unspoken request other than it was probably personal.

One night when as a teen, I was at a Bible conference in Chattanooga, Tennessee. We had a late-night prayer meeting with our pastor and I remember a young boy weeping softly during this meeting. We had just come from a very emotional service where the speaker spoke on "Having compassion for the lost."

The pastor asked the young boy if he wanted to say something. He finally spoke up and said, "I need you to pray that I can stop crying, my heart is so broken for those around me who don't know Jesus. I am really overcome."

Do you remember the story about Jesus' triumphant entry into Jerusalem before the Pass-over? In Luke 19, we find Jesus overcome with sorrow instead of the praises the people offered up. He wept over the city because He lamented over the fact that He was the long-awaited Savior, and the people totally did not understand.

God had extended His hand of mercy and grace through Jesus and the world turned away. Jesus didn't just express a few tears over this rejection, He "wept" expressing His deep grief for a lost world.

Going back to the prayer meeting, I remember as I opened up to the group, "Please pray for me to stop crying." My pastor quickly spoke up, "I pray you never stop."

Pray for me to always have a broken heart that's tender and weeps over the lost, like Jesus did. I want a heart that is able to convert my grief into pleas to God for people to wake up and see their need for an intimate relationship with Jesus Christ.

"Create in me a clean heart, O God;
and renew a right spirit within me."

— Psalm 51:10

Day 43

Feeling Contentment When Your Spirit is Down

Key Scripture: **Philippians 4:12-13**

Having a spirit of contentment is dampened when we place our thoughts and eyes on others and their success. We become curious by thinking what it would be like to have someone else's ability to live a life of good health, comfortable lifestyle, and abundant success, yet we can have days that sadness creeps in unaware and our countenance turns from feeling fully under control to an unstable heart of turmoil.

I began to dwell on what I once had, once could do, once was, and I compare them to what I am today with my limitations. Then self-pity springs forth like a monster and I'm stuck between the things I long for and the reality I'm living today.

We may face loss of loved ones, of jobs, loss of health, or abilities. Remember this; contentment is a daily battle, whether we're tempted to compare to others, or our past circumstances.

During times of significant loss, I've laid down things that were precious to me, and by experiencing these times, I find comfort in remembering that Jesus understands loss. He set aside the glory of heaven to come to earth and *"made Himself nothing by taking on the form of a servant."* (Philippians 2:6-7).

Some days it takes a stubborn courage to walk with a heart of contentment. As we face times of great loss through any circumstance, reflect and focus on what God has done in your past, trusting He'll bring you through them and give you a grateful heart, thanking Him for His faithfulness and His heart of compassionate grace. Without Him where would we be?

Is there anything at all that tends to make having a spirit of contentment difficult for you? What about self-pity?

"But godliness with contentment is great gain."

— 1 Timothy 6:6

Day 44

Do We Have a Holier Than Thou Attitude?
What Does it Mean to Be Holy?

Key Scripture: **Leviticus 11:44**

It really bothers me to see someone with a holier than thou attitude.

The only problem with this is that we are commanded by God's Word to be holy, even as Jesus is holy. This is required and apparently possible. Many have the wrong idea about what being "holy" should be and Satan has had a hay day with this. We have been taught that being holy is to be sinless and without spot or blemish, perfect in every way.

As humans, we'll never achieve this status. Only Christ Himself will fit this role. I understand that in some areas of the Bible, "holy" does mean this, but the simplest meaning is to be "set apart," meaning we are to be set apart to God and His purpose. We are in this world but not of it.

Back to the "holier than thou," we are not to be walking around with our heads in the clouds and lose touch with what is going on around us. We are to be a citizen of Heaven in a foreign country on our best behavior. Keep in mind who it is that directs our paths, leading us in His ways; we are totally accountable to Him.

By accepting Jesus Christ as our Savior, we obtain holiness, thereby putting on His perfectness and totally setting our heart and life aside for God's purpose alone. Applying this to our everyday life could be shown in many ways like: getting a grip on your temper, bitterness, and spending more time away from worldly things and investing more time in God's Word.

What is important is that we do not look or think like the world. We must ask and answer honestly this question; can others around us see that we are different, or do we blend in with the world? Do our actions cause others to wonder what we have and how they can obtain it? Remember, we must walk the walk, and talk the talk as did Jesus Christ.

"Wherefore gird up the loins of your mind, be sober,
and hope to the end for the grace that is to be brought unto you at the revelation of Jesus Christ;
As obedient children, not fashioning yourselves according to the former lusts in your ignorance:
But as He which hath called you is holy, so be ye holy in all manner of conversation;
because it is written, Be ye holy; for I am holy."

— 1 Peter 1:13-16

Day 45

God's Unseen Hand is Always Working

Key Scriptures: Romans 8:28; Genesis 50:29; 2 Corinthians 4:7; and Habakkuk 1:2

God is always near, always at work, and never sleeping nor slumbering, (Psalm 121:4). He never tires and continually works His will.

Something I read recently says: In the middle of the blessing we can find God's hand. In the midst of our questions we can find God's will. In the core of our sorrows we can feel God's hand.

As we feel blessed we see that God has provided. As we have questions about anything, God provoked them. Through the answers, God can be glorified. As we go through times of pain and sorrow, let's understand that God has allowed them so that we might learn to trust Him, increasing our understanding.

No matter who, where or what is going on in your life, God's hand is there, and He is with you NOW. He is the eternal God, always there, all knowing and Sovereign God as seen in Psalm 139:7-10.

Throughout the scriptures we see the Unseen Hand of God; the hand that provides, nurtures, and guides us each day. Maybe you have questions or are going through a difficult situation; whatever it is, ask God to open your eyes that you may see The Unseen Hand at work in your life. God will reveal Himself; just trust Him, feel Him working in your presence.

Remember how God revealed to Israel His hand as He helped Gideon defeat the Midianites; in the story of Joseph, He showed His redemptive hand, the same for Mordecai and Esther, again seen through the faithfulness of Job, Jonah, the three Hebrew children, and rewarded the stand of Daniel.

His hand is also seen in Paul's faithfulness, with Peter the faithful disciple, and the blind man from birth. Should we ever doubt that God's hand is not with us?

"Humble yourselves therefore under the mighty hand of God,
that He may exalt you in due time."

— I Peter 5:6

Day 46

Though We are Judged by Others, God is Our True Judge

Key Scripture: 1 Samuel 2:22-36

I'm sure we have heard from a friend or maybe someone else the phrase "Only God can change me." If we only knew what we're asking when we ask for God's judgment, we probably would think twice before ignoring the warnings of a parent or friend.

Eli's sons let evil abound under their leadership. In the end it proved disastrous for the entire family. Eli warned his sons to stop sleeping with women and stealing from the Lord's offerings, but nothing changed, and eventually God pronounced judgment on the entire family. Eli and his sons had been given a great opportunity and squandered it. In I Samuel 2:30, God said,

"Wherefore the LORD God of Israel saith, I said indeed that thy house, and the house of thy father, should walk before me forever; but now the LORD saith, Be it far from me; for them that honour me I will honour, and they that despise me shall be lightly esteemed."

Like Eli's sons, we ignore others' warnings and continue toward disaster. Nothing tells God we think lightly of Him like the refusal to deal with sin in our lives. God's patience is not the same as His permission. God is a loving God, but He is also just. He will not let sin go unpunished forever. Jesus warned us, *"For unto whomever much is given, of him shall be much required..."* (Luke 12:48).

When we ask Jesus into our lives, we become like Eli's sons; recipients of a position we did not earn or deserve. God is patient with us when we sin, but if we want to avoid God's punishment, we have to be willing to accept His discipline and correction.

Are we taking seriously what God tells us about sin by staying clear of disastrous situations and ignoring His warnings and not following His directions?

"For we know Him that hath said,
Vengeance belongeth unto me,
I will recompense saith the Lord.
And again, The Lord shall judge His people."

— Hebrews 10:30

Day 47

Are We Able to Change How We See Things?

Key Scripture: **1 Samuel 16:1-13**

It has been proven that people who look at the same thing and later asked to explain what they saw, came away with different views.

Not only do we see things differently, we are quick to turn perceptions on what we saw into judgments. We can be thankful God does not operate this way. To Him, our appearance neither defines us nor dictates our value.

In 1 Samuel 16, the Lord sends Samuel to Bethlehem to anoint a king from Jesse's sons. Based on appearance, it is likely Jesse's older sons would have been prime candidates for king, but one by one, Jesse's sons pass before Samuel but God rejects them all.

Samuel and Jesse were both baffled; these sons looked the part, and Samuel admits his fear, but the Lord explains to Samuel,

"But the LORD said unto Samuel, Look not on his countenance, or on the height of his stature; because I have refused him: for the LORD seeth not as man seeth; for the man looketh on the outward appearance, but the LORD looketh on the heart."

—1 Samuel 16:7

Samuel and Jesse looked at the initial seven sons and saw what we would see today; good looks, success, age, experience, strength, and authority. But then, and now, the Lord looks deeper. He looks at the condition of our hearts. Outward appearance means nothing to Him.

The Lord chose Jesse's youngest, David, who was absent, keeping the sheep. David probably looked like a messy young lad, coming straight from the fields, but that didn't matter; God saw his heart.

If God values only our character, should not this be where we should focus our eyes?

Where are you investing your time in developing your character?

"While we look not at the things which are seen, but at the things which are not seen: for the things which are seen are temporal; but the things which are not seen are eternal."

— 2 Corinthians 4:18

Day 48

Can We Find Gratitude Even Through Storms?

Key Scripture: **Psalm 40:2**

I can honestly say that I love my church, not for the building, but for the wonderful time of worship we have. I particularly love the times when the Spirit moves and God's presence is real; when a song changed the order of our service and God puts His hand directing things.

My heart breaks when songs of worship fill our hearts with His Spirit, when saints of God one after another tell a story how God has been faithful to them through heartaches. Tears of joy fill God's house because of the gratefulness that God has walked beside them through health issues or the loss of a loved one. God has remained steadfast when they are lonely, desperate and broken-hearted. Even when the storm is still raging, they feel His presence.

We all encounter the storms of life, and as threatening as they seem at first, we will soon realize that storms bring with them a unique pathway to a spirit of thankfulness.

I myself have experienced storm after storm in my life, and although my faith was not what it should be at times, God always remained faithful. By relying on His strength and not my own, was a blessing in disguise. I was able to accept God's will and be thankful for it.

When life is easy, gratefulness is easy; but not in the midst of storms. Gratefulness hinges on our ability to place the brokenness, loneliness, the pain from illness or the loss of income, and accept God's will over our own. Accept that He is in control, and our trust in Him is sufficient.

In our key passage, 1 Thessalonians 4:16-18 we see God's instruction to always be thankful. In storms of life, God is our hope, even through the darkest times, we find His faithfulness and goodness are present. It may not happen immediately, but thankfulness grows as we cling to Christ alone.

We'll always be grateful for joys of restored health, overcoming grief, and for any sorrows that brought us to the place of utter dependence on Christ. We are then able to offer up gratitude for the easy blessings but also for the storms throughout our life.

"O give thanks unto the LORD;
for He is good;
for His mercy endureth forever."

— 1 Chronicles 16:34

Day 49

Who Do We Know Who has Our Back?

Key Scripture: 1 Samuel 14:1-23

In our own relationships, we expect to be able to count on the other person. In my own life while growing up, I was bullied at school, and also at home. I never depended on my brothers or cousins to have my back; I just found ways to get the bully down to my size and earned a little respect.

As we turn into adults, we use relationships to help us learn how to pick good people to be in our lives. Everyone needs someone to have their back. A word of wisdom here is to be certain those you choose are who they say they are. If not, they "will prove" their self-centeredness, by turning their backs on you instantly.

We see a great trusting relationship between Jonathan and his armor-bearer. Their bond was so strong they were able to tackle a large army as our key passage reveals. Jonathan's armor-bearer may not have been exactly sure of how he could help, but he knew that if Jonathan needed him, he would be there. We see his promise in 1 Samuel 14:7:

> *"Do all that is in thine heart; turn thee; behold, I am with thee according to thy heart."*

This certainly exemplified what we all want in a relationship; one who is with us in heart and soul.

We may not be able to do something to help a friend as they go through certain issues, but sometimes our presence is enough. When things get tough, it is comforting to know someone is there; it gives us courage to keep moving forward. Just like the armor-bearer, who was all in for Jonathan, we can do the same for others. His promise spurred Jonathan to carry out his plan.

Is there one certain person that you're confident has your back? Do they feel the same about you having theirs?

"Let your conversation be without covetousness;
and be content with such things as ye have:
for He hath said, I will never leave thee, nor forsake thee.
So that we may boldly say,
"The Lord is my helper,
and I will not fear what man shall do unto me."

— Hebrews 13:5-6

Day 50

A Jealous Spirit is Dangerous

Key Scripture: **1 Samuel 18:1-16**

At first glance, jealousy may not seem like a major sin in our daily lives. We may get a little jealous of people here and there, but that's not dangerous, right?

In our key passage, Saul shows us that jealousy is actually one step short of murder. Saul reacted in extreme jealousy against David. David was so successful in any mission Saul sent him on and the people started singing; "Saul hath slain his thousands, and David his ten thousands." (1 Samuel 18:7). That's enough to make anyone angry or jealous. Saul was King and yet his people were praising David instead of him.

Saul's jealousy stemmed from fear and insecurity. He was afraid because David was closer to God than he was, which worried him by thinking David would take over as king of the Isra-

elites. Saul fed his own insecurities and let his jealousy grow, and in doing that, he gave Satan a foothold in his life. Saul's jealousy grew so deep that he actually attempted to kill David on several occasions. (1 Samuel 18:10-11).

We all experience jealousy, but as we see with Saul, it's dangerous to let this jealousy fester and grow in our lives. When we are confident who God made us to be, we stop comparing ourselves to other people and focus on what God is doing in our own lives. Instead of letting Satan use jealousy against us the way Saul did, let's submit our anger and envy to the Lord and watch Him take the burden from us.

Are you spending time daily reading God's Word so you can be confident who God made you to be? Make it a priority.

"For where envying and strife is,
there is confusion and every evil work."

— James 3:16

Day 51

Is Being Sorry Repentance?

Key Scripture: 1 Samuel 6

When Jesus began His ministry, the first word of action put before His followers was "repent."

Repentance is more than just guilt or regret. We can be sorry for the consequences of our actions, but not change our heart, or examine how we think and believe. Our thoughts and convictions produce our actions, for good or evil.

In 1 Samuel 6, a group of Philistines chose a path, faced the consequences, and turned a different way. These Philistines changed their behavior, which was admirable, but they weren't motivated by genuine repentance. They changed because they were afraid of the consequences.

The Philistines were motivated by fear of God, but they didn't know God, however, they did three things that we can do when we know we are wrong:

- Admit we are wrong.

- Try to make it right.

- Don't do it again.

Genuine repentance, motivated by a desire to please God and turn away from sin, will lead us to ask for help - "I know I've done wrong, so how can I make it right?" Genuine repentance also leads us to do everything we can to right our wrongs.

Genuine repentance is about changing your mind, moving away from thinking that leads to sin and moving toward thinking that aligns with God's Word. Repentance causes us to learn from mistakes so we're less likely to repeat them in the future.

The Philistines were motivated to change because they feared a God they were far away from. As Christians, we are motivated to change because God draws close to us in our need, and is always willing to help, mend the relationship, and equip us to live an abundant life, serving a Holy God.

Are there any mistakes that you've made that motivated you to make a change? Was there a genuine repentance that took place?

"He that covereth his sins shall not prosper:
but whoso confesseth and forsaketh them shall have mercy."

— Proverbs 28:13

Day 52

The Word of God Was Important to Josiah

Key Scripture: 2 Kings 22-23

This week I finished the book of 2 Kings and this time through I did a short study on Josiah. Several questions came to mind like in our current wicked world, how can we remain faithful to God? How can we tune out the sins of our world? Is there really any hope for us in our struggles? The answers to these questions can be found in the Bible if we read it and obey it.

Josiah was appointed king at 8 years old. Behind him was a family of evil kings. His grandfather and father were evil, but he was righteous in a time of wickedness and remained faithful.

In 2 Kings 23:25, the scripture says his righteousness was unsurpassed by any king before or after him. He was righteous even though the Judean society was evil, promoting idolatry, and child sacrifice; they were worse than the nations God had destroyed.

Josiah's faithfulness was seen in many ways in his life. In the eighth year of his reign "he began to seek after God" (2 Chronicles 34:3). In his twelfth year he began purging Judah of "high places" and idols; along with the breaking down the altars of Baal and punishing the idolatrous priests. His faithfulness was seen also in his tender-hearted reaction to the Law of God. (2 Kings 22).

While work was going on in the temple, the book of the Law of God was found. He recognized the value of this book; he had godly sorrow over Judah's sin, and had a desire to learn more about the Word. In God speaking to him in regards to his tenderness toward the Word of God, He said in 2 Kings 22:19: *"because thine heart was tender, and thou hast humbled thyself before the LORD, when thou heardest what I spake…"*

He tenderheartedly recognized the importance of the Word of God. Oh, that our hearts could feel this way toward God's Word. Josiah sought to know as much of the will of God as he could by walking in the ways of God and humbly obeying His commands. (2 Kings 23:3).

Something we fall so short on is sharing the Word of God with others. Josiah again knew the value of this book; in 2 Kings 23:2 it says; *"The king went up into the house of the LORD, and all the men of Judah and the inhabitants of Jerusalem with him and the priests and the prophets, and all the people, both small and great: and he read in their ears all the words of the book of the covenant which was found in the house of the LORD."* Because of his influence *"all the people took a stand for the covenant."* (2 Kings 23:3).

The life of Josiah is a great example for us; it demonstrates how we can find favor with God with the right attitude toward the Word of God, a desire to know more and share it with others. We can take a stand for God and His Word.

"Humble yourselves in the sight of the Lord, and He shall lift you up."

— James 4:10

Day 53

Doing the Right Thing, Because It's the Right Thing to Do

Key Scripture: **Titus 2:11-15**

I'm sure we all have seen movies where one character saved another character from a potential tragedy, and the one saved from the tragedy spends the rest of their life serving the one who saved them. This may be portrayed as a comedy of sorts, but one thing for sure; the deeds done are not for show, or because it's the right thing to do, but are given because of true awe, and thankfulness.

In our relationship with God, what is the motivation behind our behavior? The Bible clearly calls followers of Jesus to serve people, care for the poor, and keep ourselves from sin. What motivates you to do these things? Do you do the right thing because it's what you're supposed to do; or because people are looking; or as the character in the movie who serves their Savior out of thankfulness?

In our key passage, Titus 2:11-15, we see how the scripture so beautifully speaks of grace being our motivation for living a righteous life.

"For the grace of God that bringeth salvation hath appeared to all men, Teaching us that, denying ungodliness and worldly lusts, we should live soberly, righteously, and godly, in this present world; Looking for the blessed hope, and the glorious appearing of the great God and our Saviour, Jesus Christ; Who gave Himself for us, that He might redeem us from all iniquity, and purify unto Himself a peculiar people, zealous of good works. These things speak, and exhort, and rebuke with all authority. Let no man despise thee."

Grace is getting what we do not deserve. It is forgiveness, freely given and poured on us, (1 Corinthians 2:12). It asks nothing and is not earned (Ephesians 2:9). When we understand salvation is nothing we can do for ourselves and most definitely nothing we deserve, it brings us to a place of true thankfulness for what Jesus did. In realizing this, we want to live godly lives pleasing the One who saved us from death. Just like the character in the movie, we want to spend our lives serving our Savior.

Have you experienced the grace of God, so that you can serve Him out of a heart of thankfulness?

"For God so loved the world, that He gave His only begotten Son, that whosoever believeth in Him should not perish, but have everlasting life."

— John 3:16

Day 54

Trust—A Word We Should Begin Our Day With

Key Scripture: **Proverbs 3:5-6**

Have you ever faced a situation when just before a very important event, things seemed to fall apart?

I remember years back, just before an important championship game, a key player of mine got terribly sick. My wife and I stayed up all night nursing our son, trying to get his fever down and frantically doing everything we could to find help for this sick child. The most critical game of my son's baseball year was two days away, and he, being an important part of the team, meant we had to do everything imaginable to help get him ready if at all possible. Through our efforts, we had to embrace whatever it was God wanted to teach us in this situation.

The title of this post starts with the word "Trust." Trust sometimes is a very difficult pill to swallow, especially when you're faced with having to make a change that affects your child, as well as others, taking a different approach to the game ahead. That's why we must choose to trust, despite our feelings.

Even when our feelings beg us to experience confusion and uncertainty, we must remind ourselves of our key passage and stand on God's promises and "Trust." I have walked through enough disappointments to know His paths are best, regardless of our wants and desires. Our answers to situations may not be the path we choose, and God's path may be the opposite path we're expecting.

His "no" could be for our protection. Trust Him. His "no" could be for our provision, providing something better, Trust Him. His "no" may be a part of the process, growing us closer to God; when we are weak only then can we fully understand how God can be our strength.

Through our "Trust," in Him, we were able to find God's strength though His provisions. It's comforting to leave what we cannot control in the hands of God, who is completely capable.

"Commit thy way unto the LORD;
trust also in Him;
and He shall bring it to pass."

— Psalm 37:5

Day 55

Put the Glass Down

Key Scripture: **1 Peter 5:7**

A professor began his class by holding up a glass of water in his hand. He held it up for all to see and asked the students. "How much do you think this glass weighs?" Various answers came from 6 ounces to 20 ounces. "I really don't know unless I weigh it," said the professor, "but my question is: What would happen if I held it up like this for a few minutes?"

The students said, "Nothing."

"Okay, what would happen if I held it up like this for an hour?" the professor asked.

"Your arm will begin to ache," said one of the students.

"You're right. Now, what would happen if I held it up for a day?" asked the professor.

"Your arm would go numb, you might have severe muscle stress paralysis and have to go to the hospital for sure!" ventured another student, and all the students laughed.

"Very good; but during all this, did the weight of the glass change?" asked the professor.

"No" was the answer.

"Then what caused my arm to ache and the muscle stress?" The students were puzzled. "What should I do now to come out of pain?" asked the professor.

"Put the glass down!" said one of the students.

"Exactly!" said the professor.

Life's problems are something like this. Hold it for a few minutes in your head and they seem okay. Think of them for a long time and your mind begins to ache. Hold it even longer and they begin to paralyze you; then you will not be able to do anything.

It's important to think of the challenges or problems in your life, but even more important is to: "put them down" at the end of every day before you go to sleep; that way you wake up every morning fresh, unstressed, feeling strong, and able to handle issues or challenges that come your way. Now is the time to put your glass down.

Ultimately, we need to learn to trust our life to God in all circumstances. Philippians 4:6-7; Matthew 11:28-30.

"Casting all your care upon Him;
for He careth for you."

— 1 Peter 5:7

Day 56

Forever Changed

Key Scripture: **1 Samuel 10**

Change is something that's a part of everyone's life. Some thrive for change while others get stressed out and despise change. No matter how we respond to change, one thing will always remain true, whenever God is involved we are always changed for the better.

In our key passage, Samuel informs Saul that he will be Israel's next king. When the Spirit of the Lord came upon Saul, he became a new person. In order for him to step into his calling, he had to be changed from the inside out. Saul's heart was changed, and he was enabled, through God's Spirit, to do what God asked him to do. The difference in Saul was evident to his friends after the Spirit of God changed him. The Bible says they almost didn't recognize him because of this change.

The same thing happens to us when we surrender our lives to Jesus. People see the change. Imagine our world is a dark room, and Jesus, the light of the world, is now part of us. The Spirit of the Lord is like a bright shining light in the dark, and that is hard for others to miss.

Often in the Old Testament, the Spirit of the Lord temporarily empowered people. When we ask Jesus Christ into our heart, we become a new person forever. We find hope, security, and freedom when we are surrendered to our Savior. The Lord sets us free, gives us purpose, and through His Spirit, enables us to do what God has called us to do. Now, because of the change God has given us, we can do whatever He sets before us.

What a wonderful change in our life has been wrought, since Jesus came into our hearts.

"Therefore if any man be in Christ, he is a new creature;
old things are passed away;
behold, all things are become new."

— 2 Corinthians 5:17

Day 57

Is All Anger Sinful?

Key Scripture: **1 Samuel 11**

Everyone has been angry before. We've all seen injustice, felt pain when wronged, and felt as though we could pinch someone's head off. Anger is hurtful, but not all anger is sinful.

In 1 Samuel 11, with fear, the people told Saul that their enemies, the Ammonites, threatened to gouge out their right eyes. "And the Spirit of God came upon Saul when he heard those tidings, and his anger was kindled greatly." (1 Samuel 11:6). The Spirit of God allowed him to feel the injustice and respond appropriately.

Righteous anger, (what we see with injustice, from hate speech and feel when wounded); is not a sin. How we respond to those feelings can be. Ephesians 4:26-27, gives us a short anger management lesson. "Be ye angry, and sin not: let not the sun go down upon your wrath: neither give place to the devil." So how do we experience anger and not sin?

- Wrong actions can make bad situations worse if we choose to hurt someone physically or verbally, hurt ourselves or destroy property.

- Ask the Lord to give you strength before acting upon your anger. Ask for forgiveness or the ability to forgive. Never hold on to anger.

- Don't let Satan get a grip on your anger and cause harm. Ask the Lord to let you see your actions through His eyes, not your own. Draw close to Him and He will draw close to you (James 4:8).

Saul "burned with anger," but took the necessary steps to listen, evaluate, plan, and then take action. How he handled his anger saved his people. How we handle anger will determine if our anger is righteous like Saul's or has a Satan label stamp on it.

What could you do to prepare for any anger moments that may come your way? We don't always have time to consider the situation logically or with compassion when we are hurt and become angry.

"Wherefore, my beloved brethren,
let every man be swift to hear,
slow to speak,
slow to wrath."

— James 1:19

When Our Goals and Longings Seem Impossible

Key Scripture: **1 Samuel 1:1-18**

Being loved by her husband, Hannah's longing was for a child. Her prayers went unfulfilled while others around her had their prayers answered. Still she waited, asking, "When will it be my turn?"

Our desires might not be for a child, but still we find ourselves longing for something, like a different meaningful job, a happy marriage, a renewed chance on life itself. Often the Lord plants these yearnings in our hearts, just like Hannah's desire to be a mom. One important fact about these yearnings is that the Lord may also be the only one who can fulfill our desires.

Sometimes we're plagued with a lack of patience and want things in our time frame. When this doesn't happen, we feel frustrated, isolated, ignored, and even misunderstood. Hannah felt all of these. Even though her husband loved her, he didn't understand the weeping, but still showed her his love daily, but it wasn't enough.

Others may see you weeping in weakness and not understand, so instead of showing compassion, they use it against you. In 1 Samuel 1:6-7; Hannah's rival "kept provoking her in order to irritate her." This went on year after year and every time she went to the house of the Lord her rival provoked her to tears.

What can we do when longings go unmet? Philippians 4:6 gives us the answer...Prayer. It doesn't always bring immediate resolutions, but it always brings immediate relief.

Hannah turned her problem over to God, though her situation had not changed, her heart did. (1 Samuel 1:8-11). Because of this, she now had hope restored by placing her trust in the Lord.

The same is true for us, when we take our troubles and longings to the Lord, our prayers may not change things immediately, but they will change us.

Can we take our burdens to the Lord, and leave them there?

"Now unto Him that is able to do exceeding abundantly above all that we ask or think, according to the power that worketh in us."

— Ephesians 3:20

Day 59

Blending in with the Crowd

Key Scripture: **1 Samuel 8**

Samuel was a judge in Israel that led the nation back to the direction of God. When Samuel was at the end of his years, the nation demanded a king like the surrounding nations instead of a judge. God was not in favor of this idea because demanding a king meant they were rejecting Him as their source of leadership. Nevertheless, God told Samuel to anoint Saul, a successful soldier, as Israel's first king.

Like the nation of Israel, we tend to want to go our own way; rejecting the Lord's ways and ignoring His promises. Even though we know the promises of God are true and His ways are greater, our selfishness gets the best of us as we try to blend in with our culture.

The Bible admonishes believers to stand strong against the patterns of this world and not conform to everyone else's way of thinking. (Romans 12:2). We have a real enemy who wants us to blend in and forget who we are in Christ. Staying focused on Jesus requires us to put on spiritual armor every day. (Ephesians 6:10-18). Blending in might be easier, but is blending in worth it if it causes us to settle for less than God's best?

Jesus said God knows every strand of hair on our heads. (Luke 12:7). So even if we think we know ourselves best, God certainly knows us better. When we choose God's way, we gain happiness, peace, and joy along with a life of greatness that is unmeasurable. God's strength and promises are the only thing than can make us flourish as a set apart child of God.

How much of your ability to feel content is based on how your life compares to others?

Do you have tendencies to measure yourself against others?

"It is better to trust in the LORD than to put confidence in man.
It is better to trust in the LORD than to put confidence in princes."

— Psalm 118:8-9

Day 60

Don't Allow Negative Thoughts to Run Your Life

Key Scripture: **Proverbs 4:23**

Life has been somewhat difficult for me over the last few years due to painful circumstances, causing negative thoughts to literally run my life. These negative thoughts weighed heavily, not only on my emotions but also my outlook on life. At times the negative thoughts made me feel drained mentally and emotionally, and sometimes spiritually.

In our key verse, Solomon gives wise advice on dealing with thoughts, and was written for the benefit of his own sons. Solomon did not write concerning royal matters or how the kingdom should be run; he wrote on important matters such as the value of controlling their thoughts which determined how they felt about life's circumstances.

The quality of our thoughts will always determine the quality of our life. Our thoughts turn into feelings that have the power to control our lives, slowly steering us, and possibly our faith, in an undesirable direction.

King Solomon warns us to be careful of what we think and feel, because he knew it's often our thoughts, not our circumstances that weaken our faith.

Our thoughts have the power to run our lives if we let them. Feelings of anger, despair, broken dreams, or anything that becomes overwhelming can cause us to get caught up in a web of negative thoughts. When we think those thoughts, our feelings become negative, leading us to believe life overall is exactly that.

During my years of painful circumstances, I was made aware that my thoughts were running my life. I sought the wisdom of God and asked for His help to not allow these thoughts to take my joy, my hope, and my faith. I'll have to admit my feelings wavered, however, I committed to embrace His truth and just because my circumstances were not positive, didn't mean my thoughts couldn't be. When I intentionally changed my thoughts, my life changed as well.

"For the LORD giveth wisdom:
out of His mouth cometh knowledge and understanding.
He layeth up sound wisdom for the righteous:
He is a buckler to them that walk uprightly.
He keepeth the paths of judgment, and preserveth the way of His saints."

— Proverbs 2:6-8

Day 61

"Nevertheless"

Key Scripture: **Proverbs 3:5-6**

Have you ever thought what are some of the most important words in the Bible? Maybe faith, love, and hope, and we could add the word "holy." While doing my reading I write things down that inspire me in some form, and some time back I wrote this word down: "Nevertheless." I hope when I'm done with this post you'll understand why.

In Luke 5:1-9, we find the account where Peter and some others fished all night and caught nothing. Jesus saw them as they neared the shore, and seeing they had nothing, He told them to let the nets down again. About half way through this passage Peter answered Jesus and said:

> *"Master, we have toiled all the night and have taken nothing: "nevertheless" at thy word I will let down the net."*

We know what happened; their nets were so full they broke.

Has the Lord ever urged you in some way to do something that you did not want to do? Maybe you just thought it was not necessary or needful at the time, and you might even have argued with the Lord about it. "Nevertheless," you did it anyway, and the Lord revealed to you why it was important to Him.

Someone in your path that day may have needed prayer, someone was in your path that needed to receive a tract, or even someone may have gotten saved because of your "nevertheless."

Look what happened in verses 10-11 in Luke 5; Peter and his followers forsook everything and became fishers of men, following Jesus.

"Nevertheless" is a powerful word that shows a yielding to God's ways and releasing of our own. It's the doorway to faith in God apart from faith in ourselves. "Nevertheless" is a simple word that is more powerful than I ever knew. This verse shows us just how powerful this word really is: Matthew 26:38-39:

> *"Then saith He unto them, 'My soul is exceeding sorrowful, even unto death: tarry ye here, and watch with me' And He went a little farther, and fell on His face, and prayed saying. 'O my Father, if it be possible, let this cup pass from me: "nevertheless" not as I will, but as thou wilt."*

Our very salvation, and the salvation of all mankind, was dependent on this simple but powerful word. **"Nevertheless."**

"Thy Word is true from the beginning: and every one of thy righteous judgments endureth forever."
—Psalm 119:160

Day 62

We See Through a Glass Darkly

Key Scripture: **1 Corinthians 13:12-13**

The more I walk with the Lord and study His Word the more examples I see where we see through a glass darkly. The disciples had the same problem. Half the time they questioned Jesus' words, not knowing what He was talking about. Jesus patiently got through by explaining over and over through parables and simple explanations.

Today we live in times where we have all kinds of means at our disposal to understand God's Word and should know what every Biblical text means, but we don't. It's amazing to me that every time I read through passages I've read repeatedly, the Holy Spirit reveals things I've never seen before, simple things that blow me away. The Word of God is amazing and miraculous; it's quick and alive and written by the men anointed by the Holy Spirit. He's the best One to explain it. (1 Corinthians 2:9-10).

In our key passage (verse 13) is the key to revealing so many hidden truths in the Bible, love being greater than faith and hope. The Lord has never revealed to me anything when I was not seeking Him with all my heart. In some ways loving on Him like reading, praying and worshiping, bring us closer to God. Guess the best way to explain this is when I love on Him, He loves me back.

The Bible is, as you might say, a personal love letter to us. We can't live on someone else's revelations; we have to spend close time with God ourselves. We must put on our own armor personally, we can't wear somebody else's; it only fits them. The more we develop that personal relationship with Him, the clearer our spiritual eyes will become, seeing the light through the glass darkly.

All it takes is "Love," falling deeply in love with who Christ is and what He has done.

"But God commendeth His love toward us,
in that, while we were yet sinners, Christ died for us."

— Romans 5:8

Day 63

Managing Your Tongue

Key Scripture: 1 Samuel 14:24-52

Undoubtedly many of us have said out loud something that after it was said we realized how stupid it was and wished then we were a computer keyboard and could push the backspace bar to make it go away.

We, as parents, have said threatening words to our kids, knowing all along we could never follow through with the threat. Even we ourselves have been on the other side and received cutting statements and remarks from someone really getting under our skin.

Proverbs 15:4 says, "A wholesome tongue is a tree of life; but perverseness therein is a breach in the spirit." Our decisions, and especially our words, don't affect just us.

In 1 Samuel 14:24, Saul commanded the Israelites to eat no food before their attack on the Philistines or they would be cursed. He was in such a haste to win the battle he disregarded the welfare of his men, forcing them to battle while famished and weak.

Ultimately, Saul risked his son Jonathan's life, who knew nothing of the vow and he ate honey while he passed through the forest. Can you imagine how Saul felt when he realized his son may lose his life because of the oath, or how Jonathan felt knowing he may die over his father's emotional order?

We are human and our emotions can get the best of us. When faced with challenges we must always ask for God's guidance. Our answers may not come immediately, but that does not give us permission to make decisions that impact others based on our own knowledge and assumptions.

Saul made a terrible decision by not listening for God's guidance. He was oblivious to the pain he caused to those around him, even his own son. To avoid facing similar pain, let us remember to examine ourselves and humble our hearts when making decisions, and ask for God's grace to help us with our words and choices.

I pray God will give us all wise words and not impulsive remarks as we face hurdles in our lives, not forgetting the most important step to include God by asking for guidance in every decision.

"Thou will show me the path of life:
in thy presence is fullness of joy;
at thy right hand there are pleasures for evermore."

— Psalm 16:11

Day 64

Walking Forward in Faith

Key Scripture: **1 Samuel 7**

No one is perfectly brave at every moment of their lives. Fear is a real emotion we all feel from time to time. Fear can be particularly strong when we are facing an unknown future or when something unexpected happens in our lives. Being afraid often leads us to believe that the Lord has abandoned us in our current circumstances, leaving us weak and vulnerable.

In 1 Samuel 7, Samuel assembled the nation of Israel in a field in Mizpeh. While the people were gathered, an enemy nation, the Philistines, got word that the Israelites were gathered in an open field, completely vulnerable to attack.

When the Israelites heard the Philistines advancing toward them, "they were afraid." (1 Samuel 7:7). Even so, the Israelites begged Samuel to call out to God for them. (I Samuel 7:8). Armed with the prayers of Samuel, they moved forward to the battle against their enemy, even though they were afraid. (1 Samuel 7:11).

We are not promised a life without fear, but Jesus does promise to hear us when we pray (Psalm 34:17), and to be with us as we walk through life. (Hebrews 13:5). We can move forward in faith, in spite of any fear we may be facing, knowing we are never meant to face any battle alone.

The battles we face in life may not get easier, but our trust in the Lord will grow if we cry out to God and walk forward in faith.

"There is no fear in love;
but perfect love casteth out fear:
because fear hath torment.
He that feareth is not made perfect in love."

— 1 John 4:18

Day 65

Overnight Success Requires a Long Road Traveled

Key Scripture: **1 Samuel 17:1-17**

David was not an "overnight success." The young shepherd boy laid the groundwork for his victory against Goliath long before the showdown that made him a legend. In 1 Samuel 17:15, we see that David was a shepherd, tending the flock. Not a very heroic position, and the assignment was mostly unremarkable. His responsibilities required him to fend off bear and lion attacks, and with God's help he was able to defend the sheep. (1 Samuel 17:34-36).

Following God's direction in the not so glamorous moments is what prepared him for the bigger challenges. Over time, David grew to trust God's help so completely that he didn't hesitate to believe that God would give him victory over Goliath as well. (1 Samuel 17:36-37).

How often do we face situations we consider too trivial for God to help with? Whether it's our self-sufficiency or our busyness, too often we call on God only when a challenge is too big for us to handle ourselves; our perspective shifts by inviting God to be involved with the details of our lives.

Everyday obstacles become opportunities to see Him work. By experiencing God's provision and protection in the small things, we learn to trust Him in everything. Then when we face overwhelming trials, God's past faithfulness can secure our hope in His present promises.

If you are facing a major challenge today, what's keeping you from praising God for his past provision and trust Him to come through again?

"I can do all things through Christ which strengtheneth me."
— Philippians 4:13

Day 66

Does God Reward Revenge?

Key Scriptures: **1 Samuel 25:23-44; Romans 12:19; Deuteronomy 32:35**

Have you ever wanted to take matters into your own hands, and even plotted revenge, when you have been mistreated? In 1 Samuel 25, David found himself in this position. Nabal threw insults at David. David sent his servants to ask Nabal for whatever he could find to give him, since he had protected Nabal's shepherds. Furious, David gathered 400 armed men to kill Nabal and everyone under his authority.

We're a lot like David. Our natural instinct is to take matters in our own hands when we feel we've been wronged, instead of doing the right thing, taking the matter to God. Nabal's wife, Abigail, was aware of David's plan. Behind the scenes, Abigail had already prepared all the provisions they could spare to set out and meet David, warding off his attack.

At their unexpected meeting, David graciously said to Abigail, *"blessed be thy advice, and blessed be thou, which hast kept me this day from coming to shed blood, and from avenging myself with mine own hand."* (1 Samuel 25:33).

Shortly after, the Lord struck Nabal and he died. David thanked God for bringing him justice and keeping him from sin. Then David took Abigail as his wife.

Something we should always remember; when we seek to hurt others in an effort to get revenge, the only one we actually hurt is ourselves. God is constantly at work on our behalf. Like Abigail, working behind the scenes, God does the same thing in our lives.

When we choose to take things in our own hands, we ultimately give up blessings from God, leaving us unaware of what He had for us. We're trading short term satisfaction, for long term good.

Instead of seeking revenge, let's determine in our hearts that we'll forgive and trust that God, in His timing, will set things right.

"Say not, I will do so to him as he hath done to me;

I will render to the man according to his work."

— Proverbs 24:29

Day 67

Deceitfulness Leads to Death

Key Scripture: **Esther Chapters 7- 8**

This morning as I finished reading the book of Esther, I could not help my mind from thinking how terrible the act of deceitfulness really is. Not only is it terrible, but we see it in the hearts and lives of so many people today. In our passage we find that Haman, a man trusted by the king, had a bitter and deceitful heart against the Jews and especially Mordecai.

The decree that Haman deceived the king into backing him was targeted against God's people to be killed, even the king's own wife. Through the story we see that Haman's deceitful heart caught up with him and he was hanged in the very gallows he had prepared for Mordecai.

People today don't realize how bad and destructive deceitfulness is. Every sin committed starts with deceit. From the beginning when Satan was cast from Heaven, then to the fall of man, deceit has been prevalent. Even today we find those trying to destroy others in order to cover their own sin. They try to misuse the power of God's grace by implying they can do and say anything they want because they call themselves a Christian, and the grace of God will cover their sin. Grace certainly is not used this way.

I would humbly ask that we all examine our intent concerning God's grace. Grace is real and there for each of us as we seek God's favor and forgiveness, bringing us back into fellowship with Him.

In our story, we see that Haman's sin of deceit was revealed and that the king dealt harshly because of that sin. He lost his life. But, what will it take for those who have committed acts of deceitfulness to turn their lives around? Will it result in death or cause you to turn your life over to God's mercy and grace, asking through repentance and trust in God Almighty for forgiveness rather than the sentence of death? People don't realize that God will deal with sin, because He will not always strive with man, especially when deceit is committed against His children.

"He that worketh deceit shall not dwell within my house:
he that telleth lies shall not tarry in my sight."

— Psalm 101:7

"Deliver my soul, O LORD, from lying lips, and from a deceitful tongue."

— Psalm 120:2

Day 68

Our God Can Turn Curses into Blessings

Key Scripture: Nehemiah 13:2

God has many characteristics that for me is hard to fully understand and wrap my head around. He is an amazing God and one of these characteristics that is beyond my comprehension is the way He redeems what is lost or broken. When something in our house gets damaged or broken, most of us toss it out.

Yet, God takes what is broken in our world and in our hearts and weaves His beauty into it. This morning in my reading in Nehemiah there was a phrase that jumped off the pages; in Chapter 13:2, God said this, *"But our God turned the curse into a blessing."*

Looking into this, I found that the backstory of this passage was found in Numbers 22-24. There was a king named Balak who reigned next to the land where the children of Israel lived. He felt so threatened by the obvious blessing that was on the people of God, he hired a prophet named Balaam to place a curse on God's people in exchange for a great financial reward.

Balaam asked God if he could place a curse on His people and God answered, "No." Balak persisted and Balaam agreed to meet with Balak under the condition he would only say what God told him to say.

During the meeting Balak asked again if he would curse Israel. Each time he asked, Balaam would put a blessing on Israel. This infuriated Balak, but the blessings continued to come. Three times God turned the curse into a blessing.

See what God does? No weapon formed against us shall prosper. For every curse, He's the cure. His love and devotion to us as His people is to turn curses, (what is broken in our lives), into a blessing.

So next time you face a difficult decision such as a need to seek medical treatment for some illness, or any circumstance that may cause you to feel like you've been cursed, remember this; God turns curses into blessings.

Remember His redeeming character. When we become overwhelmed by our surroundings, we can call on God, and believe He will turn our curses into blessings.

"Every good gift and every perfect gift is from above,
and cometh down from the Father of lights,
with whom there is no variableness,
neither shadow of turning."

— James 1:17

Day 69

Never Let Failure Determine Who You Are

Key Scripture: **Isaiah 14:2**

If we're honest, no one wants to be associated with the word "failure." Remember the days when you got a test paper back and on the upper right corner was the big red letter "F"? Whether we have control over our success or not, the pain of failure is certainly hard to swallow.

The results of failing may take a long time and maybe never overcome. But, failure does not keep us from reaching our potential. Though the enemy wants us to believe we are a failure, one thing we must remember; just because we fail, we are not failures.

Let's ask ourselves, who defines who we are? God has much to say in the matter. Take a look at just a few instances from His Word:

- Psalm 139:14 - Fearfully and wonderfully made.

- 2 Corinthians 5:17 - A new creation.

- Romans 8:1 - Accepted.

- 1 John 1:9 - Forgiven.

- Colossians 3:12 - Holy and Beloved.

If you're currently dealing with feelings of failure, these words may not be a reality in your life.

As a Christian we are supposed to let the truth of God define who we are, but are we doing that? We all have good days, at home, at work, or our marriage, where everything just seems to click. Then there are days when nothing on earth goes right and you wonder why you were even born. "Who defined us then?" People, our past, or success/failure?

Our failure is never more powerful than our God. This is what should define who we are.

God can take our mess-ups and turn them completely around and make them work for our good and for His glory. The key is that we must believe what He says completely and not miss out on seeing Him work in and through us. Our failure has no footstool in God's hand basket. No matter how great our failures are, they can never redirect God's plans for each of us. (Isaiah 14:27).

If failure causes you to drift away, stand firm on God's truth; He has the power to redirect your plans and make His plans yours. Nothing we could do will keep us from the presence of God and nothing we have done or will do can remove His hand on our life by erasing the potential He sees in us.

"For we are His workmanship, created in Christ Jesus unto good works, which God hath before ordained that we should walk in them."

— Ephesians 2:10

Day 70

What Do You Do
When Your Check Engine Light Suddenly Comes On?

Key Scripture: **Proverbs 4:23**

Other things in life may be as equally unnerving to us but, when our check engine light on our dashboard comes on, it certainly takes the cake. One simple, small lightbulb has the potential to ruin our whole day.

This is nerve-wracking, and causes multiple unanswered questions. Will we even make it there? What will this cost? Ignoring the issue could cause even more damage, so the easiest thing to do is bite the bullet and go to the mechanic.

Our heart is the like the engine in our car—the driving force behind our thoughts, words, and actions. Impure thoughts, harsh words, and selfish actions are like the check engine light on the dashboard of our lives.

As our key scripture written by King Solomon says in Proverbs 4:23; *"Keep thy heart with all diligence; for out of it are the issues of life."* The way you live is determined by the condition of your heart.

That's why it is important for us to memorize the Word of God. Psalm 119:11 says, *"Thy Word have I hid in my heart, that I might not sin against thee."* By hiding God's Word in your heart you're giving yourself a "truth tune up" to the engine that drives your whole life.

"My son, give Me thine heart, and let thine eyes observe My ways."
— Proverbs 23:26

Day 71

We Sometimes Make this Simple Truth Hard

Key Scripture: **John 5:24**

Sometimes our thoughts on how our lives will unfold does not always turn out the way we planned. Life offers us disappointments and we must search to find where the mystery piece of our puzzle will fit.

God's timing and plan does not always align with ours, so we find ourselves somewhat defeated and unsure of what God is doing in our life. We must realize that what the world says our lives should look like is rarely what God has in His mind.

In John Chapter 5, Jesus healed a man who had been disabled for almost four decades. The Jewish leaders tried to condemn Jesus for healing the man on the Sabbath. Instead of celebrating the miracle of healing, they objected to the miracle because of what day of the week it was done.

It's easy for us to see that the leaders were wrong and wonder how they couldn't see what Jesus did was miraculous. We could even say that we'd never react the way they did, but the truth is we often lose sight of what is important.

Do we not often act in some ways as the Jewish leaders did by getting all caught up in how we think or want Jesus to act? In doing so we lose sight of what God has done for us. We simply miss out on what Jesus has for us because we fail to see His plans; all we can see is the way we think things should be.

Jesus wants us to each experience His gift of salvation, rewarding us an eternal home in Heaven. By wanting to do things our way and not Gods, we must be warned; if we try to make things too hard, we'll miss the simple truths God offers. He always does what He says He'll do; therefore, we can place our hope and trust in Him to meet our every need.

"And ye shall know the truth, and the truth shall make you free."

— John 8:32

Can You See What Causes Distractions In Your Life?

Key Scriptures: **Hosea 9**

Looking back at the nation of Israel, we see that they managed to fall from God's grace and favor to God's wrath. Remember at Mount Sinai, they promised God they would do everything He asked and follow His commandments (Exodus 19:5-8). During their journey, the Israelite men became distracted by Moabite women. They accepted these women along with the worship of their gods, the Baalpeor, thus breaking their promise to God. (Numbers 25:1-3).

Much like the Israelites, we allow our own self-doubt, along with the distractions we face, to be enticed to sin by: maybe a promise of a good time, harmless fun, or persuaded to do something, thinking no one will ever know. Over time, continual sin causes us to lose focus on God, the same way Israel was distracted. We fall into a trap and before long we are doing and saying things we promised never to do.

God describes His desire for His chosen people in Hosea 9:10, "*I found Israel, like grapes in the wilderness; I saw your fathers, as the firstfruits in the fig tree.*" The children of Israel were special to God, despite their ungrateful spirit, he always accepted them back into His care. (Hosea 14:4).

God's grace was abounding then just as it is today. God is a loving, compassionate and forgiving God, and does not change. If you have been distracted and swayed from God, be assured that His arms are open wide, welcoming you back into His care. He wants us to refocus our attention on Him today and take that first step by asking God's forgiveness and surrendering our life to His control.

God extends His grace to each of us today. Are there any distractions you need to remove from your life and ask forgiveness for? Put these distractions behind you and refocus on living in God's will for you.

"And all things, whatsoever ye shall ask in prayer, believing, ye shall receive."
— Matthew 21:22

Day 73

God Walks with Us Through the Fire

Key Scripture: **Isaiah 43:2**

No one likes going through trials and conflicts in their life, but the truth is we all do. Perhaps we are pressured because of deadlines, or maybe a relationship is crumbling, and nothing you do seems to work. Regardless of the circumstances you face, the intense heat is turned up.

Daniel had three friends who experienced the heat turned on them; both figuratively and literally. (Daniel 3).

When these three men would not bow and worship a statue of King Nebuchadnezzar, the king had his men cast them into the furnace and turned it up seven times hotter than normal. Now the heat was literally turned on, but God walked with them through it. In Daniel 3:24-25 the scripture says,

"Then Nebuchadnezzar the king was astonished, and rose up in haste, and spake, and said unto his counsellors, "Did not we cast three men bound into the midst of the fire? They answered and said unto the king, True, O king. He answered and said, Lo, I see four men loose, walking in the midst of the fire, and they have no hurt; and the form of the fourth is like the Son of God."

It was Jesus, the only Son of God, walking through the fire with them.

Friends, He will walk through our fires with us also. Jesus tells us in Matthew 28:20b, "... *lo, I am with you always, even unto the end of the world.*"

The Bible says we will never be alone; God will always be there for us. (Isaiah 43:2, our key passage). Scripture does not say if we pass through the waters; it says when we pass through the waters. We will experience troubles.

I would like to draw your attention to the furnace, as the king stated, he saw four men walking about. They removed the three men that were cast into the fire; where was the fourth man that had the form like the Son of God? Could it possibly be that the Son of God is still in the fire, waiting for each of us when we are cast into the furnace ourselves? In our times of need, He promised He will always be there, never leaving us to walk through the fire alone.

*"The LORD also will be a refuge for the oppressed,
a refuge in times of trouble."*

— Psalm 9:9

Day 74

A True "But God" Story

Key Scripture; **Romans 5:8**

As a young boy I loved sports, but because of my living situation I couldn't play organized ball. My dad was not interested in me playing and my mother couldn't help me get to practice or games. One day on the school bus some of the guys were talking about their baseball team and they spiked my interest. I listened to their stories and was really jealous and saddened that there was no way possible that I could be a part of an organized team. I tried to settle in my mind that this is the way it must be.

One day one of the guys asked me to come to church with him and somehow things worked out so I could. There was a club of boys in the church that gathered at night during church called the RAs. I went that night with him, not knowing how God was at work in my life. The teacher and his wife were extremely eager to reach out to those in their class.

After a while the teacher started a conversation with me about their baseball team and asked if I would like to play. I explained to him my situation about no transportation and told him it was not possible. He decided to visit my home the next day and ask my parents if he came to pick me up, would they consent to letting me play. They agreed.

I lived about twenty miles from him and at the time I was grateful, but did not realize the sacrifice this man made in order for me to be part of this team. Seeing him being a strong Christian man and willing to do all he did for me allowed me to witness first-hand the real love of God.

It wasn't until the age of sixteen that I gave my heart to Christ and this key verse became a reality in my heart. *"But God commendeth His love toward us, in that, while we were yet sinners, Christ died for us."* (Romans 5:8.)

This coach influenced my life and showed me that I too must be willing to sacrifice myself that others may see the love of God through me. God certainly is a good and gracious God.

Now I ask that God will complete my "But God" story and give me a compassionate heart to live sacrificially, serving Him by being an example to others, like my willing coach was to me.

"As every man hath received the gift,
even so minister the same one to another,
as good stewards of the manifold grace of God."

— 1 Peter 4:10

Day 75

Do You Feel You Have Gone too Far?

Key Scripture: **Hosea 7**

Sometimes as a Christian we commit sin, and at this point we remove ourselves from the fellowship we have with our Father. We may feel that because of the sin it may be too hard to return to God; or, we may be enjoying the sin we are living in. Like Ephraim, in Hosea 7:10-11, we experience the consequences of our sin, but we refuse to return to God because of our pride.

We like our plans, so we assume we can manage our consequences. By returning to God we would have to submit to His plan for our lives. On the other hand, we may feel desperate to return to God, but we're afraid we have gone too far, thinking that the sin is too big for God to forgive. That mentality and thinking in itself is a sin and holds no water with God.

In Hosea 7:13, we see that God longs to redeem Ephraim, just as He longs to redeem any child of His. There is no sin too big for Jesus to forgive, nor is there any place too far that His arm will not reach, to bring you back into fellowship.

As in an earlier chapter, God told Hosea to go find Gomer, his wife, who had run away into sin again and love her again. This is a story of God's love. God will pursue us; He longs for a child in sin to return to Him. He will forgive you, heal you, and show you His amazing plan for your life. You cannot out-sin the grace of God. All you need to do is humble yourself, return to Him, and allow your change of heart to lead you to a change of behavior.

Are you willing to face the consequences of the sin you're living in? Is pride stopping you from returning to God? He knows everything you have done; hiding is not an option; He'll pursue you and bring His child home.

"If my people, which are called by my name, shall humble themselves,
and pray, and seek my face, and turn from their wicked ways;
then will I hear from heaven,
and will forgive their sin,
and will heal their land."

— 2 Chronicles 7:14

Day 76

Do We Know What God Wants from Us?

Key Scripture: **Hosea 6**

Many of us have had jobs where at the time you're hired, you are issued an employee handbook that describes what you can and cannot do, as well as a job description. When we were in school we simply asked our teacher or maybe read the student code of conduct.

Understanding what God wants for us works the same; if we want to know what God wants for our lives, we pray and read His Word, because every word was inspired by God to help us know Him and His desire for our lives.

Many seek guidance through unbiblical sources and that only sets you up for failure. We must seek the Biblical authority for our lives and this will only happen when we recognize God's authority in our lives. In Hosea 6:3, the prophet tells God's people to "acknowledge the Lord." Properly understanding our role is the key to having a healthy relationship with God.

God is God, and we are Not!

Since the beginning of time nothing has changed. What God wants for us is to have a healthy and strong relationship with Him. To accomplish this, we must determine within our hearts to do the right things the right way. (Hosea 6:6). If we desire a thriving relationship with God, it's imperative we spend quality time together with Him.

To trust someone, we must get to know them well, and our obedience to someone comes from trusting that they will lead you in the right path. The same is true with God. When we find ourselves praying and reading His Word, we'll find ourselves submitting to His desires, not because we have to, but because we want to.

Let nothing stand in your way of having a consistent relationship of love with God.

"And be not conformed to this world;
but be ye transformed by the renewing of your mind,
that ye may prove what is that good,
and acceptable, and perfect will of God."

— Romans 12:2

Day 77

Never Forget How You Got to Where You Are

Key Scripture: **Deuteronomy 6:10-12**

"And it shall be, when the LORD thy God shall have brought thee into the land which He sware unto thy fathers, to Abraham, to Isaac, and to Jacob, to give thee great and goodly cities, which thou buildedst not, And houses full of all good things, which thou filledst not, and wells digged, which thou diggedst not, vineyards and olive trees, which thou plantedst not; when thou shall have eaten and be full; Then beware lest thou forget the LORD, which brought thee forth out of the land of Egypt, from the house of bondage."

Great things are happening, and you are in a promised place. Increase is coming and you may even now in your own life say that it's already here. God has been good to you. But remember this; once you have eaten and are full, don't forget God.

The child of God that remembers God, remembers where God brought him from. It was the Lord that kept you going when you needed

Him. It was the Lord who gave so you could pay a bill just in time. It was Him who gave you wisdom. He gave you what was needed to keep things together while you learned how to become a faithful, obedient, fervent prayer warrior, along with a heart of compassion to be the child of God you are today. It was and has been God's goodness all along.

As God blesses you more and more, walk in the principles of humility and wisdom more and more. Keep Christ as who you obey and serve. The obedient Christian that remembers God is the Christian that the Lord will continue to bless.

Our church is going through a transition period because of blessings from God. The Lord is allowing us to go through a period of growth. Let's please not forget what God has brought us through and remember that collectively we are a blessed people. May we give all the honor and glory to God.

"Remember the former things of old: for I am God, and there is none else; I am God, and there is none like me."

— Isaiah 46:9

Your Past is Behind You; Leave it There

Key Scripture: **Psalm 103:12**

A statement made by Corrie ten Boom, a great missionary woman, has deep meaning with profound truth. She said; "When we confess our sins, God casts them into the deepest ocean, gone forever. He then posts a 'no fishing' sign"

Now when we sin, it becomes needful that we ask God for forgiveness. God has a big eraser, and forgives and forgets our sins. In Jeremiah 31:34, God says; "...*I will forgive their iniquity, and I will remember their sin no more.*"

As we run our race in life, we should not look back, as Paul wrote in Philippians 3:13:

> "*Brethren, I count not myself to have apprehended: but this one thing I do, forgetting those things which are behind, and reaching forth unto those things which are before.*"

Having the assurance that your sins are forgiven, never again carrying the burden and guilt of iniquity, is what God desires for each of us, while living a life resting with our Lord and Savior. God wants us to live free from the bondage of sin. He offers forgiveness and promises your sin will be forgotten.

Jesus warned His disciples to remember Lot's wife in Luke 17:32; "*Remember Lot's wife.*" God delivered them from Sodom and Gomorrah, and they were told not to look back. Lot's wife couldn't leave things behind, and when the judgment of God came upon the city, she looked back, resulting in her becoming a pillar of salt.

How often do we look back on our past sins? We must learn that old sins will cripple us if we keep bringing them up. They will do nothing but drag us down if we allow them. Leave your past behind you. Live in the present, and move forward toward the future.

"Leave it there, leave it there,

Take your burdens to the Lord and leave them there."

"And Jesus said unto him,
No man, having put his hand to the plough, and looking back,
is fit for the kingdom of God."

— Luke 9:62

When We Can Finally Say, "Enough Is Enough"

Key Scripture: **Judges 2:1-3**

Enough is enough; a statement we finally make when we reach the end of our rope. When can we say we want God's best more than we want the temporary pleasures living outside His will? We never like to acknowledge sin in our life; we'd rather keep it hidden, but eventually we must confront it, or live a miserable, bitter life, consumed with the effects of living outside of God's will.

Sin, unrepentant and unconfessed leads to a dangerous cycle of worldly desires, defiance and destruction, totally sending us on a path against God's instructions. This is what the enemy had in mind all along as seen in John 10:10, *"to steal, kill and destroy."* Sin appeals and allures to our flesh, but we must understand that it eventually leads to an ending of suffering and weeping.

In our key passage we find Israel also had the full promise of God, yet because of sin, they faced the wrath and consequences of their sin. God had remained faithful and brought them out of captivity, to the land promised to their forefathers, only to see their unfaithfulness and defiance to Him. Through their disobedience, they now faced the inevitable: God removing His presence and protection from them. Now enslaved to the very idols they thought would satisfy their needed desires, their sin ended in despair and weeping.

The story doesn't end in gloom; God declares in this passage that the established covenant would never be broken. There are consequences to sin, but God remains faithful to His promise and leaves His chosen people hope. Sadly, the Israelites failed to show any repentance that marked a change of action nor a change of heart, so they experienced destruction.

Sin starts with misplaced desires. The Old Testament scripture and accounts of Israel should remind us that we must make a choice today; Are we entertaining with our heart and lives any misplaced desires apart from the will of God? Are we carefully asking that our hearts be cleansed and made pure, resulting in following God's desired plan and will?

This is where we must say that "enough is enough," and stop sin in its tracks, humbly bowing our heads, surrendering our hearts to a Holy God and say, "I only want Your heart O Lord, and I surrender my desires to You, prayerfully asking that You remove any desire within me that could lead to defiance, disobedience and destruction."

Is there any area of sin in your life that you know God wants you to deal with, but you keep trying to ignore it?

"Search me, O God, and know my heart: try me, and know my thoughts: And see if there be any wicked way in me, and lead me in the way everlasting."

— Psalm 139:23-24

Day 80

Old Hymns Inspire Me, "He Leadeth Me"

Key Scripture: **Matthew 10:39; Proverbs 3:5-6**

Sometimes God directs us to make a change in our direction, something new. When He does this, He's asking us to let go of something else; and this at times may be very difficult. That something or someone may have been a good gift; maybe a connection or commitment that gave us peace in a time we needed it most; a time of uncertainty, or possibly a time when healing was needed.

It's tough to imagine we could willingly let go of something that has given us comfort, but trusting God's judgment is what is now His plan. We can't see His plan, but assuredly whatever new connection or commitment He is leading us to will certainly be for our best interest.

If we are going to allow God to lead us on a new journey, we must submit to His choosing our companions, the people He knows that will bring about our greatest good and His glory. We can't possibly know today what He'll ask us to leave behind tomorrow, but one thing we can always count on is this: He will always be with us every step of the way. He is always preparing our way, leading our way, making it easy for us to follow.

Staying sensitive to His Spirit, we'll know when He is nudging us to loosen our grip on things in our life He wants to change. He never promised that letting go would be easy, but the promise He does give is that He'll be with us if we submit to His leading.

In the end we will see that we have learned through the process that we'll grow closer to Him and hold fast to His leading. The question is: Will we trust that the new connection or commitment He's calling us into is far greater than what He's asking us to give up? Will we let Him do what He does best, leading us to become more and more like Christ, even when we don't understand His ways? If we can answer "yes," then we'll find great comfort in knowing that we are always led by His loving hand.

He leadeth me: O blessed thought!
O words with heavenly comfort fraught!
Whate'er I do, where'er I be,
Still 'tis His hand that leadeth me.

"Thou wilt shew me the path of life;
in thy presence is fullness of joy;
at thy right hand there are pleasures for evermore."

— Psalm 16:11

Day 81

Burdens are Lifted at Calvary

Key Scripture: **Matthew 11:28-29**

This passage of God's Word is among one of my favorite scriptures in the entire Bible. God shows us His unwavering love and a heart of compassion. Oh, that everyone who believes in Christ as their Savior should etch these phrases in their hearts and minds. Repeat them over and over until they become a part of your life as John 3:16. God's Word is there to pull us from fear, anxiety and worry, into peace and rest in Christ.

We spend time bringing our burdens to mind like; burdens of financial, physical, emotional, weariness, grief or guilt; all are yokes that weigh upon us as if we were a working ox. Everyone labors under some load of burdens, and at times they seem unbearably heavy, and other times, not at all.

God does not intend us to go this way through life; He desires that we give our heavy burdens up and find rest for our souls. This means whenever we are heavily burdened, we never have to carry them alone. Someone much stronger than we are will never be broken by our load.

As you name your burdens, close your eyes and imagine these words by Christ, "Come to me," and there is Christ standing before you with open outstretched arms accepting your heavy burden unconditionally. As we give this load to Him, we will say as He did:

"Come unto me all who are weary and heavy laden and I will give you rest. For my yoke is easy and my burden is light."

"And it shall come to pass in that day,
that his burden shall be taken away from off thy shoulder,
and his yoke from off thy neck,
and the yoke shall be destroyed because of the anointing."

— Isaiah 10:27

Day 82

Can He Still Feel the Nails?

Key Scripture: **Matthew 27:35**

Have you ever thought about the possibility that each time we commit a sin Jesus could still feel the pain? I Peter 2:24 says *"by His stripes ye are healed."*

In Isaiah 53:5, the prophet says:

"But He was wounded for our transgressions, He was bruised for our iniquities: the chastisement of our peace was upon Him; and with His stripes we are healed."

This is a thoughtful question and I believe only you can answer it. As for me, whenever I read about the account of the crucifixion, my heart becomes so heavy, thinking that my Savior endured this suffering for me. Humbling, but it also helps me to think about my daily actions. Could Christ feel the pain when I commit a sinful act?

I have my own thoughts about this question, as well as many others. Remember in the Old Testament, God commanded that the sacrificial lamb was brought to the altar once a year to reconcile His people to himself. (Leviticus16:34).

What makes the sacrifice of Jesus significant is that He rose from the dead, the animals did not. Jesus' blood was shed once, never again needed to be slain as the sacrificial lambs were; once for "All." (Hebrews 7:27; Romans 6:8-10).

Christ definitely never has to go through this again, but thinking about what He went through should deter any desire to commit a willful sin. With a grateful heart, filled with love and respect, we should always put Him first and foremost in our thoughts and actions.

Surely if we do sin, we know that fellowship should be restored, and God desires that we walk close to Him with a clean heart. A remorseful attitude toward any known sin has to be resolved to regain that fellowship.

To answer our question, does He still feel pain when we sin? I would say that He surely feels hurt when we do, because we were made for Him and for His pleasure. There's a song written about this subject, "Can He Still Feel The Nails?" one worth listening to.

"But God commendeth His love toward us, in that, while we were yet sinners, Christ died for us."

— Romans 5:8

Day 83

Sunlight Brings Happiness; Sonlight Brings Rest

Key Scripture: **Isaiah 55:13**

Some people have a natural instinct as to where they can plant fruit, flower and vegetable plants. I think some simply buy plants to see how long it takes for them to die and others truly pay close attention how and where, along with the care needed to best care for each plant they place into the soil or pots. To get the best results for each plant, they must be planted according to the directions given. Some need direct sunlight, others partial and even some more shade, but all need to be nurtured.

In our key verse, the prophet says that instead of briers the myrtle tree will grow. Briers in the scripture most often refer in the life of a Christian as sin or something evil or bad. Isaiah said they will be replaced with myrtle, a budding, beautiful flower budding tree.

Why? Because careful direction was taken to get rid of the briers, by giving attention to the reason why the briers are growing. Turning from sin to Jesus Christ and His perfect will for your life will certainly clean a sinful heart. Christ will give you a tender heart, leaving no room for the evil briers of sin to enter.

As the briers are replaced with myrtle trees in your life, seek the abundant life in Christ, budding, blooming and living for the glory of Jesus Christ. Nurture that life with the Word of God, prayerfully giving your days, living no longer for sin, but flourishing, following the Professional Gardener's carefully planned path for your future, living for Him.

The more Sonlight given to the myrtle, the stronger the root system, and it will choke out any brier, giving life free to serve as a beautiful blooming plant nurtured by the Master Gardener. The Psalmist said that pain comes in the night, but joy comes in the morning. As a final result, the blooms that follow will show forth the power of life in the Son.

I pray that the briers of your life will be removed, giving room for the myrtle, the fullness of Christ and His abundant life for any that will follow His directions.

"Come unto me, all ye that labour and are heavy laden,
and I will give you rest.
Take my yoke upon you, and learn of me;
for I am meek and lowly in heart;
and ye shall find rest unto your souls.
For my yoke is easy, and my burden is light."

— Matthew 11:28-30

Day 84

Love Comes Calling

Key Scripture: **Mark 10:49**

I was introduced to a song carrying this title by a dear brother in Christ a few years ago. The song and the words have been a blessing since, and the thought behind this post comes from you, Brother Lee. I believe you're the real deal, a humble man of God with sincere convictions for Jesus Christ. Stay faithful brother.

The word "calling" scares many people because they think it refers to a special person who is paid to do a certain ministry. The definition of this word in one resource states that calling is a "profession or occupation," but another makes it real to me and says it is "a strong urge toward a particular way of life or career."

As a Christian, I would believe the latter would be the one we'd most likely rely upon as what a "calling" would refer to. In the story of blind Bartimaeus, he sought the mercy of Jesus and when Christ got closer he was heard above the crowd. Jesus stopped and called him to come to him. The story ends as Jesus healed his blindness.

In our own walk with Christ, we are sometimes confused or maybe we doubt that God is "calling" us to do His will. We think we are not worthy, making excuses as to reasons why God would never call us.

There may be hardships and difficult circumstances to overcome, but throughout God's Word many ordinary individuals have been greatly used for God's glory. The biggest obstacle to fulfilling our call is we often misidentify what our call is; it's not at all what we think, not a particular job or title. Our first calling is to respond to Jesus and go to Him.

Like Bartimaeus, we are called to come close. Jesus then draws us near and calls us brothers and sisters (Matthew 12:50). He erases the barrier between our humanity and His divinity by calling us friends (John 15:15).

While our faith leads us to answer His calling to follow His will, our first and highest call is to simply listen to His love come calling, by coming near to Jesus Christ. By doing this, we can answer that voice to accept His call and follow His will.

"The LORD is nigh unto all them that call upon Him,
to all that call upon Him in truth."

— Psalm 145:18

Day 85

Running from God Brings Hardship; Running to God Always Gives Opportunity for Winning

Key Scripture: **Jonah 1:1-5**

Have you ever noticed the simplistic mind of a child? They are indeed precious and innocent. Like during a game of hide and seek, they will hide behind something and even though their entire body is exposed, their eyes are hidden, therefore they believe they cannot be seen.

As adults, we are in some ways like a little child. We ignore God when we realize that we are in danger of being exposed for something we have wrongfully done. We forget about the easy way out and choose to follow a path of misery, heartache and loneliness by running from the truth, instead of running to a loving, forgiving God.

We forget 1 John 1:9; it's too hard to face truth and accept the fact that we are human and will fail. God desires and longs for us to take that step of faith and seek His forgiveness and avoid the slow death of hate, bitterness and loneliness that consumes our sin-darkened heart.

Like Jonah, he boarded a ship heading the opposite direction from where God wanted him; risking his own health, along with others, as he ignored following God's command. Did he really

think God would ignore the sea; or did he think that he was invisible from God? Or maybe he just didn't care. How one can ignore the scripture is beyond me.

In Psalm 139:1-3; God says:

"O LORD, thou hast searched me, and known me. Thou knowest my downsitting and my uprising, thou understandest my thought afar off. Thou compassest my path and my lying down, and art aquainted with all my ways."

Hiding and running from God is not an option for a child of God.

Running from God always brings pain and misery for us as well as others. Most importantly, it denies God His glory that can be accomplished through being an obedient child of His. Always remember this one thing; running to God will always give you the opportunity to become a winner.

How can we expect our life to go in a different path that honors God if we continue to run from the truth and not ask Him for help?

"For as by one man's disobedience many were made sinners, so by the obedience of one shall many be made righteous."

— Romans 5:19

The Significance of the Napkin in the Tomb

Key Scripture: **John 20:7**

Why did Jesus fold the linen burial cloth after His resurrection? In John 20:7, the Bible tells us that the napkin which was placed over the face of Jesus was not thrown to the side like the grave clothes; it was neatly folded and placed separately from them. Simon Peter noticed this as he came into the tomb; the napkin was folded and lying to the side. You might think this was not significant, but it certainly was very important.

In order to understand the significance of the folded napkin, we need to understand a little about Hebrew tradition of that time. The folded napkin has to do with the Master and the Servant, and this was understood by every Jewish boy.

When the servant arranged the table for the master, he made sure it was as the master wanted it, perfect as he desired. The servant would then wait out of sight until the master was finished eating; never touching the table until he was absolutely sure the master was finished.

When the master was finished, he would rise, wipe his hands and his beard with the napkin, and then wad it up and throw it on the table. The servant would know it was permissible to clear the table as the wadded napkin meant, "I'm done."

On the other hand, if the master got up from the table and folded his napkin and laid it beside his plate, the servant would dare not touch the table because the folded napkin signified that, "I'm coming back!" This is a picture of the resurrection of Christ and we are indeed grateful, building our hope.

We await Christ's return in the air to bring those who have trusted Him as their personal Savior to Heaven. Please examine your heart and if there is any doubt about your relationship with Christ, surrender to Him and ask Him to come into your heart and save your soul. Tomorrow may be too late.

"For the Lord himself shall descend from heaven with a shout,
with the voice of the archangel, and with the trump of God:
and the dead in Christ will rise first:
Then we which are alive and remain shall be caught up together with them in the clouds,
to meet the Lord in the air: and so shall we ever be with the Lord."

— 1 Thessalonians 4:16-17

Day 87

As a Christian, We Have a Command to "Pray Without Ceasing"

Key Scripture: 1 Thessalonians 5:17

Praying without ceasing as commanded by God is a continuing act of releasing your cares into the care of God. In 1 Peter 5:7 we are to cast all our care on Him, for He cares for us. He is at our disposal around the clock in all places, and for all people.

As we are driving, walking, working, or even sitting watching people, we must learn to pay attention to our surroundings and understand these things will trigger a thought, or a tranquil prayer as your heart is opened up to God's hand working through you. We might see a pair of child's shoes on a porch; we can simply pray that God would bring that child up to serve and be used mightily for the Lord.

God will give us these one line prayers throughout the day for whatever enters our minds. Seeing a mother holding a child: "Lord, help this mother; give her the provisions needed to raise that child, strong and faithful in Your Word." Seeing a group of homeless people standing around a fire seeking warmth, you may ask: "Lord protect these homeless, encourage them and provide a warm place for them to stay."

The days are filled with endless opportunities to pray for others and situations you encounter. Let this sink in as we become a faithful prayer warrior, used unselfishly for God. There is no telling what God could do through you giving your time by lifting up others in prayer throughout each day.

Ask God to give you this burden. We have His tools, His promises, and His command to pray without ceasing. His hand will guide each prayer lifted up. God uses what we have for His glory; He used Moses, he carried a rod; He used David, carrying a sling, and he used a little boy carrying a small lunch to feed over 5,000 people.

God will place His hand upon you as you seek to pray without ceasing. To God be the glory. May God burden our hearts for others, open our eyes that we may see opportunities as He does, and faithfully do our part.

"I can do all things through Christ which strengtheneth me."
— Philippians 4:13

"And He spake a parable unto them to this end, that men ought always to pray, and not to faint."
— Luke 18:1

Day 88

The Word is Alive

Key Scripture: **Hebrews 4:12**

In this passage of Scripture, we see that God refers to His revelation in a general sense, meaning whatever way God chooses to illuminate the Word to us humans He will. The written Word of God is our primary exposure, and we learn that the Bible is alive and active; it is not only alive, but also works. The original Greek word translated here as "living" means "to have life" or "alive." The Word is made alive because God is a "Living God." (Hebrews 3:12). Jesus said, "… *The words that I speak unto you, they are spirit, and they are life."* (John 6:63).

Christians are made alive spiritually and eternally because we are born again, not of perishable seed, but of imperishable seed, through the living and enduring Word of God. (1 Peter 1:23). Believers enter God's eternal rest (receiving God's free gift of salvation by grace through faith alone and not of works) (Ephesians 2:8-9) through the life-giving power of the living Word of God.

A number of years back while in college, I was busy on a hot, steamy Saturday, passing out tracts and information regarding our church's upcoming revival. A dear old lady working in her yard stopped me as I was returning to my car, waving the information I had left in her screen door. She said, "Young man, I want you to know that I believe every word in this brochure you left." I didn't have much time to chat and told

her I would come back another time and we'd discuss them in depth.

A few weeks went by and while making visits on a Saturday, I found myself with no set appointment and remembered this elderly lady. I drove to her neighborhood, and seeing her sitting on her porch, I stopped. She remembered me, and we chatted a while and I started sharing Scriptures about salvation.

While reading her Romans 10:9-10, she jumped up and said, "I don't think my Bible says it like that." She hurried inside and returned with her old and very large family Bible pressing against her thin body. The book probably weighed 20-plus pounds.

This is when it gets good, and I first-hand saw God reveal to me that His Word is "Alive."

Mrs. Thompson sat her Bible on a table in front of me with the bounded end down and let it fall open. Tears filled my eyes and chill bumps ran up my spine as the large Bible fell open to the very same Scripture in Romans 10:9-10. Feeling the powerful presence of God at that very moment assured me that He was in charge of the moment. Within a few minutes, this dear lady accepted Jesus Christ as her personal Savior. God's Word is "Living and Alive" and no one could ever convince me any different. I pray you can feel the same about the "The Living Word of God."

"For whosoever shall call upon the name of the Lord shall be saved."

— Romans 10:13

Day 89

Will We Choose to Wear the Coat?

Key Scripture: **Isaiah 61:10**

This scripture in Isaiah has a powerful message and really and truly everyone needs to read, understand and examine their own heart as the picture of the redemptive, worshipful plan of God is revealed to them. I just finished reading this book and the Lord opened again my eyes to see and feel His Word richly bless my heart.

Growing up as a kid, I loved the fall time of the year for many reasons, but as a tradition, I usually got a new pair of shoes, and a new coat. We feel special when we get something new, but this has no comparison to the new wardrobe God has prepared for us. We may not fully understand what this means, but as a Christian, we are indeed, the best dressed people.

The taking off and putting on of clothes becomes a reality of positional truth. I am listing some references of scripture pertaining to this truth; (*Laying aside or taking off*); Romans 6:6-11; Ephesians 4:22; Philippians 3:12-13; Hebrews 12:1; 1 Peter 2:1. (*Put On*); Romans 12:1; 1 Corinthians 15:53; 2 Corinthians 6:7; Galatians 3:27; Ephesians 4:24; and 6:13; 1 Thessalonians 5:8; Revelation 19:14.

Remember the rebellious son in Luke 15? He came back home and immediately the father placed on him a robe. It marked the end of his sinful self and the surrender of his will. This symbolizes the clean new life in relationship with his father; once dead, and now alive. The placing of the robe allowed him to stand in righteousness, giving him the reputation to stand alongside his father. The father's robe was an outward sign of the heart transformed.

In reality, the robe has to be "put on" from the inside. We have to choose to put it on. By accepting from God the Father, His Sacrifice of His Son on the cross, we can choose to "put on" the robe provided by the Father. We receive the incredible benefits of sonship and new life.

To have that continuous relationship, we must choose to surrender daily, putting on Christ and laying aside sin, dying daily. Those choosing not to, will hide sin within and bow to the temptations of the enemy, living in broken fellowship with the Father.

Christian, it is your choice. What will you choose today? Will you stay in your sinful state or "put on" the robe of righteousness that God the Father has offered?

*"Finally, my brethren, be strong in the Lord,
and in the power of His might."*

— Ephesians 6:10

Day 90

Down in the Valley I Grow

Key Scripture: **Psalm 23:4a**

Unless you have been in the valley, it may be hard for you to understand this post. I myself would love to know what it's like to not live in the valley for a while. For more than 10 years now I have experienced difficult times in my Christian life. Guess you might say I expect to be in this state.

We will always find things in our life that make us feel tangled in a web, afraid and confused about what's going to happen next. Maybe a difficult relationship, discouragement, health difficulties or a fatal diagnosis, or just painstaking memories. These are things I call valleys.

Whenever we find ourselves in the valley, we search for some sort of rescue, a shelter; a Shepherd, the Lord. This Shepherd will always be with us no matter what. The valleys may bring out our fears, but they also bring us closer to the Shepherd. As our key passage states that as we walk through the valley, God is with us.

There are ways to get through our valleys:

- **Look to the Shepherd** — Always look to the Shepherd first, He promises never to leave nor forsake us.

- **Listen to the Shepherd** — His voice is His Word. In our darkest valley, the light of His Word gives us comfort. As we listen to Scripture we are comforted by His presence and promises.

- **Lean on the Shepherd** — Valleys make us weak, but He is our strength and our refuge. Sheep are usually classified as being weak, but that's alright, sheep need a Shepherd. Nothing we face is too hard for Him. We are not to lean on our own strength; but lean on God's instead. He will walk through the valley with us, and if we can't walk He'll carry us.

"For He is our God; and we are the people of His pasture, and the sheep of His hand."

— Psalm 95:7a

Day 91

How Should We Serve Our Lord?

Key Scripture: **Luke 17:5**

The disciples asked Jesus to increase their faith. Truth is they desired a large dose of Holy Spirit anointed faith that would make them super powerful disciples. Like the pastor says, "when you ask something, ask big."

Jesus surprised them as He told them that even small faith would be enough to accomplish great things. I wonder if Christ had a mustard seed in His hand, explaining the power of smallness in bringing others into His kingdom. He chose the little seeds like them to harvest the fields of new believers as their Lord and Savior.

As a servant of Christ, He encouraged and expected them to go beyond; to exceed expectations out of loyalty and love for their Master. Christ expected to further His kingdom.

What examples should we take from this? Not being the average Christian for sure, who attends church and does nothing at all. We should serve Christ faithfully with love, expecting no reward, having a thankful heart to our worthy Master who has done so much for us.

There is always something we can do; serving Christ is to glorify Him, lift Him up and magnify His kingdom by bringing others into the family of God. Can you think of some areas that you can glorify Christ? They are not hard to find, you just gotta have the want to.

"Only fear the LORD, and serve Him in truth with all your heart:
for consider how great things He hath done for you."

— 1 Samuel 12:24

Day 92

Overcoming Obstacles Requires Persistence

Key Scripture: **2 Corinthians 3:5; 4:8-18**

Have you ever noticed that people with the same teaching and training; one will become successful and the other will not? I believe the successful person found the secret of turning the obstacles into opportunities by being persistent.

We see this often in sports, one athlete makes it and another does not. Also, in business, two receiving the same training, one becomes rich and the other goes bankrupt.

The main factor is "persistence." People who achieve stay focused and never give up. They are never intimidated by obstacles; they use them as opportunities, gaining confidence. In our text, Paul wrote about the importance of persistence in a Christian's life. In 2nd Corinthians 4:8-9, Paul tells us if we get knocked down, we must get back up without excuses.

In verses 10-12 Paul sees himself as expendable so others could come to know Christ. We may not be called to be a martyr, but an important question we must ask ourselves; is our devotion to Christ greater than any other single thing in our life?

Our allegiance to Christ must supersede everything else in order for us to persevere in the Christian life. Christ is our strength.

In verses 13-15, Paul tells us that we are to believe what we say we believe. God's Word is spiritual truth and we are to stand firm on these truths. Paul believed his life had an eternal purpose, a life of helping others.

In verses 16-18 he encourages us to keep our eye on the goal, meaning those obstacles that seemed so huge are going to seem small and momentary as we look back some day. We are not to lose heart, for inwardly we are being renewed day by day because our light and momentary obstacles are achieving for us an eternal glory that outweighs all those obstacles.

Remember the song "Great Is Thy Faithfulness?" I love the phrase: "strength for today and bright hope for tomorrow." That's what Christ brings to our lives; not exemption from life's obstacles, but strength for today, and hope for the next.

"Therefore, my beloved brethren be ye steadfast, unmoveable,
always abounding in the work of the Lord,
forasmuch as ye know that your labour is not in vain in the Lord."

— 1 Corinthians 15:58

Day 93

Counterfeit Christians

Key Scripture: **2 Timothy 3:1-13**

I recently listened to a report about how our government trains employees who work specifically with counterfeit currency. They do not train a new employee by getting them familiar with the different counterfeit bills that are being distributed, but they train them by studying the real currency until they know everything about it. Then when they see a fake bill, immediately they can tell the difference.

In our churches today, we have to guard against Satanic attacks. The enemy is here with us to steal and kill our testimonies. We, as a born-again child of God, can learn a huge lesson from the ones that deal with counterfeit currency. We can become so familiar with true Christianity that when a counterfeit steps into our church, we will be able to distinguish between the real and the fake.

In our passage, Paul warns us that there are counterfeit Christians. A true Christian should indeed be able to spot them. They may look like normal religious people, but understand this: that's the problem, they are normal religious people (not Christians at all.)

Outwardly they look the part, they attend church, go through the motions but in reality, they are self-centered manipulators who take advantage of other people in the name of God; deceivers. They deny the power of God, concerning miracles, signs and wonders. They have no desire to be born again for fear of losing their freedom and they fear losing control of their own manipulative lives.

Being a Christian is a valuable position; the counterfeit Christians know this and what they are counterfeiting is highly valued. I pray that we as true Christians will realize this and see how valuable our relationship with Jesus Christ is, and will not be blinded by acts of selfishness by the hypocritical counterfeit Christians. Guard against them and learn to spot them immediately.

*"Be ye not unequally yoked together with unbelievers: f
or what fellowship hath righteousness with unrighteousness?
and what communion hath light with darkness?"*

— 2 Corinthians 6:14

Day 94

Focusing on the Wrong Direction Matters

Key Scripture: **Daniel 3:16-17**

Facing adverse circumstances day in and day out can cause us to focus on the negative possibilities in every direction; altogether leaving out the fact that God holds the power to change either my attitude or my circumstances. We may be facing trials like: a loved one whose health is failing, a breakup of a relationship or marriage, or financial difficulties. By dwelling on the negative, we fail to see God's possibilities in our circumstances. God will always be faithful, and that will never change.

In our key passage we read about the three Hebrew children who refused to follow the king to bow down and worship the golden image or be thrown into the fiery furnace. This would be a horrible death, yet, instead of keeping their eyes on the negative, they chose to keep their eyes on God.

To choose to do wrong even for a moment certainly does not please God. They faced death, but welcomed the power of God to deliver them. They stood firm on their convictions and trusted in God.

This story challenges me to consider the direction of my focus when things get difficult. Focusing on God's power seems to lighten the gloominess of my problems. Always remember that God has the power to save us from darkened paths and He will help us change the direction we are looking in order to change our perspective.

What problems are you facing today that have taken more of your attention than they deserve?

"In every thing give thanks; for this is the will of God in Christ Jesus concerning you."
— 1 Thessalonians 5:18

"I will lift up mine eyes unto the hills, from whence cometh my help."
— Psalm 121:1

Day 95

Our Desert is Blooming

Key Scripture: **Isaiah 35:1**

Churches need great leaders, those who take church seriously and sacrifice their time to see that church matters are following God's order. Pastors and staff meet faithfully to discuss the needs and assure those needs are carried out for the glory of God. Looking around different areas, we see many churches struggling to keep their doors open. It's sad but true.

Their attendance has fallen, causing financial needs to accelerate and the pastors and leaders are becoming discouraged. Many elderly members find it hard to attend on a regular basis. They try, but their bodies will not let them. Some of the original leaders and decision-makers are now gone on to be with the Lord. New, younger members are now given the opportunity to step up and take on the role as leaders.

I remember an old friend told me a story. Many years ago he worked in a desert town and one day the heavens opened up and flooded the area with a tremendous storm. Roads were washed out and the terrain was changed instantly. In two days, the desert was covered with little flowers; billions of seeds, lying dormant for months, now sprouted and bloomed. The desert was in full bloom.

Churches need to understand that as we remain faithful and sow the seeds of faith in various ways, God, in His plan, will bring about change. The rain of faith will come. Just as the desert bloomed overnight, churches seeking God's righteousness will flourish.

Right now, our church is experiencing the power and faithfulness of our Almighty God. Miracles that we usually see elsewhere are happening now in our midst. We must stay humble with a grateful heart for the goodness of God's love, mercy and grace. We must keep sowing seeds of faith and reap the blooms in our desert. God will remain faithful as we continue seeking His righteousness.

May we all stay faithful, sowing the seeds of faith and wait on God to water those seeds, seeing our desert blossom.

"Lord, lay some soul upon my heart, and love that soul through me; and may I ever do my part to win that soul for Thee."

"Set your affection on things above,
not on things on the earth."
— Colossians 3:2

Day 96

My Prayer is to Be More Like You, Lord

Key Scripture: **Galatians 3:27**

One of my biggest prayers is to be more Christ-like every day. You may ask; what is that like? In a nutshell, it is to show more grace to others; helping someone in need, having more patience with those you are around each day, being a demonstration of love to all. being sensitive to those who may be grieving, and most importantly, forgiving, even when it's hard.

Christ demonstrated His love and amazing grace when He was sacrificed on the cross, taking upon Himself our pain and suffering, that we could be free from the bondage of sin. During our time here on earth, we are called to be the hands and feet of Christ and the salt and light of the earth. (Matthew 5:13-16).

What could we do to show others Christ, and to be more like Him, and to glorify and further His kingdom? First, we can live our lives in ways that glorify Him. We can show others the fruit of the spirit within ourselves like: love, joy, peace, patience, kindness, generosity, faithfulness, gentleness, and self-control. (Galatians 5:22-23). Guided by the Holy Spirit, we are to share these gifts with others. My prayer for myself and others that are surrendered to being more Christ-like is that we live our lives reflecting 'Who' we live for.

This brings to mind the lyrics of the chorus of the song: "A Little Less of Me." Look it up.

"For even hereunto were ye called:
because Christ also suffered for us, leaving us an example,
that ye should follow His steps."

— 1 Peter 2:21

Day 97

This is the Day that the Lord Hath Made

Key Scripture: **Psalm 118:24**

The latter part of Psalm 118:24 says; *"we will rejoice and be glad in it."* I have, and I'm sure you have as well, heard this phrase and this entire verse over and over throughout our lives. But often, with some of the verses we hear frequently, they become so familiar to us we may miss the deeper meaning and context under which they are written.

We may question about the word "day" in this verse and ask exactly what does it refer to? Does it mean the general "every day" that God gives us, or is it referring to a specific day in history?

The author is writing about incredible adversity, not when times were good; but when they were extremely difficult. The situations were changing, yet the Psalmist cried out to God in anguish, being surrounded on all sides by the enemy. He felt pushed back and about to fall, yet in the midst of these huge struggles he started and ended this chapter with the same verse: *"O give thanks unto the LORD, for He is good, for His mercy endureth for ever."* Psalm 118:29.

True joy never depends on our circumstances. Learning to choose joy in hard times takes effort along with action on our behalf; it requires our heart to be set and focused on God. He is faithful to help so we can choose well.

We can be assured that in His grace, He has made every day, and for that gift itself we can "rejoice and be glad in it." No matter what we face, we can still believe in the goodness of God and His unwavering love. That's what carries us through our most difficult circumstances.

A song by the Perrys, "Walk Me Through," has a great message about bringing us through difficult circumstances.

"I have set the LORD always before me;
because He is at my right hand, I shall not be moved."

— Psalm 16:8

Day 98

What Happens When You Choose to Run from God?

Key Scripture: **Jonah 1:3**

God gives all Christians a unique mission along with a choice whether or not to fulfill that mission. God's mission for Jonah was to warn the people of Nineveh of the coming judgment. Jonah faced consequences for his decision, much the same you or I would if we try to run from God's will for our lives.

The Bible says in verse 4 that he boarded a ship to get away from following the plan of God and the Lord sent a great wind pushing it back; giving Jonah another chance to do the right thing. God loves each of us the same and will provide opposition to our wrong decisions, trying to encourage us to follow His right decisions.

When we run from God, innocent people around may get hurt in the process. Jonah's disobedience threatened the lives of those aboard the ship because of the great storm. Think about those close to you that could possibly suffer by you not following God's will for your life.

Jonah shows us that when you run from God, your life begins to spiral downward. Your disobedience will cost you financially, physically, and relationally.

Jonah tried running to Tarshish, instead of following God's path to Nineveh almost 2,000 miles in the opposite direction. Truth is, there is no place we can run to avoid God. He knows exactly where we are at all times. He's everywhere we are and knows where we should be.

He gives us choices because He wants us to willfully surrender to His will and follow Him voluntarily showing our love. He has our best interest at heart, why run the other way?

When running from God, Satan will always be there to provide a boat; trouble is, God still knows what's best. Learn to trust Him.

"But they that wait upon the LORD shall renew their strength;
they shall mount up with wings as eagles;
they shall run, and not be weary;
and they shall walk, and not faint."

— Isaiah 40:3

Day 99

Is Your Time Running Out?

Key Scripture: Isaiah 55:6

There is nothing more certain in my mind that Jesus is coming again. All the promises about His first coming were all precisely fulfilled. There are more promises about the second coming than there were about the first. The world is on notice and as every day passes we get closer and closer to the day Jesus will return as King of Kings.

As today's news events are unfolding around the world, many people are forced to ask questions and search the scriptures about the prophesies Jesus made about His return, looking for answers.

The significance of the scriptures for today is this; "Time is running out." It is an urgent matter for all; if we do not know the Lord as our personal Lord and Savior, we must humble ourselves before the Savior, the Lord Jesus Christ, and accept His gift of salvation.

Scripture says that no man knows when Jesus will come again, so we have to prepare ourselves to meet our Maker now, before time runs out. The events of the world are a huge wake-up call for us all. Please understand that time is "RUNNING OUT." Come to Christ today, delay no longer, seek ye the Lord while He may be found. One day it will be too late.

Lord, thank you for your gift of salvation. My heart is heavy because I know many right now are without the assurance of a Heavenly Home. Lord, I humbly pray that people would understand they are a sinner, and the only way to Heaven is to confess their sin to a Holy God and ask forgiveness, repent of their sin, and ask Jesus Christ to come into their heart and save them.

By doing this they will assure themselves a home in Heaven.

"And if I go and prepare a place for you,
I will come again, and receive you unto myself;
that where I am, there ye may be also."

— John 14:3

Day 100

We All Need a Clean Heart

Key Scripture; **Psalm 51:10-11**

David asked God to create a clean heart within him, one free from the lust and lies as a result of that lust. Not stopping there, David went on to ask the Lord to *"renew a right spirit within me."* David desired to love the Lord and His people.

David wanted to live in obedience to God; and love the things that God loved, honoring and glorifying Him in everything he did. He wanted these things and sought them only from God and not within himself. He needed God's power and presence to have his spirit renewed.

We can acknowledge that we don't always love God as we should, nor His people; we don't always follow Him with all our hearts, and we repeatedly miss the mark of holiness. God understands this and sees our grief by His mercy and grace. The Lord sees our repentant heart and quickly comes to restore fellowship with Him with the fire of the Holy Spirit.

In Matthew 3:11, John the Baptist is foretelling of the coming Lord and said of Jesus, *"He will baptize you with the Holy Spirit and fire."* This fire is sanctifying, cleansing, healing and renewing. Then we'll find the old ways of the flesh fading away, giving room only for the renewed life of the Spirit within us.

When we have the presence of God's Holy Spirit burning in our lives, we also experience His abundant joy as we walk in fellowship with Him.

To keep this fire burning, we must be an individual of light, willing to see our sin, confessing it to the Lord, and always allowing His mercy and grace to cleanse our heart, restoring us into His righteousness. Our spirits are renewed as God's presence is manifested in us and through us, giving us the assurance that our joy rests in Him and the promise that eternally we are His.

"Verily verily, I say unto you,
He that heareth My Word, and believeth on Him that sent me, hath everlasting life,
and shall not come into condemnation;
but is passed from death unto life."

— John 5:24

Day 101

Expect Great Things; Attempt Great Things

Key Scripture: **Philippians 1:20**

This statement can really make one wonder in many ways. Over 200 years ago a missionary wrote a sermon and this was his title. At the age of 21, William Carey answered God's call to the land of India. He was concerned about global missions and even though others tried to discourage him, he taught that Jesus' Great Commission applied to all Christians.

Millions of people around the world have confessed Christ as their personal Savior due to his mission-minded heart for evangelism. His inspiration moved others like Adoniram Judson, Hudson Taylor, and David Livingston to all surrender to the mission field.

We also can be inspired, even in our immediate surrounding by accepting the call of God to go and tell others about God's mercy, grace and love. Your neighbors, friends, co-workers, fellow students, and family; they all are part of God's Great Commission. We expect God to save them, but maybe He wants to use you as the very one to attempt to reach them.

We expect God to answer prayers for these; we expect Him to prepare their hearts; we expect God to give us His words and use them with His guidance. We expect God to give us opportunities to be a witness for Him, yet do we have the faith and trust in God that, as we attempt these things, His hand and Spirit will give us the confidence needed to be that witness?

I would like each of us to write our own sermon with the title "Expect Great Things, Attempt Great Things." Pray that God soberly gives us the heart to do this and as He does, remember that we always can "expect great things from Him" and He will empower our faith to "attempt great things for Him."

"Call unto me and I will answer thee,
and shew thee great and mighty things,
which thou knowest not."
— Jeremiah 33:3

(This should always be our personal phone call to God.)

Day 102

Whatever Situations We Face, God is Still on the Throne

Key Scripture: **Psalm 103:19**

A few years ago, our nation was in turmoil over the presidential election. Many were upset their candidate was not chosen the winner, and some were jubilantly proud. Those who voted were willing to take a risk by standing up for what mattered most to them, regardless of the outcome.

It's not easy to accept losing; it leaves a feeling of discouragement and disappointment. You may experience feelings of defeat and wonder why others were not able to see things as you did. Truth is, every time we're willing to have a voice and take a stand for what we believe, "we win." We win with anything in life when we do what God asks, so we trust God with the results.

We win by living wisely and by obeying God's Word. There is great freedom in doing this: freedom from fear, worry, defeat, even from anger and hate. We must be reminded that nothing takes God by surprise. He's on the throne and over all. He has a plan and works on behalf of His children. (Philippians 2:13).

Our prayers and voices matter as we choose to live in God's grace and make a difference in our world. We must always be faithful to pray for those in authority, speaking with wisdom and discernment and having a heart of compassion and love.

We can be strong by following God's voice, even though it may not be the most popular. Remember Proverbs 21:1; God says even *"the king's heart is in the hand of the LORD and He directs his ways."* God is faithful and His power, peace and presence rule above all; this includes our day to day situations. Trust and believe Him; He is in control and nothing is impossible for Him.

What we do matters to God. Let's leave a legacy of trust in a God who is always on His throne.

"Whether therefore ye eat, or drink, or whatsoever ye do, do all to the glory of God."

— 1 Corinthians 10:31

Day 103

Our Past is Meant to Be Purposely Used for God

Key Scripture: **Luke 8:39**

I remember after the Lord saved me how grateful and overwhelmed I was that Christ had given me a new beginning, a fresh start, to live for Him and not myself. How I wanted the world to know what had transpired. I remember clearly these words that the Lord gave to me after He saved me: "Go share and tell others."

What exactly did that mean? The Lord wanted me to share my past and my newly acquired membership into the family of God. My heart wanted to, but my will was holding me back. I accepted Christ as my Savior but, simply wasn't ready for my past to be purposely used for Him.

In our key passage, this verse is talking about the manic of Gadara. He was a tormented man who lived many years as an outcast. When he saw Jesus, he fell to his knees and cried out begging for mercy from God.

Jesus commanded the demons to leave his body and they were cast into a herd of swine that ran down the hill into the water and drowned. This man was healed physically and most impor-tantly, spiritually. He immediately was over-whelmed with gratitude for what Jesus had done and begged Jesus to let him become a follower and stay with Him.

Jesus told him he needed to go and tell his story; and he did. How many people believed the story of this man and now will spend eternity in Heaven because this once demon-possessed man shared what Christ did for him? No one can ever deny God's power and witness of a transformed life.

We all have a testimony to tell others; we have a past to purposely be used for God's glory. Go share it! Live it! God would never waste our pain and suffering, but we do by withholding from others what Christ did for us. Because of our past many could receive God's redemption. Let's be faithful and let God's Spirit purposely lead us.

Are we thankful enough for the Spiritual healing given to us to go share our past with oth-ers, bringing them to Christ?

"I will speak of thy testimonies also before kings,
and will not be ashamed."

— Psalm 119:46

Day 104

Doing Things The Right Way — God's Way

Key Scripture: **Joshua 6:14**

There is a saying: 'Plan your work and work your plan.' Organized people do this successfully and it's not a bad practice at all.

Whenever we bring our petitions to the Lord, is this a practice we should follow? We must learn that our ways are not God's ways. In Isaiah 55:8-9, God tells us that His ways are not ours and our suggestions and plans have no bearing on His will for our lives.

Remember in the book of Joshua when the Israelites faced the massive wall of Jericho? I can imagine that God's people murmured and complained and had their own ideas as to how they could take this city, but God never asked their opinion, not even Joshua. All He asked was for their complete unwavering obedience. God knew that His plan would not make any sense to the Israelites; His plan was to simply "obey" with no battle.

The story goes on and a faithful, obedient people marched as God said, and on the seventh day they were to end with trumpet blasts and shouting. I'm sure the Israelites had doubting thoughts of God's plan, but with their faithful obedience, they saw a great victory.

What do we do in times when God wants us to follow Him and the plan does not make sense to us? How can we stay faithful and obedient? In 2 Corinthians 5:7 we find our answer; *"we walk by faith, not by sight."* In Hebrews 10:23 we take God at His Word and trust in His promises. He promised in Joshua 6:2 that He would deliver Jericho. Without the Israelites plans, God honored their unwavering obedience to His plan.

We don't always have to understand why God chooses certain ways to do things, but we do have to keep choosing to be obedient and follow His ways and not our own. His plans are always good and are to be trusted.

"Trust in the LORD with all thine heart;
and lean not unto thine own understanding.
In all thy ways acknowledge Him,
and He shall direct thy paths."

— Proverbs 3:5-6

Day 105

Why Do We Make Trusting God Hard?

Key Scripture: **1 Peter 5:7**

I remember years back I loved planting a garden. I loved working with the ground and nurturing the plants as they grew and harvested the vegetables as they ripened. One year my brother-in-law wanted us to join forces and plant the garden together. He said he would get the ground broken up and ready for planting.

Time was slipping away and all I heard was, "Don't worry; I'll get it done" and the ground still was not ready, so I took it upon myself to cultivate the ground and start planting on my own. This annoyed him and my lack of confidence in him showed. A trust issue evolved. After all we started this relationship to do this together because of trust.

Throughout the scriptures God asked His children in different ways, "Do you trust me?"

The Israelites were to gather manna for the current day only (Exodus 16:15-20); they were not to collect the spoils of the land of Jericho (Joshua 6:18). Gideon, was told to stop hiding in the wine press (Judges 6:11), and Joseph, was told to marry a woman with child that was conceived by the Holy Spirit (Matthew 1:18-25).

It's easy to say on Sunday that we trust God and lay the cares of this world on the altar, only to get up on Monday and have the weight of those trust issues again on our shoulders. In our key verse we see God wants us to *"cast all our cares upon Him,"* but we have to be willing to hand them over to God and let go.

Scripture tells us that God's ways are different than ours. His ways are higher. That's just one of the ways He offers hope, even when trusting Him is hard. (Isaiah 55:8-9). If there is anyone we can place our trust in to handle our cares, it is God.

Cast your cares upon the Lord, and leave them there.

"A man's heart deviseth his way;
but the LORD directeth his steps."

— Proverbs 16:9

Day 106

A Lie is a Lie and Dishonors God

Key Scripture: **Proverbs 12:22**

No one will ever secure a relationship with God by simply living a good life. God's standard for your life is not as easy as avoiding the "major sins." His ninth commandment alone is sufficient to keep all of humanity forever separated from Him. If you have ever told a lie, you have fallen short of God's standard of holiness. (Romans 3:23).

Having this knowledge, it is amazing that we, as Christians, continue to lie. Not only do we do so, we dismiss it as if it's not sin at all. Why do we approach sin this way, knowing that sin is sin and in order for one to experience a relationship with Christ we must confess our sins and ask for forgiveness?

Our eternal security with God does not exclude us from temporal consequences of our sins. Never should we assume that God takes lying lightly because we have accepted Christ as our Savior. Confession and forgiveness is still required. Proverbs 19:5 teaches us that *"A false witness shall not be unpunished, and he that speaketh lies shall not escape."*

Those who lie, gossip, and withhold the truth from others are condemned by God in Exodus 20:16. Jesus said He is the way, the truth, and the life in John 14:6. Lying and tainting the truth is not a part of the nature of God. On the other hand, we see in our key passage in Proverbs 12:22 a reminder that *"those who act faithfully are His delight."*

Commit to being a delight before the Lord each and every day. Ask Him to keep you sensitive with His convicting Spirit of sinful thoughts before they manifest in the form of lying lips, which dishonors God.

"But the fearful, and unbelieving, and the abominable, and murderers, and whoremongers, and sorcerers, and idolaters, and all liars, shall have their part in the lake which burneth with fire and brimstone: which is the second death."

— Revelation 21:8

Day 107

What if the Hearing of God's Word Became a Famine?

Key Scripture: **Amos 8:11-12**

There is so much going on in our world today and we see a drastic decline in our church attendance. What are we to expect? Our pastor eluded to a statistic recently that made me want to cry. He said one third of our population age 35 and under do not believe there is a God. Shocking!

In our key passage in Amos, it expounds on our need for the words in the Bible. Imagine a time that God's Word had disappeared like crops during a famine. The time would come when God would be silent toward His people Israel, because of their sin. At this time, even the prophets would not hear from Him.

What about us today? Many find it difficult to get into God's Word, because of the pressures and demands of a busy lifestyle that edge God out. Even though we live in a time where God's Word is so abundantly available, we find ourselves in a time of self-imposed famine. Just think, if the number of people that do not believe there is a God would faithfully read the Word of God and sit under the voice of a Godly pastor, preaching the truth, would not those statistics change?

In verse 11 of our passage, God declared to Israel that the days are coming that He will send a famine, not a famine of bread nor thirst, but rather for "hearing the Word of the Lord."

A hunger and thirst to learn the truth of God is needed today; spending time in His Word, with deep fellowship with our Savior and Lord; spreading His Gospel with compassion to others will give us assurance that we will always be able to hear God's Word.

Lord, increase our hunger for Your Word, our desire to stay faithful serving You in whatever capacity You chose.

"…man doth not live by bread only,
but by every word that proceedeth out of the mouth of the LORD doth man live."
— Deuteronomy 8:3b

Day 108

What Matters Most is the Condition of Your Heart

Key Scripture: **2 Chronicles 30**

As a child I remember times when I really tried hard to seek the favor of my teacher or my parents, eagerly doing things I thought that needed to be done and taking the initiative to do it. Once I ran into a situation and did something that I thought was totally right and found out later it was totally wrong.

My parents knew what I was trying to do and that my heart was in the right place, so they overlooked the mistake and forgave me of my blunder. God does the same for us by caring about the motivation of our hearts, not just what we do.

In our key passage, we see Israel during the time of the Passover celebration, totally dropped the ball, even though this law was to be sacredly upheld. Some people did not purify themselves and Hezekiah delayed the Passover one month so all Israel could observe the Passover together. (2 Chronicles 30:18)

The Lord heard the prayer of Hezekiah and healed the people. In God's eyes, faith and obedience always come before ritual. In other words,

God saw the condition of their heart. 1 Samuel 16:7:

"But the LORD said unto Samuel, Look not on his countenance, or on the height of his stature; because I have refused him; for the LORD seeth not as man seeth; for man looketh on the outward appearance, but the LORD looketh on the heart."

This brings up a valid question; how is your heart? Are we motivated to please God, yourself, or someone else? Our hearts are easily led astray. (Jeremiah 17:9). But as we read our Bible, talk with God, and share life with other believers, we must understand the importance of protecting our hearts and keeping our motivations pure. In guarding our hearts, we protect the motivations that drive us to do what we do to honor God with all our heart, soul and mind.

God is more interested in the state of our hearts than our outward actions.

"Create in me a clean heart, O God;
and renew a right spirit within me."

— Psalm 51:10

Day 109

Are We Peacemakers?

Key Scripture: **Matthew 5:9**

As a young boy, I learned quickly who was the peacemaker in my house. It was my mother. She made the decision who was wrong in any dispute that took place between us children. We got under each other's skin so easily. Believe me, there were many disputes and our peacemaker was always there to bring justice.

Still today, I meet people who get under my skin so easily that it feels impossible to get victory over my feelings toward those that bring out the worst in me. We are born into a world of sin and we don't always have that peacemaking mentality.

Sometimes we may allow our defense mechanism to take over when we are provoked. Another way we may react is to withdraw to ourselves and shut down, refusing to work things out. This is why parents and schoolteachers attempt to train us to work out our issues peaceably.

As an adult now, sometimes I still feel it difficult to respond correctly when aggravated by someone; knowing what to do inwardly and simply not complying.

Our key scripture says; *"Blessed are the peacemakers."* Knowing what to do, we find it easier to be a peacemaker toward others with their conflicts and not our own. We determine in our hearts that we will do what's right and soon find out that at times we fail.

Perhaps we need a deeper understanding what a peacemaker is? The word "peace" in the above scripture means harmony, security and rest. We find throughout scripture how Jesus took those that sought to do injustice to Him and turned the situations around peaceably. As our example, we too must realize that He gives us the ability to make peace. When we do, He promises that we "will be called the children of God."

So, when Jesus said we are "blessed" when we bring peace, it's because being a peacemaker allows us to follow Christ's example and represent the reality of who He is as His children.

Being a peacemaker is challenging and may not come naturally. May we all be reminded that in every conflict that comes our way, we have the capability to bring resolutions of peace. We can bring harmony, security and rest because the promises in His Word are real in our lives and we have peace, knowing that He gave Himself as a ransom, endured the cross, and rose again, giving us everlasting hope.

"The Spirit itself beareth witness with our spirit,
that we are the children of God."

— Romans 8:16

Day 110

God Throws Curveballs; They Will Humble You

Key Scripture: John 5:30

While coming up I loved to play baseball. I remember several pitchers that threw a good curveball and at first, they made me look terrible at the plate. I did learn to hit that pitch, but can say that before I did, the pitch humbled me without question.

Many of us remember Sandy Koufax who played for the Dodgers; he was a master of the curveball. Curveballs are tough and the ability to hit one is perhaps the deciding factor if a player makes it to the majors or not.

God has the greatest curveball, even better than Sandy Koufax. Here are a few examples: Abraham had his life planned out and God threw him a curve; *"Pack up your belongings and follow me to a place where I'll tell you later."* Again, he told Abraham to: *"Take your only son and offer him to me as a sacrifice on an altar."*

Daniel was a noble in his own country and God threw him a curve, placing him in exile in Babylon. Moses struggled with the curveball sent to him at first, but he did recover very well. Peter struck out on three pitches before he finally learned to hit.

One thing we can count on is that God will allow us to receive a curveball in our lives. Ever thought why? In baseball, every hitter in the majors can hit a straight fastball. In life if all we see is a straight fastball, (the same thing over and over) then we would become confident in our own abilities. It's when the curves come we soon realize that we are not great hitters.

What makes us a good player in life is learning to lean on Christ—not looking to ourselves for the answers or leaning on our own understanding, but trusting He will direct our paths.

Jesus Himself never did anything on His own; He relied on His Father. So should we. God will send us a curveball; they all have a purpose. Let's learn from them.

Take my life and let it be, consecrated Lord to Thee.

"Those things, which ye have both learned, and received, and heard, and seen in me, do: and the God of peace shall be with you."

— Philippians 4:9

Day 111

God is Always Near

Scripture: **Psalm 16:8**

Sometimes even a strong Christian can become overwhelmed by their busy schedule. A pastor, torn between family and ministry, a business man or woman pulled from one meeting to another, traveling from one motel room to another. What about a student, covered up with deadlines of exams and projects that keep coming; or a mother, juggling the kids and home and at times not able to realize whether they are coming or going?

All these situations can create stress so that even while sitting, your heart is racing out of control. Things build up and all of a sudden you have to stop and bury your head in your hands and say; "Lord I am tired. I need to release all these burdens, relax and clear my mind and consider adjusting my days ahead." Most of all we need to feel the presence of God beside us.

As a Christian it is always comforting to know that God is near. Remember back as a child you started learning about Christ. Knowing about Him caused that knowledge to become an indwelling of Jesus Christ. At times when I stop to really let this sink in, I become teary-eyed just thinking that Christ is living inside me. He has made a home inside and has set me apart for a purpose.

It is then we can feel the key verse come alive; *"I have set the LORD always before me: because He is at my right hand, I shall not be moved."* Knowing that He is at our right hand comforts us, relieving the stress and giving us a new spirit to carry on. The busy life is still there, but we have stopped to focus on Christ. He is, and we now understand that walking in the knowledge that God is right beside us makes us unshakable.

Lord, help me to always feel your presence right beside me and experience Your peace in my life as I go through my busy days; always remembering the many ways You have been with me.

"And the LORD, He it is that doth go before thee;
He will be with thee, He will not fail thee,
neither forsake thee: fear not, neither be dismayed."
— Deuteronomy 31:8

Discipleship Costs

Key Scripture: **Matthew 16:24**

Someone said the mark of a great leader is the demands he makes upon his followers. An Italian freedom fighter Garibaldi offered his men only hunger and death to free Italy. Winston Churchill told the British people he had nothing to offer them but "blood, sweat, toil, and tears" in their fight against their enemies.

Jesus talked about the necessity of total commitment, even to the point of death; *"For whosoever would save his life will lose it, but whosoever will lose his life for my sake will find it."*

The cost of discipleship is high. Jesus Christ demanded our obedience when He said: *"Take up your cross and follow me."* He asked nothing of us that He Himself would not do, for He took up the cross that He was sent to earth to carry, and that was to bear our penalty of sin by shedding His blood, dying in our place, for the entire world.

Jesus made extreme demands of us, to take up our cross and follow Him. We must never forget that He made the extreme sacrifice for us. He said to His disciples: *"What shall it profit a man if he shall gain the whole world, and lose his own soul? Or what shall a man give in exchange for his soul?"* (Mark 8:36-38).

We all should understand and accept the fact that it is far better to deny ourselves, take up our cross and follow Christ. Our eternal offer is to spend eternity with Him.

Discipleship costs...are you willing and ready to take up your cross and follow Him?

"And these words, which I command thee this day, shall be in thine heart."
— Deuteronomy 6:5

Day 113

Are We Doing What We Can?

Key Scripture: **Mark 14:8**

There is a mindset among the world today that literally attacks our good intentions and causes our heads to turn from that which is unpleasant, causing discomfort. It's the mentality that the needs of this world are so great, and our personal ability to make a difference is so tiny and insignificant; what we can do to change anything just doesn't really count. So, the end result is that we do "Nothing."

"Nothing" does not change the darkness or make a difference in anyone's life. Christian, the fact is that we can't do everything, but we all can do something, and that something we can do will make a difference to someone.

Think about the thousands of missionaries that have followed the call of God to go into the most remote regions around the world. Where would that poor starving homeless child be today had not someone accepted the call to be used of God to help them? The mission trips are set up to provide medical care, assist in building needs, and to share the Gospel of Christ to those who may otherwise perish without being given the opportunity to accept Jesus Christ as their Savior. "Nothing" is not the answer. We all cannot go, but everyone can help support and pray that God's will be done through those who are sent.

What about those less fortunate ones that are next door or in the neighborhoods near us, desperately in need of someone reaching out to make a difference in their lives? Doing "Nothing" certainly does not meet the needs of the homeless, the poor, sick, or elderly that awake every day without someone to help them to get through another day. There is always something we can do.

What about within our own churches? There are so many areas of service and yet we sit back and let those overworked Sunday School teachers, staff members, and the few willing to go the extra mile to get to church early, and stay longer doing all the work, while we fail to serve the Lord in some capacity.

We must reach out to those who may need help getting to and from church and determine to make a difference in someone's life. Doing "Nothing" is not an option.

Check out a song sung by Steve Green, "The Mission."

"As every man hath received the gift,
even so minister the same one to another,
as good stewards of the manifold grace of God."

— 1 Peter 4:10

Day 114

The Lord Despises a Lying Tongue,

Key Scripture: **Proverbs 12:22**

Satan was exposed as the originator of lies. He lied to Eve, bringing death into the world, (John 8:44), causing sin, pain, and destruction to become a reality. (Romans 5:12). A single lie can cause many problems for both; the one being lied about and the liar.

A lying tongue can destroy one's testimony, doing irreparable damage. Though the lying tongue is but for a moment, (Proverbs 12:19) its affects can last a lifetime. It's so important that we keep our tongue under subjection.

We must think before we speak by asking ourselves, "How is what I am about to say going to impact God's Kingdom?" Will what I'm about to say defame someone's character or will it help this person and please the Lord? (1 Peter 2:12).

Many of us only think the tongue is an instrument used for evil. Not so, if it is controlled by the Holy Spirit, then it becomes an instrument with great impact for service to glorify Christ. It can be used to edify, encourage, uplift, teach and counsel, doing good fruitful things for the cause of Christ.

Through our controlled tongue, we are made witnesses, bringing the lost to Christ; however, if used for deceitful malicious purposes, the tongue will destroy not only the one spoken about, but also the one speaking the lie. We are to remember that we always are to be slow to speak and slow to wrath, thinking prior to letting our tongue control what we say or do. In the long run, it will help us and please the heart of God.

Seeking God's favor is essential; speaking lies will cause God to despise our sin. The old saying still stands true; If you can't say something good about someone, say nothing at all.

"I said, I will take heed to my ways, that I sin not with my tongue;
I will keep my mouth with a bridle,
while the wicked is before me."

— Psalm 39:1

Day 115

A Tree is Known By the Fruit it Bears

Key Scripture: **Matthew 12:33**

Someone said: "Your outer world will always be a reflection of your inner world," meaning that your actions are driven by what's going on inside of you. Our lives produce fruit that is a reflection of what's going on in our hearts. We question whether it is good fruit or bad fruit. Our spiritual state reflects the fruit we bear, which means to have better fruit, we must maintain our spiritual state.

I love planting a garden and enjoy watching the plants take root and grow, maturing to produce tasty vegetables. This is God's order of things, and it works in plants and also works in the life of a child of God.

With plants, they have to be nurtured in order to produce. I have noticed that when plants lack water, they grow and produce much slower than when they have abundant rain. As long as we keep plants nurtured and watered they will continue to produce and bear fruit.

This is much the same in the life of a Christian; if we are not continuously being watered by the Word of God, we risk the same thing as our plants. We will reflect a dry spirit and the fruit will not mature as it should. We must nourish our spirit through reading God's Word and prayer.

In order to escape a chaotic life and not produce a fruitful Christian life, we must focus on what is going on inside. Our heart must reflect the Lord Jesus Christ in everything we do, His will, His ways, His desires, His promises, His love, His compassion for others, and a clean heart always seeking to glorify Him.

In time our lives will bloom and produce the fruit that's tasty to others and to God.

"Ye have not chosen me, but I have chosen you,
and ordained you, that ye should go and bring forth fruit,
and that your fruit should remain:
that whatsoever ye shall ask of the Father in my name,
he may give it you."

— John 15:16

Day 116

The Raging Storms We Face Shatter Our Faith

Key Scripture: **Hebrews 6:18-19**

I just recently read the events in Luke where the disciples were on a boat with Jesus and a great storm arose. The disciples were so afraid and looked to Jesus for help. They found Him at peace, sleeping. The disciples walked daily with Jesus, saw His many wondrous miracles of healing, and heard the parables, yet were not able to rest in troubled times.

Should they not have followed the example of Christ? He was not afraid; He was aboard the same boat as they were, and would to God they should have realized that with Jesus, they would be perfectly safe, even in the midst of a storm. After the storm was calmed, He asked them where was their faith?

We ourselves do the exact same thing; we call out to Jesus in desperation when our lives are filled with problems, one after another, and although we are a child of God, we become afraid of circumstances. We ask the Lord, "Why does it have to be so hard?" We seek an answer, but if we are truthful, our answer comes back to us as a question: "Where is your faith?"

We should ask ourselves where are we putting our trust? When the storms rage and winds blow, and they will, our faith needs to be in Jesus, not the outcome of life's circumstances. Within each and every child of God, we have the Holy Spirit to help calm our storms, we have God's Word to help us find answers, and we have a Heavenly Father that hears our prayers. Our faith and trust in the all-powerful God will help keep us safe and calm during storms.

"Now faith is the substance of things hoped for,
the evidence of things not seen."

— Hebrews 11:1

The Right and Wrong Way for Guarding Your Heart

Key Scripture: **Proverbs 4:23**

Putting on a false face of security is something that we do in order to let others and even ourselves feel the necessity to guard our heart. We all have been through circumstances that have caused us to build walls of protection because of a lack of trust, fear of being rejected, being betrayed, or being hurt by the deceitful intent of others.

Our self-confidence gets shattered and we feel unloved, unprotected and therefore place walls of protection, guarding our heart. These walls are stealing our peace and joy, and sometimes draw us away from God instead of drawing us to God.

Our scripture passage tells us to guard our hearts above all else. So, exactly what are we to do? This passage, written by Solomon, gives us an important aspect of our Christian life. The status of our heart effects who we are, how we feel, what we do, and how we live.

Solomon's description of guarding our heart differs from the way we view guarding our heart. Through a scriptural perspective it means for us to be alert, through the power of Christ within us, to what enters and dwells in our hearts. Biblically guarding our heart exists because of consistent communication with our Lord for direction, conviction and peace. In essence, putting up walls does more harm than good because we are looking to self rather than God to help protect our hearts from harm.

Again, scripturally guarding our hearts help keep our faith on track, but those self-built walls keep people out by protecting our emotions which become walls that keep us bound in insecurities, fear, unhappiness and loneliness. We were never created to live in prison of our own making within ourselves. God is the only One who can protect our hearts from pain. It is our choice to live behind those restricted walls of imprisonment; so therefore, we must understand that God created us for companionship and love.

God wants us to live free, full of joy and with peace in our hearts, not fear. These are indeed accessible if only we would ask.

"Hear thou, my son, and be wise, and guide thine heart in the way."

— Proverbs 23:19

We Should All Want God's Will; Not Our Own

Key Scripture: **Luke 22:41-42**

I believe that many of us have different views about the will of God. At times we get in God's way as He attempts to show us His will, and it does not align with our thoughts on how things should go. If we see that Christ was obedient in seeking His Father's will for His life, should we not equally feel the need to know God's will for our life?

We would rather question God's methods, timing, and plans. This is far from being obedient. We all struggle somewhat with praying for God's will to be done. We offer up prayers asking God's will to be done, only to retract them when God's way doesn't fall into our thinking, our goals, and our anticipations of where our lives are heading.

I'm not sure where Mary and Martha's thoughts were as their brother was on his death bed; probably that Jesus would rush to give help to His friend. They questioned Jesus' urgency because He, as they thought, took His time getting there.

They didn't understand that the Father's will was Jesus' priority. Seeking our own approval and the approval of others is not desiring the will of God. Jesus was serious as we see in our key passage; He wanted His Father's will and not His own.

Our prayers go up and I wonder how many are sent seeking our own will and not the Fathers. Is it no wonder that our prayers seem to not get answered?

We must have a surrendered life, our will, our wants, our prayer life, and our plans; they all have to be totally given over to God, having no reservation to control our future; that everything is in His control, and we must wait on His answer.

God may want to give us our desires, but we must trust Him, knowing that His will and ways are best. In John 5:19 we are reminded that whatever the Father does, the Son does also. So, we see our greatest example is to follow Jesus. His continual and humble submission to the will of the Father is our example, which means we are to fully obey, and as we do, we bring our heart's petitions to the Father, remembering to willingly say, *"Not my will, but Thine be done."*

What would happen if we opened our hearts and humbly prayed to God like Jesus did?

"Father, if thou be willing, remove this cup from me; n
evertheless not my will, but thine be done."

— Luke 22:42

Day 119

What Do Others See When They Look into Your Face?

Key Scripture: **Act 6:15**

While in Tennessee Temple College, I had a never-forgetting experience. My father had a stroke and I was left with a dilemma of staying in school to finish my exams or leaving to be near my father. Through the registrar's office, I got a message to meet personally with Dr. Lee Roberson right away.

I went to his office and knocked on his door to hear a strong voice answer to enter. Upon walking into his massive office and seeing first hand this man of giant faith sitting at his desk, witnessing a look I'd never seen before; a shining glow of God's glory in the face of this dear saint. God, may I never forget this moment.

Once again God gave me someone in my life that caused my eyes to see the angelic face of another dear saint, my late wife, who in her later years went through a trying time with cancer. I do so vividly remember the events of her last days with us. I first-hand saw her surrender to her loving Heavenly Father, that beautiful angelic face along with her sustaining strength of her unbroken trust in God.

Some days, as those events flow through my heart and mind, the tears flow as praise and worship flood my soul with a deep sense of our Lord's love, comfort, and pleasure forever etched into my heart and mind of that beautiful angelic face.

In our key verse we see Stephen, known as the first martyr of the Christian faith. He was described by his persecutors as a man with the face of an angel. Stephen was also in scripture described as a man of faith and power, though stoned because of his unwavering faith, we find by his persecution, the Christian movement was accelerated, thus proving that the Christian movement cannot be destroyed by stoning an angelic-looking leader. The Rock, who is Christ, cannot be moved by man's secular stones.

We must ask, what facial expressions do others see when they look at us? Joy, because of gratitude to God? Peace, because of our Heavenly future where there is no more sorrow, nor tears? Love, because of Christ's love for us and our love toward Him? Is there enough evidence in our countenance to connect us as a faithful follower of Christ? Facial expressions reveal a lot, and we must learn to reflect the Lord Jesus Christ on our face.

Our face is the first indicator of Christ in us.

"The LORD bless thee, and keep thee;
The LORD make His face shine upon thee, and be gracious unto thee;
The LORD lift up His countenance upon thee, and give thee peace."

— Numbers 6:24-26

Day 120

Eyes are a Window to the Soul

Key Scripture: **Matthew 6:22-24**

This popular phrase comes from Shakespeare and in reference to Biblical Scripture, it carries great truth and meaning. I am legally blind in one eye and for a period of time used this as an excuse to not read God's Word on a regular basis. I still loved to hear preaching and the Word being read, but I myself could not read for any length of time because of the hurting in my eyes. A major change in my life came months ago and the need to lean on Christ was more apparent in my life than life itself.

God has now given me the hunger and thirst to seek Him and study His Word in depth as I never had before. His Word has illuminated my heart to a new prospective and I yearn to know more each and every day. It is not easy to read, but God has put a new strength in my one eye and I am forever thankful. I pray it will last.

Reading, studying, and seeking God's will through the Bible is without a doubt the most important part of growth as a Christian. The eyes are an important member of your body. (Matthew 6:22-24.)

John Bunyan said; "Sin will keep you from this Book or this Book will keep you from sin." To have an abundant Christian life, it is imperative that God's Word is read, studied, and your life's desire is to fashion your walk with Jesus Christ each day. The Bible has much to say about the eyes as an important member of your body, for your eyes are the eye gate to your soul.

"Open thou mine eyes, that I may behold wondrous things out of thy law."

— Psalm 119:18

"If my step hath turned out of the way, and mine heart walked after mine eyes, and if any blot hath cleaved to mine hands;"

— Job 31:7

"The eyes of your understanding being enlightened; that ye may know what is the hope of His calling, and what the riches of the glory of His inheritance in the saints."

— Ephesians 1:18

Many verses are found in the Bible about the eyes and they are to be used as a tool for growth in our Christian life by reading and studying God's Word.

Your eyes are necessary to follow God's path; use them wisely.

"Thy Word is a lamp unto my feet and a light unto my path."
— Psalm 119:105

Day 121

Little is Much When God is in It

Key Scripture: **John 6:9**

In my mind I see in this world many different supposedly spiritual materials written, and it scares me to think where the false doctrines and lies of Satan end. To keep from getting discouraged I have placed my focus on the hope that as I seek to serve, whether in speech or writing, anything that comes from me will have the hope attached with it that one more seed planted in the right soil will be used by the Holy Spirit to bring forth fruit for the glory of God.

In our key verse, Andrew asked, *"What are they among so many?"* He was speaking about the five loaves and two fish; God was testing their faith. They compared the ratio of food to the 5,000, and what they had was nothing.

The disciples were about to learn an amazing truth that would be demonstrated time and again in their ministry. That is: when little is put into the hands of the Lord, it becomes sufficient. God chooses to use the small insignificant things of this world rather than the great.

As we surrender our lives to do some service for the Lord, He never says "What are they among so many?" Rather, He takes each of us to fulfill His plan, no matter what our abilities may be. When you put yourself in the hands of God, you will be sufficient. He'll take the two and the five and multiply His blessings through a surrendered heart.

As long as we surrender our hearts in concentration to Him, we never will have to wonder if we are sufficient. May we also learn as the disciples; "Little is much when God is in it."

"Better is little with righteousness than great revenues without right."
— Proverbs 16:8

Day 122

God Does Care—
He Sees Our Weakness and Knows Our Infirmities

Key Scripture: **2 Chronicles 16:9**

We say that our faith and trust in God is unwavering today and yet tomorrow we struggle finding peace. Today we rely on God's strength and then tomorrow we flip the script and begin to search for answers within our own self and not God. We are not the only ones who waver, but we can look into God's Word and find encouragement.

In 2 Chronicles 14 &15 we find King Asa in a restful state because of his dependence on the Lord. God gave him victory while facing the massive armies. Now moving on to Chapter 16, we see a sudden shift in his behavior as he finds himself facing a battle with King Bassha of Israel.

Asa now turned to his own means in handling this situation by misusing the treasures of the temple and placing his hope in unwise alliances. This resulted in his unrest and King Asa, a once faithful, trusting king who was led by God, is now facing battles in his own strength, refusing to trust God.

Just like Asa, our past victories by faith and trust in God have no guarantee that in the future we will rely on God. We feel sometimes as if God may be blind to our present circumstances; but looking at our key verse, we see that as our hearts remain blameless toward Him, we have His total support and strength. God will strengthen each of us if we are willing to wholeheartedly place our trust in Him.

God has been faithful in our past and will continue to do the same. Fear makes us forget, as we see in the life of Asa. Surely the outcome would have turned out differently had he not wavered from trusting God's faithful guidance.

God's faithfulness in our past is assurance that He will be faithful in our future. We must stop running to fix things on our own. We must fix our eyes on God. (Isaiah 26:3). God cares, He sees our weakness, and knows our infirmities. Trust Him today as you have in times past.

"The works of His hands are verity and judgment;
all His commandments are sure."

— Psalm 111:7

Day 123

Something We All Should Include in Our Prayer

Key Scripture: **Ephesians 5:20**

Whenever I go to a restaurant and eat, I observe others as they sit down to a meal, watching to see if they give thanks to God for their meal. Luke 9:26, God says, *"For whosoever shall be ashamed of me and of my words, of him shall the Son of man be ashamed"...* 1 Thessalonians 5:18, He also says, *"In everything give thanks; for this is the will of God in Christ Jesus concerning you."*

In my observation, I do see others praying before they eat their meal. Praise God. All I can hope for is their hearts are genuine and they most certainly mean what they pray. This is something we all should do in reference to our Holy God; always careful to give Him praise and thanks for His provisions.

Another thing that as Christians we should add into our time of giving thanks to God is to remember our waiters and waitresses. Sure, it is their job to serve our food and drinks, but let's be sensitive to these people God has placed before us. As they are bringing our food, may we all take a moment and include them in our prayer. Let them know we are about to thank God for our food and would like to know if there might be something going on in their life that we could pray with them about.

God will bless these efforts, and as they share a burden or a request you will feel a bond with that person who is now more than a waiter or waitress; they are someone who shared a piece of their heart with you. I know several folks that do this and I believe it is a great witnessing tool and shows others the love of Christ.

"Let your light so Shine before men,
that they may see your good works,
and glorify your Father which is in heaven."

— Matthew 5:16

Day 124

God's Not Done Yet

Key Scripture: **Philippians 1:6**

Yesterday, I heard a great sermon from my pastor and just would like to say thanks Pastor Brian, God has used you in my life over and over through your sermons and I look forward to many more. This title I used is from that sermon, used in a different perspective, with the same outcome.

Some years back when I was coaching kid's baseball, I had a small but loving kid on my team that was a lot of fun to coach. Even though he was a player that we always used as a sub, he accepted that role. He never stopped talking, and sometimes early in the game the other team would score first and he would automatically start saying that we were going to lose the game. Not just once, but he repeated it without stopping.

I would have to sit him down and explain that he couldn't know we'd lose, because the game had just begun. In other words, I tried to change his thinking by putting the thought in his heart and mind that "God's not done yet;" we have a long way to go.

We as Christians have to face and understand that as circumstances weigh heavily against us at times, God is still in control and He cares. (Romans 8:28). Instilling in the lives of children as well as our own, our faith and trust in a powerful God will grow as He leads us through each testing moment. Be consistent by staying faithful in God's Word, prayer, showing brotherly love, and being a faithful witness to others.

Remember, that the start of each game is no indication of the outcome. As little Brian doubted so often, his doubts were less and less as he saw God work over and over and prove that the beginning is certainly not how things end. As God proved to Brian, He also wants us to trust Him; because He is definitely not through with us yet.

Our key verse says *"that He which hath begun a good work in you will perform it until the day of Jesus Christ."* We can trust that.

Remember the kids' chorus: He's still working on me? He is! Let's stay faithful and follow His leading.

"Being confident of this very thing,
that He which hath begun a good work in you
will perform it until the day of Jesus Christ."

— Philippians 1:6

Day 125

Oh to Be a Bondservant

Key Scripture: **Ephesians 6:4-8**

Peter in his writing of 1 Peter addressed himself as a "bondservant of Christ." He could have mentioned he was an apostle of Christ, which would have given him a much higher position; but, he didn't; he humbly took the title as bondservant, meaning he was crucified with Christ, no longer he lived, but Christ lived in him.

A bondservant chooses to serve. It is voluntary submission of one's life to offer service to another. He chooses who will be the master of his life. A decision to call Jesus Christ the Lord of our life is to become "His Bondservant." To lay down our life, means to surrender our will and pick up the Cross to serve Him daily in a life of total obedience; not through force, but willingly choosing this position to follow God's perfect will.

Through the Spirit we have freedom to choose who we will serve, and by choosing Christ, His Spirit liberally gives us the fruits of His Spirit. The role of bondservant to Christ must fully consume our life. Remember the relationship of Joseph and Pharaoh? Joseph was not the ruler of the country, but was given the authority, power, and resources of the one who was.

In the same way, our life becomes subject only to Jesus Christ. The role of Christ in our life is important; He is our Master; we live in subjection only to Him. As we see in 1 Peter 2:13-16, to be a bondservant of Christ is to seek Holiness, Oneness, and Completeness in Christ-alone.

Jesus learned obedience as in Hebrews 5. Full service to Christ demands obedience. We cannot fully serve the Lord with part of us still serving self. So, there is much involved when we accept the role as a bondservant of Jesus Christ. It takes sacrifice; no more self. It takes surrender, all to Jesus, no more about me, and it takes total obedience, following His will, His Word, and His authority in our lives.

A Bondservant is one who is Subservient to and entirely at the disposal of their Master.

"I am crucified with Christ: nevertheless I live;
yet not I but Christ liveth in me;
and the life which I now live in the flesh I live by the faith of the Son of God,
who loved me, and gave Himself for me."

— Galatians 2:20

Day 126

Cultivating the Fruit From God's Orchard

Key Scripture: **Galatians 5:22-23**

Have you ever thought about how the everyday circumstances and life changes make it difficult for us to see in our own lives the evidence of the fruit of the Spirit? As a child, we are told to attend Sunday school and church, and as a teen, the peer pressure to be included is so great that it's extremely hard to focus on spiritual maturity.

As we start our careers along with a family, we seldom take the time to develop our consistent walk with Christ. For some this may come easy, but for most, they look at others and see different traits of strength and evidence of the fruit of the Spirit in their lives, and totally ignore their own.

As we see the nine fruits of the Spirit in our key verse, we must as a child of God understand that it is not us, but the Spirit of God that manifests these traits in our lives. Sure, we could be stronger in some ways more than others, but the fact that God gives them to us is of great importance.

We can't ignore God's will and it is certainly His will that these fruits are evident in our lives.

When the Holy Spirit is shaping our lives and molding us into His image, we can't help but have these fruits blossom. If they are not present, then there has got to be a heart problem.

An analogy about fruits is that a lemon tree doesn't just all of a sudden decide to grow lemons; it is created to do so, and under proper cultivation and care, it produces lots of fruit. God works in us for His pleasure, and the results of Him working means that the Holy Spirit does not produce jealousy, bitterness, and selfishness. The Spirit produces love, joy, and peace, etc.

When we are looking for hope in the world, for God's goodness, there is no purer expression than these traits placed in us by the Holy Spirit of God. When we see these traits in others, it is a gift for us to name them, because sometimes we need to be reminded that we are producing fruit ourselves, even through difficult times. God triggers in our minds that His goodness shown through others, is exactly what we as Christians should cultivate within our own lives...the blossoming of the "Fruits of The Spirit."

"For we are His workmanship,
created in Christ Jesus unto good works,
which God hath before ordained that we should walk in them."

— Ephesians 2:10

How Do You Face Criticism?

Key Scripture: **Matthew 5:44-45**

Looking at the life of Paul, it would be easy for us to lift him up as a superhero. Truth is, Paul is a mere human like you and I. Throughout his writings we get the idea that he was strong and confident and so filled with faith. Certainly, when he was stoned, he bled as we would; the times he was slandered and threatened, imprisoned, I'm sure he hurt deeply as we would.

Criticism and opposition like he took would've hurt anyone. His testimony allows us to realize that we too can reach that stage of maturity as a Christian, enabling us to manage our pain and forgive hurt and slander or criticism.

Paul looked at Jesus as a role model, and because of that he was comforted in knowing that his Lord and Savior was also constantly criticized and attacked. Look at some of the names Jesus was called by His enemies; He was called a glutton, a drunkard, a lawbreaker, a blasphemer, and a demon-possessed madman.

Satan always tries to portray good as evil and evil as good. Our enemies try to create confusion and switch the attention away from themselves and their sin. Also, our enemies will always claim that those who stand for Biblical and Godly truths are guilty of the most vile of sins, the sin of intolerance.

When Paul responded to criticism, he did it without giving in to anger or self-justification, but he focused entirely on defending the Gospel of Jesus Christ. When we are criticized for sharing our faith in God's Word, about our trust in Jesus Christ, or for our belief in the Gospel, let's react as Paul did, look to Jesus; remembering always that Christ's love and compassion, along with His unwavering commitment to the will of our Heavenly Father, is our goal as we face criticism.

"Finally, brethren, whatsoever things are true,
whatsoever things are honest,
whatsoever things are just,
whatsoever things are pure,
whatsoever things are lovely,
whatsoever things are of a good report; if there be any virtue,
and if there be any praise, think on these things."

— Philippians 4:8

Things as Small as a Mustard Seed Can Make a Difference

Key Scripture: **Matthew 13:31-32**

We have always heard the phrase "that bigger is better." Those with bigger houses, bigger bank accounts, sky-rocketing careers, and a big place in society, have the greatest opportunity to be and do something great. Most everyone wants to be part of something big. Small is not valued or taken seriously. Small is non-essential.

Though the mustard seed was the smallest of seeds known to Jesus' listeners, just what would it do? Jesus said when it grows it was the largest plant in the garden, growing into a tree. The kingdom of Heaven is like a mustard seed, having the potential to grow huge, spreading everywhere.

We must not underestimate the small things in life; when accompanied by a powerful God, can change the world. Let's consider a few instances where this could happen; what about a small child whose family has been torn apart who feels hopeless, afraid, and unloved?

How could God use something small from you to encourage and give the child a hope that someone cares and love is real, and most of all the love of Christ matters? What about a home-less man or woman who has lost everything and are without hope? A small gesture of love can fill their soul with warmth and hope that they too matter.

Just think, a small gesture from you with God's powerful anointing can make a difference. Remember the feeding of the 5,000; two small fish and five small loaves, touched by the power of God, satisfied their hunger. Let's not forget that a few men that followed Christ changed the course of history and turned the world upside down, called and sent with the power of God.

So then, maybe we can't change the course of our world in a big way, but with God's power and our faith the size of a mustard seed, we can change a little child's heart, restore hope to a homeless individual, and not forget the most important thing we can do; plant the seed in their life that they too can have eternal life by accepting Jesus Christ as their Savior.

Let's fill our pockets with the seeds of God's glorious hope and move mountains, making an impact for Christ.

"He that is faithful in that which is least is faithful also in much:
and he that is unjust in the least is unjust also in much."

— Luke 16:10

Day 129

Experience the Joy of Surrender

Key Scripture: **James 4:10**

"Humble yourselves in the sight of the Lord, and He shall lift you up."

I have heard many times that the way up is down. Humbling yourself to God, means you must step down, allowing Christ to build you up. We've got to love the Lord's faithfulness; He is never slack concerning His promises and shows us His perfect will and teaches us how we are to walk in His perfect way. Without one thing, the aforementioned praise about God could not happen and that is we learn the importance of "Surrender."

Surrender to many is not the more perfect plan they have in mind. They believe that surrender is missing out or settling for something less. That mentality is far from the truth. Surrendering to God is about living a victorious life in Christ and experiencing peace and joy.

We sometimes may think that our prayers and desires aren't met, and in all sincerity, we blame God for not answering our wants. This certainly is a bad approach to a victorious life because in surrendering to God, He may or may not give us what we want; but in total surrender, He will always give to us Himself. Much more than what we want, in total surrender, we always receive what is best; the Lord Jesus Christ.

So then, surrender is not about giving up; it's about giving in to the One who knows what is best for us, our will to be His will, our wants to be His wants, and His ways are now our ways. In summing up about surrender, total surrender is the only way to experience God's perfect peace, and also the only way to experience true lasting "Joy Unspeakable."

I recall the simple but true words in the children's song; "I have the joy, joy, joy, joy down in my heart." Where should that joy be? Down in our hearts "To Stay." which hinges on "Total Surrender."

"I am crucified with Christ,
nevertheless I live; yet not I but Christ liveth in me:
and the life which I now live in the flesh I live by the faith of the Son of God who loved me,
and gave Himself for me."

— Galatians 2:20

Day 130

Loving the Unlovely

Key Scripture: **Matthew 5:44**

We have always been told that we should never hate someone; it's not Christian-like. Truth be known, we do indeed have enemies. I believe Jesus Himself knows that there are those we just can't get along with. Someone who is a bully, an ex-boy or girlfriend, an ex-spouse or a co-worker that for whatever reason rubs you the wrong way. But, scripture does say we are to treat them with kindness, even those who make our lives miserable.

Most everyone is kind to people who are kind to them. I believe the mark of a true disciple for Christ is how we act or react toward people who treat us like enemies or have truly wronged us in some way. A true disciple of Christ involves praying for those who wish us harm, going out of our way to be friendly to the unfriendly, and even offering help to someone who has hurt us.

Why? Because we have a loving, forgiving Heavenly Father, and as His child, we must learn to show the same traits He has, and show God's love toward those who do not deserve it.

Most of all, if God did not love His enemies, where would we be today? We were once an enemy of God before He gave us life eternal. If He had not forgiven us we would be lost eternally.

God loves His enemies, so must we follow His example to 'Love the Unlovely.' May God give us a heart of love, humbling us to always be able to reach out with love and compassion to those who may be undeserving.

"Bless them that curse you, and pray for them which despitefully use you."

— Luke 6:28

Day 131

To be Chosen of God

Key Scripture: **Acts 9, key verse is 15**

Saul's conversion on the road to Damascus is one of the most powerful chapters in the Word of God. So many things about Saul's conversion remind me of just how God brings us to salvation. God always shows who He is and in the same instant, shows us our need of a Savior. We know that God is not willing that any should perish, however, not everyone will become a Christian.

Saul, after the blinding experience was led to Damascus and God sent Ananias, (one sent by God), to heal his sight. After that, the most amazing title one could ever have pinned on them was placed on Saul. In verse 15 the Lord told Ananias that Saul was *"a chosen vessel unto the LORD to bear His name before the Gentiles and Kings, and the children of Israel."* Saul was special, and probably the greatest missionary for God in the New Testament. God changed his life and his name.

Looking now at Paul, let's switch and look at our own conversion, comparing what God did through Paul. We too are "Chosen of God," maybe not to the magnitude of Paul, but each child of God has their ordained purpose. Surely, we all could think of many ways God orchestrates His purpose; just a few are: we are to walk in fellowship with Him, follow His commandments, trust His judgments, be Christ-like, be faithful, assemble together, edify Christ and others, and worship Him in Spirit and truth.

Although these are only a few, we are no different than the Apostle Paul, in that we are to be a witness, spreading Christ everywhere we go. We are called to have compassion, reaching to all the uttermost places of the world, compelling them to receive Christ as their Savior. (Matthew 28:16-20).

My prayer has and will always be that when others look at me, they will see Jesus. May we each feel this same way.

"And of some have compassion, making a difference."

— Jude 1:22

Day 132

It Takes Two

Key Scripture: **Amos 3:3**

Marriage is a wonderful institution, but at the same time, it can be extremely difficult. Couples are usually drawn together because of their similarities, but also because of their differences. Even though a couple has opposite mindsets, or personalities, committed couples can survive the most difficult times if they agree on their commitment in marriage.

Yet without the same convictions it will not work. Jesus said to the Pharisees in Matthew 19:8:

"Moses because of the hardness of your hearts suffered you to put away your wives; but from the beginning it was not so."

When one spouse or the other allows the hardness of their heart to take precedence over unity, there will be a division that could lead to a couple parting their ways. It takes both partners in a marriage to press forward through forgiveness, reconciliation, and unconditional love and respect for each other.

Even unequally yoked marriages can survive if there is unity in the other areas of their relationship. Through God's grace, a believing spouse can find the places of agreement and stand firm in the gap for the other spouse.

Unfortunately, in the body of Christ, if one spouse refuses to step up to do what it takes for the marriage to survive, division will happen. God can change a hardened heart, but this does not always happen. In this case, it is imperative that the other spouse stand faithful, seeking wisdom, guidance, and discernment from the Lord, allowing God's will for their future; God has called us unto peace. (1 Corinthians 7:15).

In some cases, there is reconciliation, but for those where there is no reconciliation, there is always healing if they place their trust in the Lord. It takes two for a marriage to last until death; however, it takes only one grain of mustard seed faith for God to do His greatest work in our lives. Stay faithful, keeping your eyes on God and allowing Him to prove there is life after your marriage breaks up.

"Faithful is He that calleth you, who also will do it."
— 1 Thessalonians 5:24

Day 133

We Must Focus on God's Promises, Not Our Problems

Key Scripture: **Romans 4:20**

Let's look at Abraham; he was 75 years old when God made the promise that he would be the father of a multitude of nations. For 25 years he continued to believe in the promise of God, even though his body was withering away.

How did he continue to believe God when he knew his physical body was waxing old and feeble? Because he kept his focus on God's promise and not the problem of his aging body. It is as we know impossible for an elderly couple to have a child except through the promise of God. (Matthew 19:26).

We, as did Abraham, have the choice to focus on the promises of God or to focus on the problems of our lives. Abraham never denied the problem; he simply did not focus on it. Certainly, we all have problems we face from time to time, but by faith we must press forward continually pointing to the cross, knowing through faith God will keep His promise.

Our problem will be with us until death and we know also this sinful world will never be without problems; however, even problems will have an end, but the promises of God will continue throughout eternity. As Christians, we know the promise of eternal life is secure and we have the indwelling presence of the Holy Spirit to stir our hearts with joy, with the promise that one day we'll be with Jesus.

Focusing on the promise and not the problem is a discipline of our hearts and minds. The enemy will tempt our hearts to focus on the problem, and think how terrible things could go wrong. Focusing on the problem will tear down our needed faith and cause us to doubt the power of God. Therefore, we must stand and refuse to waiver on God's promises; only then will we experience the joy of knowing our faith and trust in an all-powerful God we can rely on and in our Lord Jesus Christ to keep His Word.

"Behold I am the LORD, the God of all flesh; is there anything too hard for me?"
— Jeremiah 32:27

Day 134

Always be Grateful, No Matter What

Key Scripture: **Ephesians 5:20**

If you have lived for some time I am sure you recognize that life has its peaks and valleys. One minute we may be on top of the world and the next we'll be stuck in a rut, holding on by a thread. This certainly means that at some point thankfulness and gratitude is easy and then at others, we find life has thrown you a curve and thankfulness and gratitude are difficult.

The Bible says in 1 Thessalonians 5:18 that we are to give thanks in everything. How is this possible? There is only one answer; when we are at our very lowest state of mind, we still know that we have God's gift of salvation no matter what has happened or what we're going through, Jesus Christ is still our Cornerstone. That, my friend, is a beautiful gift; one we will never fully comprehend to the fullest. The sacrifice of grace that God has shown is more than our mere minds will fully understand; but we know it is possible by faith and trust in God's grace. He will guide us through any hardship that we face. We can forever be grateful for this, no matter what is happening in our lives or the world around us. God is so good.

A great old song, "He Giveth More Grace" speaks to me. I hope it speaks to you too.

"The LORD hath done great things for us; whereof we are glad."

— Psalm 126:3

Day 135

God, "Our Fortress," Makes Us Forever Strong

Key Scripture: Isaiah 61:1-3

I recently read about a piece of God's handiwork on a wooded area just outside John's Island in Charleston, South Carolina. The description of this piece of God's handiwork is impressive to behold. It is "The Angel Oak Tree," standing 65' high and also spreading out to cover over 17,000 sq. feet. This mighty tree has endured hurricanes, floods, fires, earthquakes, and people for over 1,400 years.

In our key scripture, Isaiah says that God's people will be called "oaks of righteousness." Could he possibly mean that we could stand out as the Angel Oak Tree? Could we be a testimony of God's amazing handiwork, and a masterpiece with credentials of withstanding anything the world could toss against us?

God created each of us, giving us physical life, and giving us a spiritual life to serve Him while we walk with Him until eternity calls us home. God has equipped us with His Word, the Holy Spirit, and the ability to share this with others, giving us His strength to carry out the great commission.

Because of the sin-filled world we encounter weakness, pain, suffering and death and even through all this, we can experience the goodness of God as Isaiah proclaimed that we will become "The Oaks of Righteousness." For this to happen, we must have our roots planted and strengthened through Christ and our faith increased to grow in wisdom and knowledge of God's perfect plan. He will lead us in His paths of righteousness for His glory.

We are wonderfully made as the Angel Oak for God's purpose, and as we face difficult times, let's remember our strength comes from above and in that strength, we find His power to save. God can make each of us into "The Oak of Righteousness." I am grateful my strength is found in the Lord Jesus Christ, and in Him alone.

"For we are His workmanship,
created in Christ Jesus unto good works,
which God hath before ordained that we should walk in them."

— Ephesians 2:10

Day 136

Concerned About the Sin Unto Death?

Key Scripture: 1 John 5:16

This verse really puzzled me recently to the point I stopped everything and researched what it really meant. Remember the passage in Acts 5:1-10 and 1 Corinthians 11:30; speaking about Ananias and Sapphira, the "sin unto death" is willful, continuous, unrepentant sin. God has called His children to holiness (1 Peter 1:16), and God corrects them when they sin.

We are "punished" for our sin in the sense of not losing our salvation or being eternally separated from God, yet we are disciplined. The Lord disciplines those He loves, and He chastens everyone He accepts as His son. (Hebrews 12:6)

In our key verse it plainly states that there comes a point when God can no longer allow a believer to continue in unrepentant sin. God may decide to take the life of that stubborn sinful believer. This is a physical death. God will purify His church by removing those who deliberately disobey Him.

This really disturbs me because we may know others that might be living in deliberate, continual sin as if nothing bothers them at all. As I said, God will purify His church. Another thing, God will chasten those He loves and correct those He accepts as His children. To me this says that those who have not been corrected, have not been accepted as His children.

In Acts 5:1-10, God dealt with intentional, calculated sin in the church by taking the physical life of the sinner. Not all sin is dealt with the same way because not all sin reaches the level as a "sin unto death."

God is good and just, and He will eventually make us a radiant church, without stain or blemish, and holy and blameless. (Ephesians 5:27). Remember, God chastens His children; one with no chastening certainly points to one without Christ. I do pray that the Lord preserves His children from hard-heartedness that may cause them to fall and commit the "Sin Unto Death."

"Create in me a clean heart, O God; and renew a right spirit within me."

— Psalm 51:10

Day 137

It's that Simple, "Be Still"

Key Scripture: **Psalm 46:10**

In the Hebrew language the phrase "Be Still," means to drop it. In other words, "stop" what you're doing and either do nothing or listen for further instructions. At the time our key verse was written, there was much warfare going on; battles raging with lives being lost and total destruction of cities.

As humans we find it extremely hard just to "be still." We always have to be doing something in order to appease our restless minds, hands, and hearts. God told the people to "Be Still," truthfully meaning it was "Enough." As we now look into this phrase, we too must lay down our weapons and trust God for victory in all our situations that we face; having the faith that victory will come in God's timing and His perfect plan. This means putting our rest in Him.

We agree this is what we're supposed to do, yet we hold onto concerns that should be turned over to God with both hands. We feel we must fret over our children's future, our families' health, and if we don't agonize over life's disappointments, whether big or small, who will? Simple answer to this is: God will, not I will. God really wants us to understand this; so, only when we stop striving, can we recognize the truth about God; "He is in control."

No matter how crazy things get, God is still on His throne and His good and perfect will is certain to prevail.

Another phrase in our key verse says; *"and know that I am God,"* reminds our fretting hearts just who God is and what He can do. He is the creator of all things, even humanity, and He knows how to calm our hearts and minds and guide our lives in the right direction. Be still and know!!!

When our worries come, we can lift them to God; when our adversaries appear, we can let God handle them. For God to change how we live, He must first change how we think. Our first step is "To Be Still."

"Be careful for nothing;
but in every thing by prayer and supplication with thanksgiving
let your requests be made known unto God."

— Philippians 4:6

Day 138

It's Time for All Christian Men to Stand for Their Faith

Key Scripture: **Ephesians 6:11-13**

The Bible has much to say about standing. We are exhorted to stand still, to stand fast, to stand fast in faith, to stand fast in the Lord, and then after we've done all that, "Just Stand."

Yes, men of faith, it is time to stand, to stand your ground against the enemy like never before. Do we really know what it means to stand? Several meanings of the word 'stand' from the dictionary are: to take and maintain a "specific position."

You might need to take a stand regarding your family; their salvation, or your healing. Maybe take a stand to hold your marriage together or make sure your children are following the proper paths of righteousness.

Another meaning would be to hold a course; like the idea of holding a course during a storm, refusing to allow the pressures of life to take you off course, never losing focus of God's plan for you and your family. You stay the course, walking by faith, not by sight, holding onto the straight course by the strength imparted through the Word of God, holding onto your convictions, not letting your surroundings change your heart. Never allow the forces of fear from the enemy make your heart fail under the pressures you'll face while taking your stand.

We must guard our hearts and minds through God's Word because our spirit grows stronger or weaker by what we take in through our eyes and ears. Control your thoughts by allowing only things God intended to be good, helpful, and pure; keeping your mind focused on your stand for righteousness.

Circumstances will come, and when they do, we must be firmly grounded. It is not impossible, but very difficult to establish a firm grounded stand during these times, so it is important that our faith is standing firm prior to times of difficulty. (Ephesians 6:14). Establishing a strong faith to stand is essential and a question we must ask ourselves is: will we have our feet firmly planted so that after the storms pass, will we still be standing? I pray it will be so.

"For now we live, if ye stand fast in the Lord."

— 1 Thessalonians 3:8

Day 139

We Can Find Beauty in a Broken Heart

Key Scripture: **Psalm 51:17**

Sometimes in cold or dreary rainy days we can find ourselves falling into a slumbering mood. Perhaps these days cause our hearts to remember things of our past that enhance that mood. I experience those days often because I am certainly one that has, throughout my life, seen many days of hardship through a broken heart. I have experienced broken dreams by losing a dear loved one, to having shattering moments of broken relationships, along with unfortunate life-altering health issues.

Years ago, God taught me a valuable lesson. Through any circumstance we face, always give it to God, asking for necessary grace to bring us closer to Him. God has been faithful, although these days still pop up occasionally and gloom sets in, God brings sunlight into my heart, allowing His love to overshadow the darkest thoughts and memories that may surface.

Pray: "Lord, I want to serve You more and more and show Your mighty works through me for Your glory. Please let me see Your faithfulness and purpose through this pain."

What God does show me is that the wounds from the scars of brokenness and heartache reveal these scars have made a more beautiful heart because of His faithfulness. Each and every scar is living proof that I serve a faithful, forgiving, and loving God that has given me an abundance of grace because of my broken heart experiences.

God intends for us to see the beauty of our brokenness, and as these days reappear, let us be reminded what a true wonderful God we serve; and that each scar shows us He cares.

Be still, be quiet and wait on Him; we have a more beautiful heart.

"The sacrifices of God are a broken spirit:
a broken and a contrite heart,
O God, thou wilt not despise."

— Psalm 51:17'

Day 140

Trusting in Your Own Feelings for Peace

Key Scripture: **Isaiah 26:3**

Looking to yourself for peace in life's situations is probably the most dangerous place to search for true solutions to life-changing moments we face. We all experience times when things seem to fall apart such as: major events that may occur beyond our control, failing relationships, and stressful health problems, which are just a few that cause us to search for peace.

Seeing these bombard our lives, we immediately look to our own feelings for peace and comfort, when in fact God is giving us a glimpse of the unstable feelings deep within ourselves. Lovingly, He reveals this to us in order that we can see the truth. Feelings are fragile and unstable; only our faith and trust in the truth that God is unchanging and stable will bring peace when our life feels like it is falling apart.

Our key verse is found in Isaiah and we discover that this chapter focuses on the strength that God gives His people and the ability to accomplish His purpose. Isaiah is a prophetic book that looks to the future, the end of all things. (Revelation 21-22). God promises us that His plans are good. He shows us that there will be a day that death will be swallowed up in victory and there will be no more tears from our eyes. (Isaiah 25:8). He has ordained peace (Isaiah 26:12).

In Revelation we are promised peace on the other side of eternity; Isaiah shows us that we can experience and walk in strength and peace today. The phrase "stayed on" in our key verse has deep Hebrew meaning; it means to brace, uphold and support. Powerful. Those with minds that are braced, upheld and supported by truth and trust in God will be kept in perfect peace.

This certainly does not mean that we will not face adversities any longer and that things will suddenly get better or that our prayers we pray will suddenly all get answered, but it does mean our mind can be steadied with Truth, instead of being overrun with anxiety and fear.

We cannot look within ourselves for peace; we will surely never find it. In Hebrews 13:8; we see God is now and will always be the same, never changing. In Isaiah we see the same God who delivered David, parted the Red Sea, and delivered the Israelites into His Promised Land, is the same God we can trust in, and experience strength and peace throughout our life.

Quote from John Piper; "There is no power in the universe that can stop God from fulfilling His totally good plans for you."

"Thou wilt keep him in perfect peace,
whose mind is stayed on thee: because he trusteth in thee."

— Isaiah 26:3

Day 141

Do We Really Want to be Totally Surrendered to God?

Key Scripture: **Mark 10:28**

This statement by Peter, the Lord replied by saying: *"this surrender is for my sake and the gospels."* (Mark 10:29). Surrender was not for what the disciple would get out of it. One fact we must remember and be made aware of is: personal benefits have no place in surrender. Saying things such as, "I'll give myself to God to be delivered from sin because I want to be holy." Truth is that being delivered from sin and becoming holy are the result of getting your heart right with God.

Having this kind of thinking about surrender is certainly not the true nature of Christianity. Motives for surrender are not to be for personal gain. Christians have a self-centered attitude, meaning we only go to God in order to get something from Him, and not for the glory of God Himself.

Being displayed as a showcase for God, saying this is what "God has done for me" is not what surrender to God is about. Being delivered from sin and made useful to God is not what real surrender is about; rather, genuine total surrender is making a personal sovereign preference for Jesus Christ Himself.

Total surrender will always go beyond our own self-centered natural devotion. We must give up ourselves; then God will surrender Himself to embrace those around us and will meet their needs. We must caution ourselves to not stop short of a total surrender to God. Most of us have a vision of what this really means, but have never truly experienced the reality of "Total Surrender."

Think and sing, allowing the Spirit of God to sink these thoughts deep in your heart as you close your eyes and softly sing the words of the great hymn "I Surrender All." I pray this gives new meaning.

"For ye are bought with a price:
therefore glorify God in your body,
and in your spirit, which are God's."

— 1 Corinthians 6:20

Day 142

I Desire a Good Heart

Key Scripture: **Proverbs 4:23**

From a person with a diseased heart, let me first say that nurturing your heart is important to having a healthy heart. An unhealthy heart limits your ability to function as a normal individual in so many ways; so, as we diligently attempt to nourish a healthy heart, so must we guard our spiritual heart for the purpose of living a fruitful life, centered around Jesus Christ.

Our key verse tells us that everything flows from your heart; your hopes, your dreams, your fears, your anxieties, your anger, your forgiveness, your humility, your peace, your greed, your generosity, and your love. Yes, everything that makes you who you are is in your heart.

Without a doubt, we need Jesus Christ to guard our heart. As a Christian, our hearts are emptied at salvation only to be filled by the Holy Spirit of God with the Fruit of the Spirit. Only a heart guarded by Christ can resist the influences of ungodliness. A heart submitted to Christ in prayer is protected by His peace. (Philippians 4:7).

We may experience ailments that hinder our wholehearted devotion to Christ, like: faintheartedness, or, being weary in your faith and service to Christ. Slow down and ask the Holy Spirit to restore your heart into wholeness.

Next, we may experience a loss of heart, meaning we are distracted and defer our better judgment to self and not keep our hearts focused on what Christ desires. We must keep our hope in Christ, giving us peace and reassurance.

Sometimes, we may develop a foolish heart, meaning we forget Christ as if we stop believing who He is and make uncharacteristic decisions that do not include Him. This usually occurs when we are faced with fear and anxiety. To guard against this, we must seek the wisdom of Him in all we do.

Perhaps the most dangerous ailment would be to develop a hard heart. This is usually triggered by injustice or a lack of integrity in others. Fortunately, through our faith in Christ, a hard heart can be replaced by a new heart, born from above.

As the Psalmist asked God to create in him a clean heart, we too can guard our needy hearts by taking each day, submitting to Christ, following Him, and allowing Him to control our heart and guard against any ailments that arise.

Additional reading: Isaiah 26:3; Matthew 6:25-34; John 14:27; Ephesians 3:29, & 6:18.

"A good man out of the good treasure of his heart bringeth forth that which is good."

— Luke 6:45'

Day 143

Trusting God's Will and Not Our Own

Key Scripture: **Proverbs 16:3**

Surely many of us started our adult lives as that one force in life to be reckoned with, taking on the business field we had chosen as a career, with all our efforts laid out to become the best, most valued employee that would set our careers skyrocketing to the top. Certainly, it is not wrong to dream, but several things should be considered as a Christian man or woman seeking success in a chosen career.

In our seeking success, we have ourselves focused on our own desires and not the will of God. Often, we forget as Christians, we should be asking God for His will to be relevant in each step. The more you try to follow your desires, the more your soul and your walk with Christ will suffer.

Seeking the gods of this world creates idols out of our dreams and we must guard that this never happens before something else in our lives suffers. We must recommit our heart's desires to our Heavenly Father, as our key verse clearly states. This is God's desire for us to commit our life and plans to Him while trusting His leading and guidance. God's will for our lives will always be best; taking what's in our hearts and conforming it to His.

Our desires, left unchecked, will open the door to a life fueled by pride and idolatry, taking us further away from the Lord. When we seek God in all things, we learn that our heart's true desire can only be found in Jesus. Only then as we commit to follow Him, will He lead us in the path of righteousness. (Psalm 23:3).

"But seek ye first the kingdom of God,
and His righteousness;
and all these things shall be added unto you."

— Matthew 6:33

Day 144

Who Do You Say I Am?

Key Scripture: **Matthew 16:15**

Does anyone remember to whom, and when this was said? In Mathew 16:15 Jesus asked this question to His followers. Various answers came back to Him but only one came back as a personal response. All but one said some in way or another who they thought Jesus was. Only Peter answered personally.

If this question were asked to a group of people that somewhat followed Jesus today, I am sure the response would be that he is "Jesus." Today, Jesus is a common name in the household of most everyone. In reflection to the name Jesus, I ask what and who do you say that Jesus is in your heart today?

A great songwriter, Dottie Rambo, wrote a song that best describes who Jesus should be to each of us called "I Call Him Lord." Give it a listen.

Hudson Taylor, the great missionary wrote: "Christ is either Lord of all, or He is not Lord at all."

This is the name for Jesus that stands out most to me and should be to every Child of God; meaning every Christian should say, do, or think anything that does not reflect that Jesus is truly the Lord of their lives should re-dedicate themselves to Him!

I pray that each couple would search their hearts, and if Christ is not the Lord of your life or your relationship, you would stop, turn to our Holy God, ask forgiveness and make Christ the Lord of your heart today.

"I am Alpha and Omega,
the beginning and the ending,
saith the Lord,
which is, and which was,
and which is to come,
the Almighty."

— Revelation 1:8

Day 145

As a Christian We Live a New Life

Key Scripture: **Romans 6:4**

Just a few days ago, I finished reading and studying the book of Romans. I really believe that I will never exhaust the fullness of this book in my lifetime. God is real and powerful.

Our topic today is about the new life that we may live as Christians. Most of us have stood by the graveside of a loved one and felt the weight of death. Conversations are usually silent and we experience the true reality of death.

Death separates. Anyone who has lost a close friend or family member has felt the weight of this separation. Death leaves a deep empty void in our lives where that loved one once occupied.

Through the gospel, something as terrible as death can speak a word of hope. The death of Christ separates us from the power and bondage of sin in our lives. The death of a Christian separates that loved one from the struggle with sin and brokenness in this life. Death does not have the final word.

In God's redemptive plan, resurrection follows death. Believers will live with Christ. Furthermore, all who believe in Christ do not have to wait for physical death in order to begin the new life in Christ. The power of sin has been broken in our lives, and like Christ, we begin living for God.

Baptism is a picture of what has transpired in our lives, buried the sin, and we live as different people; not as those living in the clutches of sin and death, but those destined for a life of God's glory.

By God's grace, the weight of sin and death gives way to the new life in Christ, giving hope even over the grave.

Lord, I know you suffered death on the cross for me, and rose again giving us the hope of eternal life. Break the power of sin in me and give me the hope to face my destiny.

"For the wages of sin is death,
but the gift of God is eternal life through Jesus Christ our Lord."

— Romans 6:23

Day 146

Change is Sometimes Difficult; But God Never Changes

Key Scripture: **Malachi 3:6a**

Change is hard. Sometimes change is not only hard, it is painful. But whether we like it or not, change is a part of our lives today. The longer we live, we will learn that the only thing in life that is certain is change. Whether our changes seem hard or make us happy, change teaches us that life is fragile, uncertain, and temporary.

We can then say that nothing lasts forever. However, one thing does, "God." In our key verse the scripture says that He is the Lord and never changes. God doesn't change. He has always been and will always be never-changing. (Psalm 102:27):

"But thou art the same, and thy years shall have no end."

Not only does God stay the same but so does His loving plans for us that are based on His Word found in Psalm 33:11:

"The counsel of the LORD standeth for ever, the thoughts of His heart to all generations."

Despite changes that come in my life beyond my control, I have learned to place my trust in Him who promises to carry me through any changes that I may face today. (Psalm 119:90):

"Thy faithfulness is unto all generations: thou hast established the earth, and it abideth."

If God has allowed changes in your life, let them motivate you to draw closer to Him and to His Word. Let Him be your refuge and strength in times of change.

"Jesus Christ the same yesterday, and today, and forever."

— Hebrews 13:8

All We Really Need is a Little Bit of Faith

Key Scripture: **2 Kings 4:2**

In the last six years of my life I have experienced over and over grief that at times seemed more than I could bear. I felt that each morning I woke up to expect another heartbreaking situation to arise; like Job, a season of "now what?"

Just like the widow in our passage talking to Elisha, I felt powerless to change my circumstances. Losing a wife through death and one through needless divorce, I have gone through some trying times, facing new challenges like finances, health, relationships, and emotions.

The widow in 2 Kings understood exactly the season of events as I did. Elisha asked her what could he do to help? What did she have in the house? She answered; "Nothing at all except a flask of olive oil." She awoke each day, facing the mourning of her dead husband. She felt she was alone and abandoned in her circumstances. She was without a husband to share the day, raising children, and without the means to provide. She faced threats of lenders seeking unpaid debts and losing her children to slavery, which meant she felt powerless.

Being in these situations causes us to focus on our misfortunes rather than our promises of blessings. Her misfortune was a lack of income, her blessing was a little bit of oil. We too have blessings in our season of "Now What?" They are simply harder to find when our thoughts and activities become centered around our misfortunes.

In times like these, it is difficult to look past the problem and notice the blessings. When I look beyond my own circumstances, God helps me see my little blessings. I have a "little bit of hope," a "little bit of joy," and a "little bit of energy."

We, like the widow, can look upon the little bit and think it is not enough. God looks at our little and says; "It is plenty; watch what I can do with it."

With little faith, the widow in 2 Kings 4:5-6 says she poured and poured until every jug and bowl were filled. God knew exactly what was needed to help her through this season of trial. Her little faith changed the course of her family's life. In our own season of "Now What," God knows exactly what we need; He will take our little bit of what we have and multiply it into exactly what we lack and need.

The only thing we must do is offer ourselves as **empty jugs**, allowing God to pour into us what we need during our season of "What Now." He will take our little bit of faith and produce more. He will take our little bit of hope and develop trust; and finally, He will take our little bit of joy and bring much laughter, and that little bit of energy will accomplish much.

"And Jesus said unto them, Because of your unbelief: for verily I say unto you, If you have faith as the grain of mustard seed, ye shall say unto this mountain, Remove hence to yonder place; and it shall remove and nothing shall be impossible unto you."

— Matthew 17:20

Day 148

A Choice to Have a 'Heart of Compassion' — Go, Give, and Pray

Key Scripture: **Matthew 9:36**

Many Christians have a huge misconception that unbelievers are their enemies. This is certainly not true at all. We were all unbelievers at one time. In our passage, we see that Jesus saw the multitudes and was moved with compassion. He was moved because they were weary and scattered, like sheep having no shepherd. This is where we as Christians, need to step up and understand that our role is to desire a heart of compassion.

In verse 37-38 of this chapter we hear, *"the harvest is plenteous but the laborers are few."* Jesus said, *"pray that the Lord of the harvest will send forth laborers into His harvest."* Not only should we have compassion for the sick and hurting but also for the unbelievers needing a Savior. They do not understand their need of a Redeemer unless we, as the laborers sent by Jesus, choose to have this heart of compassion to reach those wandering sheep. It is our responsibility to go, give, and pray that others will have this chance.

Some may think this is not their calling and that they should remain distant from participating in this ministry of outreach. This is like Jonah when he was called to Nineveh to preach the gospel and rebelled against it. God finally took charge of things and got him there, and the city repented toward God.

Let's not think that God will always handle things this way. When God calls, we must heed His call, and with a heart full of compassion for the lost, step up to the plate and willingly lead hurting souls to Christ.

Lord, give me a heart beating for the needs of others and an ear to hear Your calling.

"And He said unto them, Go ye into all the world,
and preach the gospel to every creature."

— Mark 16:15

Day 149

To Be Moved with Compassion

Key Scripture: **Matthew 14:14**

It is impossible to read the Gospels and not recognize that Christ was moved with compassion. The phrase "moved with compassion" is used again and again, which I believe shows His reaction to the needs of the people who came to Him. In very simple language, having compassion means to be touched by the needs of others. Christ showed that His compassionate heart was the driving force behind the miracles and healings He performed.

I look around and even in my own life, feel a need for compassion, not only for myself but also so many others who are hurting through sickness or heartache for a friend or a loved one in need. There is a genuine need for us to experience as Christ did the necessity to have a compassionate heart.

God is love, so we as Christians should allow ourselves to be moved with compassion, and by doing so, we are learning to walk with God. Allowing yourself to be used by God as a compassionate person improves your relationship with Christ and gives a peace of heart and mind knowing God is using you to perform a ministry that is close and dear to His own heart.

We can train our hearts to feel the pain of others, and once we learn to feel the pain of others, our lives will change because we can now respond and understand how to help and pray for their needs. We want the power of God in our lives, and one way to achieve that power is by opening our hearts to the needs of others while feeling their pain.

Having the necessary faith to help others is increased by love for that individual in need. Sharing and showing love will increase our ability to have a heart of genuine compassion for others.

"But whoso hath this world's good,
and seeth his brother have need,
and shutteth up his bowels of compassion from him,
how dwelleth the love of God in him?"

— 1 John 3:17

Day 150

There is No Secret to Having a Flaming Heart

Key Scripture: **Luke 24:32**

Honestly many people will never understand that having a heart desiring to stay burning for Christ is not a secret. Pastors and teachers stress the issue of the importance of keeping a fire burning and maintaining zeal. I admit that we should have a heart that is capable of going through anything. We are usually the reason our fires are smothered; however, we can also be the reason our heart stays eagerly seeking to do what is right in God's eyes. We simply must learn to "abide" in Christ.

Much of the distress we encounter in our lives is a result of sin, but we are also ignorant of the laws of our own nature. For instance, the only test we should use to determine whether to allow an emotion we have to run its course in our lives is to examine what the final outcome of the emotion will be. By thinking this through, we should be able to determine if this is something God would condemn. If so, then we should immediately put a stop to it. On the other hand, if the Spirit of God kindles an emotion, then by all means allow that emotion into your life.

As I said earlier, to maintain our steadfast zeal we must learn to abide in Christ. This means keeping up a habit of constant, close communion with God, as well as always leaning on Him, resting in Him, pouring out our hearts to Him, and using Him as our fountain of strength. To abide in Christ is no secret, simply make up your heart and mind to keep the flame in your heart kindled by abiding in Him.

This sounds simple, but with our busy lifestyles and so many things of this world distracting our hearts and minds from having a faithful, steadfast, abiding relationship with Christ, we must determine to stand with His power and keep our hearts and thoughts on Him.

Oswald Chambers said, "Defenders of the faith are inclined to be bitter until they learn to walk in the light of the Lord. When you learn to walk in the light of the Lord, bitterness and contention are impossible."

"Abide in me, and I in you.
As the branch cannot bear fruit of itself,
except it abide in the vine,
no more can ye, except ye abide in me."

— John 15:4

Day 151

God Does Mend Broken Dreams

Key Scripture: **Genesis 37:5-7**

For six long weeks, every morning I had to leave my wife in a hospital room and go to work, then each evening after visiting her, I returned home for a short rest. This was not the way I dreamt our marriage to be. I watched as my lovely wife was covered with tubes and fighting every day to beat major surgery to remove a horrible disease that had taken over part of her body. In my wildest dreams, I never imagined we would for the next five years of our marriage be faced with a battle against cancer.

My mind looks to our subject in the key passage. Joseph, I am sure felt his dreams were shattered as his brothers stripped him of his garments, threw him into a pit, and sold him into slavery. God doesn't end stories with slavery. Fast forwarding in the life of Joseph, we find him in prison for a crime he did not commit. God intervened in Joseph's life and he was freed from prison and given a position in the land, second only to the king of Egypt. Later through circumstances, Joseph was united again with his brothers and they bowed down to him, really showing how God turned this impossible dream around and made it come true.

Sometimes when it looks like our dreams are ending, it's not the ending; it's just the beginning. Like Joseph, God does not promise that seeing a God-given dream come true will be easy. However, it does mean we need to stay faithful and totally surrender to Christ, asking Him to make something out of our broken dreams and make them a reality of His divine power and promise.

God didn't send His only Son to die on a cross and buy our freedom only to let the story end with bondage.

"Ye are of God, little children,
and have overcome them:
because greater is He that is in you,
than he that is in the world."

— 1 John 4:4

Day 152

Where Did God Go?

Key Scripture: **Colossians 1:27-29**

Have you ever felt as if God was distant—like you were playing an old fashion game of hide and seek with Him? The truth is, we sometimes walk right past God, as if He were just an image blended in with our surroundings.

In our key verse, God clearly wants us to live and grow closer to Him. The passage shows us that God made Himself known to all through His Son. He wants to live through each of us, therefore we should look forward to sharing His glory with others.

To increase our knowledge and understanding of who God is and to know the heart of God, we must first stay faithful in the reading and studying of His Word.

In 2 Timothy 3:16 we see that the Bible is God's Word on paper; so, let it become real and speak to you. Through the Bible, we learn what matters to God, who He says He is, and how seriously He desires to have a relationship with each of us.

Next, we should seek friends that build our character and help us remain strong and faithful in our relationship with God. We need those who lovingly hold us accountable to truth and doctrine and will let us know if we drift away from our faith.

In our passage, Paul desired his friends to not only know Jesus, but to also grow and become mature followers of Christ. If it feels like God is hiding, just open His Book and you will find Him; He is always there.

"And ye shall seek me, and find me,
when ye shall search for me with all your heart."
— Jeremiah 29:13

Day 153

Afraid to Accept God's Calling?

Key Scripture: **Joshua 1:9**

Many times in our lives, we go through changes. While they might seem great, God steps up. I remember getting married and watching my high school sweetheart walk down the aisle toward me; also, when my first child was born, and when I started a new career. All of these were indeed changes that caused fear of uncertainty for me. I remember questioning God and asking Him, "Are You sure this is what You want for me? What if I fail and I'm not able to do what You've called me to do?"

As I decided to step out by faith and suppress my fears, I was reminded of Joshua. God put him in charge of leading His people into the Promised Land. I'm sure Joshua felt that things were impossible, and wondered how he was to bring down the walls of Jericho and leading the children of Israel.

In Joshua chapter 1, God had to tell Joshua to be strong and courageous three times. This tells us that he felt ill-equipped for the assignment. Maybe we feel ill-equipped to do things in our lives too, causing us to be fearful and unsure. I know in my own life I have felt that I was not able to do things required of me and doubted my abilities—feeling like I would fail.

Let's be reminded of what God said to Joshua in Chapter 1:5 & 9, He would be with him as He was with Moses and would not forsake him. He was the One who called Joshua and he was not to be afraid, but stand strong and God would always be with him.

God does the same for us today. When He calls us to do something, He will equip us with Himself. There is no room for failure with this promise. No matter what you're called to do, push through your fears and take that first step. God commands us to be strong and courageous, and assures us that He will always be with us through everything we face. If you are called to do something for God, put your eyes on Him and watch Him step up and show up in your life.

"And Moses said unto the people,
'Fear ye not, stand still, and see the salvation of the LORD,
which He will shew to you today..."

— Exodus 14:13

Day 154

Keep the Fire Fanned

Key Scripture: 2 Timothy 1:6

Growing up, I remember some very bitter winters and how we dealt with Old Man Winter. We lived about a mile and a half off the main road in this big wood framed house. We had one fireplace in the center room. So, you can imagine that room was constantly used for all family activities.

We learned that controlling that fireplace was a full-time job, from cutting the wood to starting the fire and maintaining the hot coals. By keeping the flame blazing, we became efficient in heating that one room.

When the fire is not maintained you can expect the flame to go out and the coals to start smoldering because they lack the necessary oxygen to keep them burning. This means you have to introduce more oxygen to bring back the flame. This is what the Bible means when it says, "fan the flames."

Look further into this in 2 Timothy 1:5-6 where Paul reminds Timothy of his calling, and encourages him to not just keep the faith but to fan the flames of the spiritual gift God gave him. Paul understood that like a fire, our faith and our ability to operate in our spiritual gifts can start strong, but through time and circumstances, the fire can dwindle down to a pile of smoldering coals, giving off little warmth or light.

The same thing happens in our own spiritual lives. For me, what feeds oxygen to my fire could come in the form of quiet, uninterrupted time in God's Word, or when hearing a favorite song of worship playing over and over in my mind. It can even happen driving down the road, praying to God for His empowering for my life. One or all these cause my heart's flame to stay blazing.

The next time you feel your flame is almost out, give it a boost of intentional oxygen that works to rekindle your fire. Keep it going by using your spiritual gifts to serve others in the name and power of Jesus Christ.

Lord, help me to keep the fire in my soul burning bright and hot for your glory.

"Wherefore I put thee in remembrance that thou stir up the gift of God, which is in thee by the putting on of my hands."

— 2 Timothy 1:6

Day 155

God is with Me Through the Valley

Key Scripture: Psalm 23:4

We have all been in situations that make us somewhat afraid. I remember when I was a teen, my father asked me if I wanted to stay home from school and go hunting with him. I jumped at this chance and we started pretty early the next morning by going down to the creek to our hunting club on the Savannah River.

It turned out to be a cloudy day, with no sun to help us get our bearings. This proved critical, and after several attempts to cut off wherever the dogs were running, all of a sudden, I realized I was lost. I made several attempts to find anything that may look familiar and failed. (This was before cell phones.)

I kept moving slowly, and after going through several extremely thick patches of cane breaks, I decided to sit and wait. After a while, my mind wandered to my key verse, and I started thinking about the Lord is my Shepherd, and we walk through valleys and really never have to fear evil, for the Lord is with us. I certainly was in a valley right then, and I had plenty of fear. I was alone, there were no sounds of civilization, and no way to know where to find a safe refuge.

This is what I should have done, and now much older and wiser, I pray that I'll always seek my Shepherd before making any moves or judgments on my own. We should look at the Shepherd first, realizing we are easily rattled, like sheep. When we find ourselves in a valley, He has promised to never leave us. This means never look for an exit; look for the Shepherd.

Next, we are to listen to the Shepherd. His Word that you have hidden in your heart will spring forth in your mind. As it does, meditate on these verses and let His presence fill your heart.

Finally, we are to lean on our Shepherd. In the valley we become weak, but in His strength, we are made strong. He will lead or even carry us through our difficult valleys. Remember, we are sheep in need of a Shepherd to help us face our fears in life of things that are above our abilities. Nothing is too hard for Him. We must learn to lean on God's strength and not our own, because He is more than enough to get us through any valley.

"From the end of earth will I cry unto thee,
when my heart is overwhelmed:
lead me to the rock that is higher than I."

— Psalm 61:2

Day 156

Thanks Lord, I'll Take Over Now

Key Scripture: 1 Samuel 23:7

Have you ever been in a situation when all of a sudden, your life changed drastically? It's not a good feeling to have a cardiologist look into your eyes and say; "You will never work construction another day for the rest of your life." This happened to me at the age of 39, and the feeling of total helplessness immediately took over my thoughts about my future.

After going through a period of depression, the Lord revealed to me the need to pray for doors to open to me. God answered my prayers and gave me several directions to pursue. I began to walk through those doors and "stopped praying." I figured I would do as I was trained to do and take on these new opportunities.

In the midst of my new beginnings, I never once questioned if God was behind the new doors opening for me. I simply took it for granted that He was, and told myself; "I can handle this from here."

Shortly after Saul became king of Israel, he took over his life and no longer humbled himself to ask God for wisdom, which caused his heart to harden. In 1 Samuel 10:9-10; we see that Saul experienced a change of heart and allowed the Spirit of God to move in his life. Then the sin of jealousy over a young shepherd boy named David took over his success, and his jealous heart blinded him from recognizing the voice of God. Saul now confused God's voice with his own jealous heart.

In our key verse we find Saul was made aware of where David was hiding and actually thought God had revealed this to him in order that he might kill David, the one God had anointed to become the next king. How did Saul slip from the place where in 1 Samuel 11:6; *"the Spirit of God came powerfully upon him,"* to the point he was now seeking to kill God's anointed one?

First, he failed to obey God fully, but in 1 Samuel 16:10, he did obey. He valued more looking into people's eyes than looking into God's. (1 Samuel 15:30). Finally, he deceived himself by allowing his jealousy of David to overtake his heart. (18:9). His heart grew cold because he lost his intimacy with God, which led him away from God.

I look back at my own situation and realize that no matter how sure I feel about my decisions, I need to hear from the Spirit of God in every aspect of my life. The moment I stop asking God for wisdom, direction, and to examine my heart is the day I will find myself taking what belongs to God into my own hands. Never again do I want this.

"If any of you lack wisdom,
let him ask of God, that giveth to all men liberally,
and upbraideth not, and it shall be given him."

— James 1:5

Day 157

God Believes in You; Believe in Yourself

Key Scripture: **Philippians 2:13**

Having control of our dreams means we are to believe in ourselves, rather than letting our fears hinder our dreams. John Maxwell wrote: "If you know who you are, make the changes you must in order to learn and grow, and then give everything you've got to your dreams; you can achieve anything your heart desires."

By focusing on particular events in our lives, we try to put things into perspective. When we do, we could have the same perspective as the apostle Paul, who wrote:

"Not that I speak in respect of want: for I have learned, in whatsoever state I am, therewith to be content."
— Philippians 4:11.

This verse says much, considering that Paul was shipwrecked, whipped, beaten, stoned, and imprisoned. His faith allowed him to maintain his perspective. He understood that as long as he was doing what he was supposed to be doing, being labeled as a success or failure by others mattered nothing at all to him. We should feel the same because God gave us unique abilities to seek the plans He has for us. Jeremiah 29:11 says:

"For I know the thoughts that I think toward you, saith the LORD, thoughts of peace, and not of evil, to give you an expected end."

"A man's heart deviseth his way: but the LORD directeth his steps."
— Proverbs 16:9

Day 158

What Happens When We Stop Living for Jesus?

Key Scripture: **2 Peter 1:3**

I am sure many of us have had times when we struggled with our walk with Christ. Seeing things in others that were real showed me my lack. I wasn't experiencing a true intimacy and peace with God like I should. Deep inside I knew there had to be more to my relationship with God than I was experiencing.

I found myself promising God I would give up some sin in my life, only to repeat that sin the next day. I failed religiously and my willpower evaded me to the point I felt worthless and defeated. I had the desire to do right, but no matter how hard I tried, I couldn't. Perhaps you can relate.

Finding myself desperate to understand what was behind my confusion, God's Word brought insight. This is where our key verse spoke to me.

Jesus had not only saved me through His power, but He had given me an inexhaustible heavenly resource enabling me to live a godly life. Only when we solely depend on God's power to do for us what we cannot do ourselves will we be able to conquer temptation to sin and gain victory over ungodly habits.

By trusting in my own ability instead of relying on God's ability to work through me, I discovered that nothing was missing in my relationship with God and He had not left me ill-equipped. Now I have what my heart longed for most; an intimate relationship with God.

I can honestly tell you that the life Jesus promised is real. A change takes place in our lives when we stop trying to live for Jesus and let Jesus live in us.

"I am crucified with Christ: nevertheless I live;
yet not I, but Christ liveth in me:
and the life which I now live in the flesh I live by the faith of the Son of God,
who loved me, and gave Himself for me."

— Galatians 2:20

Day 159

God Hates Sin

Key Scripture: **Proverbs 6:16-19**

God hates sin and in our key passage He lists seven of those sins that are probably the most prevalent in everyday life. The first one mentioned is a haughty spirit in verse 17. Have you ever met someone who in their mannerisms reflected the pride in their heart? You see in this one a proud, arrogant person with their nose and eyes in the air, showing their prideful spirit.

Ever wondered why pride is listed first? That's because it is a sin of the heart. Rebellion against God, it so happens, was the very sin of pride where Satan himself cried out against God, saying in Isaiah 14:13-14 that he would ascend to Heaven and would set his throne above the stars of God and would sit on the mount of assembly in the sides of the north. Also, he would ascend above the clouds and make himself like the Most High.

God also hates a lying tongue. Humans have tried to distort truth in order to give themselves a better advantage or promote themselves. Still, if it is not the truth, it is a lie. God does not tolerate lies of any kind, so we are to live according to His truth.

Th next thing God hates is a murderous hand. Some people would rather kill because of their greed and hatred to gain their desires than live a godly life. God ordained the sanctity of life and therefore decreed that murderers be put to death.

God also hates a wicked heart and feet that run to evil. Sometimes people fall into sin inadvertently, but here God speaks of people who plot out sinful acts, then run eagerly to execute them.

Finally, God hates a false witness and a divisive spirit. Bearing false witness is simply telling lies about someone, seeking to destroy their reputation or to obstruct justice. A divisive spirit sets out to create division where unity should be.

Certainly, these aforementioned sins characterize unbelievers, but Christians are not exempt from them. Let's learn and remember these things that God hates and ward ourselves from them along with anything else that displeases God.

"Through thy precepts I get understanding: therefore I hate every false way."
— Psalm 119:104

Day 160

Who Fills the Emptiness in Your Life?

Key Scripture: **Psalm 63:1**

The woman at the well met a stranger who asked her for a drink. He then offered her "living water," something that would satisfy her thirst, causing her to never thirst again. She asked Jesus how He was going to draw this water, because he had nothing to draw it with. She also asked where she could get this "living water." (John 4:11).

All He needed to draw the living water with was His Spirit; it would draw her to Him. As far as the depth, He only needed to reach that empty place in her heart. All who have not accepted Jesus as Savior have experienced this empty feeling. But like the woman at the well, we all have sought other means for our needs to be met instead of Him.

I've looked to people, possessions, and positions and I've said, "If only I had… or could… then I'd be fulfilled." However, I now realize these things were never enough to satisfy. No matter how much I do or get, it is never enough to fill me up, because it is not supposed to. The empty spaces in our hearts were created to be filled by God alone.

We see the deep thirst in David's life. Even though he had everything he wanted, it was not enough. (Psalm 63:1). Then David described what he experienced when he drank deeply of God's love. (Psalm 63:2-4),

The same thing happened to the woman at the well. She drank deeply of God's love and was filled to overflowing, as will be for all who ask for this water. Only His unconditional acceptance, approval, and affirmation can fill the empty places within our hearts; the deepest thirst of our souls. Until God's love and acceptance is enough, nothing else will be.

"Cause me to hear thy lovingkindness in the morning;
for in thee do I trust: cause me to know the way wherein I should walk;
for I lift up my soul unto thee."

— Psalm 143:8

Day 161

Pleasing God

Key Scripture: **Proverbs 11:20**

As Christians, we all experience joy in our lives by knowing and serving God. Our topic is "pleasing God" and we try to share several aspects of joy and the joy of pleasing God, as well as how to lose your joy.

Maybe we never focus on how we can bring joy to God, but scripture mentions several ways: for example, in Luke 15:7, God says: *"I say unto you, that likewise joy shall be in heaven over one soul that repenteth…"* Repentance brings joy to God.

In Hebrews 11:6 we see that faith is another source of joy for God. *"But without faith it is impossible to please him…"* That's the negative side of a positive principle; when we trust God, He is pleased.

In addition to repentance and faith, prayer also brings joy to God. Proverbs 15:8 says: *"The sacrifice of the wicked is an abomination to the LORD: but the prayer of the upright is His delight."*

Righteous living is also another source of joy to God, as David shared in 1 Chronicles 29:17:

"I know also, my God, that thou triest the heart, and hast pleasure in uprightness…" As well our key verse Proverbs 11:20; Solomon says: "They that are of a froward heart are abomination to the LORD: but such as are upright in their way are His delight."

Repentance, faith, prayer, and righteous living all please God because they each are expressions of love. This is the overshadowing principle: whenever we express our love to God, whether by words of praise or acts of obedience, we bring Him joy.

It should thrill each of us to know that the God of our Salvation delights in us. I pray that this motivates each of us to find as many ways as possible to bring joy to our Lord and Savior, Jesus Christ, every day.

Let's all be determined to be who we say we are, and show our love for God, pleasing the One who deserves all glory and praise.

"And He that sent me is with me:
the Father hath not left me alone;
for I do always those things that please him."

— John 8:29

Day 162

We are to Listen Twice as Much as We Speak

Key Scripture: Isaiah 50

The title for today's entry simply means that God gave us two ears and one mouth, so we are to double up on listening. Christ is thought of as the world's greatest teacher; multitudes flocked to hear Him. Even those sent out to arrest Him came back empty handed, as it says in John 46:7: *"Never has anyone spoken like this."* Something we critically miss is that the world's greatest teacher was first the world's greatest listener. Jesus often reminded people about the source of His words. They came from the Father, as spoken in John 12:49.

Jesus always spoke the right words because He first listened to the Father. The Father woke Jesus every morning to hear His lessons. He never forgot that He was first a listener, then He was a teacher. This is why Jesus made it a priority to rise early and listen to the Father. (Mark1:35).

This is a vital point in Biblical truth: "It is the ear that is the seat of intelligence." Insight for life is the ability to listen. Wisdom is something we are not born with; we must listen for it. It comes from outside us and must be daily learned from God.

As the Father opened the ears of Jesus, He also opens ours as David says in Psalm 40:6. Having the right words to say is not a matter of smarts, but a matter of first listening to God. Hearing God speak is not just for Jesus or the psalmist, but also for us. In Matthew 11:15; the Word of God says: *"He that hath ears to hear, let him hear."*

So, each day let's ask God to open our ears to listen before we ever open our mouths to speak. That's why God gave us two ears and one mouth.

"He that answereth a matter before he heareth it, it is folly and shame unto him."

— Proverbs 18:13

Day 163

Which Voice Do You Hear?

Key Scripture: **John 10:27**

When you find yourself in a situation where you have just finished a play before your family and friends, you hear words of praise and approval from those in attendance, and also maybe from your brothers a very discouraging remark that you looked dumb in your performance. There are two voices pointing out two different perspectives, so which words ring loudest in your heart and mind?

In John 10, God calls Himself the Good Shepherd, and we, His children, are the sheep of His pasture. In our key verse, Jesus confirms we can hear His voice. Jesus speaks of a stranger's voice who also calls to the sheep; a stranger likened to a thief who only comes to steal, kill, and destroy. Jesus states that the sheep will not follow the voice of the stranger because they don't know it, but His voice they know and follow.

Sometimes, the voice of God may seem faint or distant. At these times, we need to get intentional about listening to His voice. Those distant times come when we try fitting God into parts of our lives when it's convenient, like reading God's Word only when we have nothing else to do or attending social events rather than church functions.

The voice gets weaker, the closer you get to the world. Starving the soul of fellowship with the Spirit of God is not the answer. When you hear the right voice, your perspective on life changes and your course is changed to wanting to hear that strong voice of Jesus, causing that stranger's voice to become non-existent in your life. The two voices now become One.

Lord, help us to not grow weary in seeking Your voice, and learn to listen to Your voice, and as we do, may we follow You Lord.

"Therefore we ought to give the more earnest heed to the things which we have heard, lest at any time we should let them slip."

— Hebrews 2:1

Day 164

Our Goal in Life is to Love Others Well

Key Scripture: **James 1:19**

As a child I grew up with several brothers and sisters. Because of this, I feel like I missed out on some major things in life that were important, like a role model to listen to my anxieties and help me deal with my emotions. So, by the time I became a young adult, I'd had to learn about dealing with my emotions on my own.

As an adult, I feel more than anything it is important to be a person who is willing to simply listen. I am learning to lend an ear to the heartfelt rumblings of others who have no one in their life who will simply listen without giving advice. Sometimes, all that's needed is someone to listen.

It would be wise that we all memorize our key verse. Recently, I looked at this verse as instruction for my role as a Christian grandfather, father, friend and co-laborer. It is a challenge to not only talk less, but truly listen to those around me.

James gives us the wisdom and the challenge to be the emphatic listeners others desperately need. No matter what role we are filling at the moment, we need to slow down and listen. James, while reminding us we are loved, calls us to move quickly to a position of listening and to move slowly, even with caution, to a place of speaking.

I am challenged by James' words because words like these inspire me to set things right so I can move forward in setting other things right. James reminds us that getting things done is not the goal; loving people well is the goal. Listening is loving people well.

With Jesus' power in us and James' word before us, we can love people as we listen well.

"Look not every man on his own things,
but every man also on the things of others."

— Philippians 2:4

Day 165

Unfailing Promises of God

Key Scripture: **Joshua 21:45**

In Joshua Chapter 21, a very ordinary passage, we read about the division of the cities and properties among the priests. The entire chapter is devoted to this subject until the last verse, God declared that not one of good promises He made to Israel was unfulfilled. Not one promise failed. God was faithful to fulfill every promise made to His people.

Notice that the word "good" was used to describe His promises. I believe that in every promise we see the goodness of God. He has not changed since the days of Joshua, so still today we can have the confidence that He is faithful and will fulfill His promises. (2 Peter 3:9).

At times, we may lose confidence that God will not fill our promises today. But, as He did in the days of Joshua, He is still the God of this universe and remains faithful to meet needs now, just as He did back then. Be patient, God's hand is not shortened, nor is He slack as 2 Peter says.

He desires our faithful trust and support in Him; God is a promise-keeping God. Remember these thoughts:

- My God fulfills every promise.

- By faith, I will hold on to every promise God has made.

- All God's promises to me are "good".

- God will never fail to fulfill even the smallest promise made.

"And we know that all things work together for good to them that love God, to them who are the called according to His purpose."

— Romans 8:28

Day 166

When Something is Missing, What Should We Do?

Key Scripture: Ecclesiastes 3:11

Reflecting on my early years as an adult, I remember I had the privilege to coach young kid's baseball. So often certain young kids had very little ability to play ball, but they wanted to be included and be part of a team. The hardest thing as a coach was to keep a child confident so he did not give up.

Teaching children to hit a ball sometimes tried my patience. Getting a kid to stand in the batter's box, keep their head still, keep their eye on the ball, grip the bat properly, etc. was difficult. It was a lot for a kid to learn.

Many times, those big teary eyes would look up at me and he would say, "How do I do it?" It broke my heart, but I tried hard to build their confidence, and they kept trying.

Then one day during a game, suddenly this child put together all he had learned, hit the ball and was able to reach first base. The child who was not sure what to do now understood that you never give up and practice until things come together.

Sometimes in my life I feel like one of those kids—unsure. I ache and worry about the future and fret about the present. I feel close to God, but not close enough. I see glimpses of God's presence, so I ask, "How do I do it?"

Our key verse says we are made for eternity and for glory, so as long as our feet are here on this earth we will experience a glory-ache that only heaven will fully satisfy. We will always feel a certain something is missing that's hard to define. We want to live in a constant state of awe, but we can't—our minds, our bodies, our emotions can't contain it because our human limitations won't allow it.

I hope this final thought will encourage you. We are children of God who are completely loved, completely forgiven, and complete in Christ. Those days when you feel that something's missing, don't beat yourself up about it. Don't get swallowed up in guilt because you're not totally satisfied and feel like something is missing—it is. We are not home yet. Until then, let's savor the moments when God's presence is strong, and look forward to the day when there will be nothing missing at all.

"In my Father's house are many mansions: if it were not so, I would have told you. I go to prepare a place for you. And if I go, and prepare a place for you, I will come again, and receive you unto myself; that where I am, there ye may be also."

— John 14:2-3

"And God shall wipe away all tears from their eyes; and there shall be no more death, neither sorrow, nor crying, neither shall there be any more pain; for the former things are passed away."

— Revelation 21:4

Day 167

God Always Blesses When We Do the Right Thing

Key Scripture: **Proverbs 11:1**

God does not like ugly. He hates it when people are dishonest. A part of our key verse says: "He loves it when business is above board." We all have a choice to live according to the values of this world or according to the values of the Word of God. Christians should always make the decision to follow the ways of Christ, believing they will receive an eternal reward for standing up for right.

Others choose to go the way of the world by lying, cheating, and stealing every chance they get. It just simply makes sense to stay on our Christian path when we realize that God will bless us for doing the right thing. Many of His blessings are obvious, but even if you are suffering in some way for doing what is right, we have 1 Peter 2:20 to rely on: God will bless you if you have to suffer for doing something good.

Doing right may be costly at times but being a person of character does not have a price tag on it. Integrity is saying and doing the right thing, even when no one else is around. We all can choose to live consistently, and we can all decide to do the right thing in all we do. We can decide right now how we will respond to any moral or ethical dilemma that may come our way in our future.

It's easy because we already know what we will do because we have already made our choice. It is about upholding God's standards and knowing He will give us power to overcome temptation, resist ethical shortcuts, and pursue what's right instead of letting the world dictate our decisions.

With the help of God, we can do the right thing.

"Therefore to him that knoweth to do good, and doeth it not, to him it is sin."

— James 4:17

Day 168

Right Things to Do in a Separation

Key Scripture: **Proverbs 3:5-6**

What's happening in your life is more about your faith than it is about your marriage. Going through a separation can be difficult and leave one or both parties bitter and feeling hateful. It can also mean that maybe one remains faithful and the other becomes extremely withdrawn from their faith. Either way, it is a difficult situation but God desires us to obey His Word.

Often, as the events and emotions of a marital crisis unfold, our perspective becomes skewed. Instead of viewing this present situation in the perimeters of our entire faith journey, we tend to focus on the pain the crisis has created. As a result, our faith becomes distorted and ineffective.

Remember, healing is a process that requires both time and faith, i.e. God's time, our faith.

Even though we can't control our spouse's heart, the good news is that God can work miracles and wonders in the one heart we give Him, our own.

A variety of issues can lead to challenges or even hopelessness for one or both parties in a marriage. Gaining a sense of hope and direction often requires understanding underlying issues and relationship patterns that might have led to the crisis.

Taking steps toward recovery is essential and necessary. The way to do this is with a personal dedication of faith, trusting in Christ, or maybe seeking guidance through a well-trained professional that God provides. As one of my former pastors told me, which over and over echoes deep within in my heart: "Stay Faithful, No Matter What!"

"Trust in the LORD with all thine heart,
lean not unto thine own understanding;
In all thy ways acknowledge Him and He shall direct thy paths."

— Proverbs 3:5-6

Day 169

God has Us Repeat Things Until it Sinks In

Key Scripture: **Joshua 6**

God gave the army of Israel specific instructions for how He wanted them to march around the walls of Jericho. God's order was they were to march around the city once each day for six days. On the seventh day, they were to march around seven times, and at the end of the seventh time, they were to yell and blow the trumpets. Once this was done, then the walls of Jericho would fall. These were precise and uncomplicated instructions. So, why did God ask them to repeat the march for seven days?

God constantly came through for Israel, starting in Egypt. He sent the plagues so Pharaoh would release them from captivity, then parted the Red Sea for them to cross over and destroyed the Egyptian army. He fed them with manna from the sky every morning, and gave them water to drink from a rock in the desert. Even with all this, the Israelites saw the tall people and the big walls facing them in the Promised Land, and they doubted God's ability to bring them through.

As God did for the Israelites, He also will do for each of us. He uses our struggles to teach us dependency and trust in Him. Sometimes God will send us for another lap around the wall until we understand the truth He is teaching us.

Constantly through the desert, the Israelites struggled to trust God and have faith in His promises. Now at Jericho, with each circle the Israelites made, they were saying, "Yes, God, I still believe." Pushing aside their doubts and fears with each lap, they were choosing God's words over their own personal fears.

Today, through our struggles, let's ask God what He is trying to teach us. Our struggles are an opportunity to allow us to grow closer to Him. When fear and doubt creep in, ask God to give us grace and faith through our trials and give us a steadfast faith to conquer our fears.

"For we walk by faith, not by sight."
— 2 Corinthians 5:7

Day 170

Salvation is the Beginning of Lordship

Key Scripture: **Romans 14:9**, Additional Reading: **Genesis 25:26; Matthew 8:1-17**

The reason why most people become a Christian is because they become convicted of sin and desire Salvation to escape the penalty and judgment for sin. They also want a place for eternity in Heaven when they die.

Many do not understand that this salvation is only the beginning of the Christian life. Paul spoke about why Christ died and returned to life. His focus was on Christ's Lordship and not just His saving work. Over 600 times in the New Testament Christ is referred to as Lord, and 24 times as Savior, so we cannot separate Christ's work as Savior from His role as Lord, because Lord is who He is and saving is what He does.

By thinking that Christ is only our Savior, we deeply grieve the Holy Spirit, even though Salvation is an important part of our Christian life. By not bringing our lives under His Lordship, we miss out on what Christ has to give.

Remember the rich young ruler in Mark 10, who asked Jesus what he needed to do to obtain eternal life? In verse 22, Christ told him he must sell all he had and give to the poor, and he lowered his head and walked away, sad because he had great wealth. What excluded him from God's Kingdom was that he already had a master in his life, and he refused to leave his wealth and place his loyalty in Christ.

If we want the benefit of Salvation and leave out the Lordship of Christ, we are left to our own insufficient, fallible devices. To have Christ reign in our hearts requires us to leave certain habits and desires behind, with the help of Christ. This is not an overnight transformation in which we become exactly as God wills us to be. Submitting to the Lordship of Christ is what brings our transformation, enabling us to call Him our Lord and not just Savior.

Let's all ask God to cleanse us of any sin, show us anything we might hold more valuable than Christ, and fully surrender to the Lordship of Jesus Christ.

*"And why call ye me, Lord, Lord,
and do not the things which I say?"*

— Luke 6:46

Day 171

Where Would we be Without Friends?

Key Scripture: **Ecclesiastes 4:9-12**

Rolling back the tears, I found myself stretched very thin some days when my four children had ball games going on the same day and at the same time. I remember having friends help out as I stood between two fields trying to watch two different kids play on different fields.

My friends stood with me and were able to relate what was happening on one field as I watched the other. I remember how blessed I felt to have such good friends helping, standing in the middle for me. We all need friends like this to help us see the games of life and stand in the middle, helping us to focus on things we can't do ourselves.

Our key verses tell how important it is to have friends; to bind ourselves with other Christians in friendship so they can love, support, and encourage us in our day-to-day struggles. Take time to thank those who stand in the middle with you. Determine to do the same for others.

Remember, no matter what, as Christians we all have the One who stands in the middle for each of us. Christ is always in the middle of life as a Friend who is closer than a brother. We are not alone.

So, let's take comfort in knowing that Christ is always in the middle of our circumstances, but also look for ways we can stand with others in the middle of their lives. Let's be the friend others can count on to help them see the game of life.

"Fear thou not; for I am with thee:
be not dismayed; for I am thy God:
I will strengthen thee, yea, I will help thee;
yea, I will uphold thee with the right hand of my righteousness."

— Isaiah 41:10

Day 172

Real Christianity, What Does it Mean to You?

Key Scripture: 2 Corinthians 5:15

Many people have the idea that legalistic religion has a list of "Dos" and "Don'ts." Sad, but some think the same about Christianity. But, as we know, real Christianity is a relationship of love with God, through His Son, Jesus Christ.

If you are in a loving marriage relationship, you want to make your spouse happy because you love them, not because that's the rule. If you're a parent, you are devoted to your children's well-being, not because some parenting book may say this is how you are supposed feel, but because you love them.

This is how our relationship with God should be. We should be devoted to Him. We should obey Him and serve Him. We should want to accomplish God's purpose for our life. We should do these things not out of commitment to a set of rules, but because of our love and devotion to Him.

Consider this: God sent His Son to suffer and die for us. Why? Certainly not because we deserved it, as every one of us is born with a sinful nature. The Bible tells us we have all sinned. God is holy, and there can be no sin in His presence, but He loves us and desires that we spend eternity with Him. He provided a way for this to happen by Jesus paying the penalty for our sin. That is incredible love!

When we receive Jesus as Lord and Savior, He loves us, guides us, strengthens us, and comforts us. How can we respond in any way but devotion to Him? We are no longer living for ourselves, but for Him. That's *real* Christianity.

In a true relationship there is a complete commitment to that relationship. In true Christianity, there is a true commitment of love to our Lord and Savior.

"A man that hath friends must shew himself friendly: and there is a friend that sticketh closer than a brother."

— Proverbs 18:24

Day 173

Lack of Repentance Brings Our Downfall

Key Scripture: 2 Chronicles 8

If you have ever built anything like a house, then you fully realize that nothing is placed by accident. Everything has a purpose and each stage of building is carefully planned and executed.

Solomon seemed to make a deliberate decision to marry Pharaoh's daughter. Solomon knew that he could not allow his wife to live in the palace of David because it was a holy place that could not house an unholy marriage, so Solomon built a separate house for his pagan wife. (2 Chronicles 8:11).

The marriage was a military alliance; he deliberately ignored God's command and married a woman who worshiped other gods. His solution was not to repent and ask for forgiveness, but to place his sin as far away from the holy city as possible. This brought the downfall of Solomon because of his unrepentant heart.

No matter how hard we try, we cannot separate ourselves from our sins. Solomon was repentant in most areas of his life, but his refusal to surrender this one eventually led him away from the Lord. (1 Kings 11:4-6).

Lack of repentance is nothing more than sin allowed to simmer. We can cover it with all the righteous acts in the world, but at some point, it will boil over and begin to affect every area of our life.

God is not blind to our sin, but our sin can make us blind to Him. If we want to experience the fullness of God's grace and healing in our lives, we have to understand "Repentance." We're not giving up something good; repentance is turning to something better.

"If we confess our sins,
He is faithful and just to forgive us our sins,
and to cleanse us from all unrighteousness."

— 1 John 1:9

Day 174

Balancing Act: My Independence vs. Dependence on God

Key Scripture: **Hebrews 4:16**

Most of us are considered to be independent people. I understand that some are forced to become that way, but for the majority, myself included, grew up being completely content doing our own thing.

As children, we learned to keep ourselves entertained and out of mom's hair. As we grew older, we still wanted to do things our own way, like keep our own schedule and spend our time as we wish. As we grew even older, circumstances seemed to strip us of our free will and we lost some of our independence. For me health issues like heart issue, failing eyesight, and joints wearing out have caused me to accept the fact that I can no longer be independent in some things.

We can lose our independence in another sense as well. This occurs when life becomes too hard for us to handle emotionally on our own. I am experiencing this now after losing my ability to do things I have always been able to do. After spending most of my life being able to handle emotional trials, I find myself in my current circumstances trying to still handle things alone. We finally do learn that our limitations of the emotions and tasks we try to accomplish are just too much.

Thankfully, through all these trials—whether losing our independence physically or emotionally—we have a God who does not want us to walk alone. He doesn't want us to be independent, but rather He wants us to run to Him and be dependent on Him for His guidance and His mercy.

How can we learn to balance the need to be independent with the need to also be dependent on God? We must pray that God will give us the ability to accept things as they are and trust Him to get us through. (Matthew 6:8).

God will use others to help balance our independence with dependence by losing our pride and allowing others to lend a helping hand. (Galatians 5:13-14). Lastly, God uses His Word to help balance our independence and dependence by giving us direction through the scriptures and seeking His will for our lives.

Nothing takes God by surprise. He knows our needs and promises to meet those needs as long as we stay faithful to Him. Being independent may feel like a great accomplishment, but the blessings we can receive from submitting to His guidance far outweigh what we can accomplish by our own hands.

"But seek ye first the kingdom of God, and His righteousness; and all these things shall be added unto you."

— Matthew 6:33

Day 175

Is Your Name Written in Heaven?

Key Scripture: **Luke 10:20**

Have you ever had plans to fly and upon getting to the airport and checking in found your name was not on the manifest? What a surprise! Even though you did everything you were supposed to do, you won't be getting to your destination as planned.

This is like our key passage, God has a manifest, "The Book of Life." Jesus sent His disciples on a mission journey and on their return, they happily reported their success. Jesus told them not to rejoice in their success, but rather to rejoice that their names were written in Heaven. Focusing on our joy is not merely that we are successful, but that our names are written in God's Book.

How can we be sure? Romans 10:9-10 says:

"if thou shall confess with thy mouth the Lord Jesus, and shall believe in thine heart that God hath raised Him from the dead, thou shall be saved. For with the heart man believeth unto righteousness, and with the mouth confession is made unto salvation."

In Revelation 21, John makes a breathtaking description of the Holy City that awaits those who trust Christ. He writes that nothing impure will ever enter there, nor will anyone who does what is shameful or deceitful, only those whose names are written in the Lamb's Book of Life will enter. (verse 27).

The Book of Life is God's heavenly manifest. Is your name written there?

I pray that all will search their hearts, not trusting in religion or doing good deeds, but by faith, trust in Jesus Christ to save you.

"Notwithstanding in this rejoice not, that the spirits are subject unto you; but rather rejoice, because your names are written in heaven."

— Luke 10:20

Day 176

God Places Others in Our Lives for a Purpose

Key Scripture: **John 12:25**

God opened my eyes a few years back about being vulnerable—something I never thought I wanted. While growing up we're taught to protect ourselves, never admit to anything, and to hold back the tears. If we didn't learn these things before high school, we were in deep trouble. Sadly, this resulted in many of us wearing different masks to cover up our moods and we never learned how to be real.

Now, it blesses my heart when others are authentic and stand up and share their unguarded hearts. As Christians, we need to support one another's creative efforts to be human. Be honest. Be real. Lord, help us to be sensitive and pay attention, remembering everyone has something to offer.

I, myself, was an introvert for years, not getting to know other people and putting on a mask so others were not able to see the real me. Imagine if Christ thought this way! Thank God He didn't, because He came forth to be really seen and people loved Him enough that they dropped everything and followed Him, and today still do.

Sure, He wants us to step out, be seen, and shine the light of His Gospel to others. How can we achieve this if we remain behind a mask? Christ Himself is to shine forth through your words, your life, and your actions. See what others are really made of and be real enough yourself that others are able to see the real you.

"And whatsoever ye do in word or deed,
do all in the name of the Lord Jesus,
giving thanks to God the Father by Him."

— Colossians 3:17

Day 177

We Have a Message of Hope

Key Scripture: **Romans 10:14**

"Why should we hope?" asked the king of Israel in Elisha's day. (2 Kings 6:33). Why? Because God can send an army away in fright. God can use unseen things to overcome the things that are in our path. (2 Kings 7:5-7).

God will turn away evil to rescue us and can prepare a lavish banquet in the presence of our enemies. He can bring the light of Salvation out of darkness, comfort in grief, peace in bitterness, and strength in weakness.

Still, why we should hope? Because we have a Shepherd who has laid His life down for His sheep's protection. Because there isn't a single valley in the shadow of death that our Shepherd cannot walk us through. Because we are His children, protected in the palm of His hand. Because of all of this, we can hope.

We have been given the message of hope to share with fellow mankind so they too can experience this hope. How will they hear unless we tell them? We all have been summoned to take this good news of hope to the world.

"Now the God of hope fill you with all joy and peace in believing,
that ye may abound in hope,
through the power of the Holy Ghost."

— Romans 15:13

Day 178

Tears are Necessary

Key Scripture: Psalm 56:8

Over the past few years, I have learned a lot about tears. Mainly they are normal and they are necessary. They're certainly nothing to be ashamed of and they are noticed by God.

In our key passage, we're reminded that God is intimately concerned with every aspect of our lives. His overwhelming compassion is shown, no matter what size the situation where each tear is shed.

David expressed his grief over the situation he was in because Saul was trying to murder him. This meant David had to constantly be on the move to hide from Saul. He was fearful, grieved, and unsure about his future. I can imagine the tears shed agonizing on his knees, pouring his heart out to God—I can relate to those feelings.

Yet David was comforted, knowing God was with him no matter what was going on. (Psalm 56:9). He believed his tears did not go unnoticed. Tears are normal when our hearts are broken or fear consumes us. Never should we be ashamed. Holding back tears causes stress and keeps us pretending that everything is fine when it is not.

Tears are necessary because God created us as emotional humans. Tears are much like a relief valve for stress, sadness, anxiety and grief. Crying is not a sign of weakness, but studies show that it is a sign our bodies are needing to excrete toxins that have built up during times of immense stress.

Remember this; our tears are normal and necessary, and are noticed by God Himself. Let yourself heal by letting your tears flow, because God is there to catch every tear and hold them and you, close to His heart.

"He healeth the broken in heart,
and bindeth up their wounds."

— Psalm 147:3

Day 179

Do We Believe We are Worthy?

Key Scripture: **John 14:1**

Many of us go through changes in our lives that cause us to feel inferior or unworthy. I have been there, and even though I knew I was a child of God, these doubts hovered over me like a big, dark cloud. We let circumstances dictate and suppress our relationship with Christ; when in fact, at these times our relationship should be strengthened.

We wallow in feelings of doubt and worthlessness instead of doing what is right in God's eyes. We have a help basis to prevent these feelings of unworthiness, yet we stray away when we should be seeking the mind of God by praying fervently. We must stay faithful and hold fast in God's Word, where we can truly find any answer we could possibly need.

I know that some think it is wrong to seek help from a pastor or a strong Christian, but it is scriptural to do so, because we are to seek Godly counsel. It's very easy to say that you can handle things on your own, but in doing so we try to minimize our problems and will never conquer this monster within.

God knows the aching in our hearts and our desperate need to know we are worthy of being something meaningful and useful to God. We need to get on track, with clear minds, and focus on being a fruitful vessel used of God. He needs prayer warriors to get answers. He needs faithful Christians studying His Word, helping others to find their way from the doubts and feelings of unworthiness.

Finally, God needs us all serving Him by sharing the Light of Jesus Christ to a lost and dying world. You are "Worthy."

"Let us therefore come boldly unto the throne of grace,
that we may obtain mercy,
and find grace to help in time of need."

— Hebrews 4:16

Day 180

Following Hard After God

Key Scripture: **Mark 12:30**

I heard a prayer of song today that really spoke to my heart called "One Pure and Holy Passion." It has great lyrics involving a prayer asking God for a pure and holy passion. Used the proper way, passion and ambition are not bad, though they are often misplaced and can destroy us.

Our passions and ambitions could sometimes lead to an obsession and ultimately to sin. We rush to meet our ambitions and never slow down to check our hearts, and look to God and say: "Give me one pure and holy passion. Give me one magnificent obsession. Give me one glorious ambition for life—to know and follow hard after You."

What are your passions, obsessions, and ambitions in life? Are you so consumed by your passion that you've lost your compassion? Has your driven passion caused you to hurt others? Do your obsessions cause you to turn your eyes from Jesus? Do your ambitions in life cause you to be greedy?

Our heart, soul and mind are God's; let Him have control of each. Where do you want your passion to lead you? Are your obsessions affecting your focus on God? What do you think the key to reaching your ambitions without becoming greedy is?

"My soul followeth hard after thee:
thy right hand upholdeth me."

— Psalm 63:8

Day 181

We are Not a Mistake

Key Scripture: **Psalm 139:15-16**

My mind recently was taken back a number of years in time to when I was in college. My wife and I helped out in a local church, teaching and doing anything the Lord led us to do.

During this time, we met a single lady with three kids who were in our Sunday School class. We became close to this family. One night, we got a call from her that was extremely emotional. She said she had come to the end of her rope and wanted to end her life. We told her we would be there as soon as we could.

When we arrived, she was semi-conscious. We were able to wake her enough to talk, and I opened my Bible. It fell open to our key passage. What a blessing it was then and still is today to know we are not here by mistake.

Our friend survived and was able to get some much-needed help, thanks to our Lord. I'm sure there are many like our friend who need help, and God's Word will show us that He cares enough about each of us. He cares enough that He has written each of our days in His book.

We all need to be wanted and have a purpose in life. Emotional abandonment can steal what is rightfully ours: our destiny and sense of purpose. I believe that it is God's desire to let us know that our lives are not a mistake, and we are not just a number in His eyes. Every one of us is an incredibly unique individual with a special purpose. Someone is watching over us who loves us more than we could ever know.

"Fear ye not therefore,
ye are of more value than many sparrows."

— Matthew 10:31

Day 182

What Others Intend as Hurt; God Intends as Grace

Key Scripture: **Psalm 27:5**

Many have heard of or experienced the pain of families being torn apart because of sin. This could involve mothers pulling themselves together and struggling to make a home for themselves and innocent children, or perhaps a father doing the same because of a wayward wife. Sin has destroyed many homes and has hurt the hearts of many battered or abused people through reasons which all point back to sin.

God strengthens and encourages those willing to listen and follow the redemptive plan for their lives. God's picture of grace transforms them from despair to masterpieces of His Almighty hand. When sin threatens to take everything comfortable away, God offers the grace, mercy and comfort we truly need.

People will make mistakes and hurt your heart deeply, but remember, "God didn't bring you this far to leave you." His plans are far greater than yours. Don't let the mistakes of others make you something other than what God desires of you. He mends our hearts and offers His grace even if we think we no longer can handle our hurts.

Our key verse tells us that God is not done in our lives and He can take the most broken and bruised people and transform them into the most beautiful, loving, caring children of God imaginable.

"God is our refuge and strength,
a very present help in trouble."

— Psalm 46:1

Day 183

That's Not the God I Know

Key Scripture: 1 John 2:10

A note to every Growth Teacher, Pastor, or anyone who wants to get through to their audience: have your message speak to the hurting souls because there are some in every pew.

I just heard a song by the Collingsworth Family called: "That's Not the God I Know." When you hear this song, you feel the magnitude of pain that is before our eyes, and realize some people have hardened their hearts to those experiencing difficulties in their lives.

Abraham Lincoln said something pertaining to this belief: "I am sorry for the man who can't feel the whip even when it is laid on the other man's back." Much of the world is calloused and indifferent toward other's poverty and distress. This is mainly because they have not experienced the rebirth of their souls and the love of God has never been shed abroad in their hearts.

We must be redeemed. We must be made right with God before we can become sensitive to the needs of others. Divine love shines down on us before it radiates out. Let's be determined to allow the Holy Spirit to reflect the warmth of God's compassion, for without it we cannot love our fellowman as God desires us to.

Help me, dear Lord, to share Your love, and feel the hurt of others, that I might shed the light of Your love to an uncaring world.

"Bear ye one another's burdens, and so fulfil the law of Christ."

— Galations 6:2

Day 184

Cherish Every Moment — They Matter!

Key Scripture: **James 4:14**

The book of James tells us that life is like a vapor, here one minute and gone the next.

I have been away on vacation out of town and seen a wreck with a family standing on the side of the road. Their vehicle is destroyed beyond repair, and they're hundreds of miles from home. With only minor injuries, they were stranded.

Wondering how this could happen caused me to wake up and say, "This could have been me." It was a sobering reality to see this family's world instantly changed. I stared in the rear-view mirror after passing them and could see the children's sad faces.

I immediately thought of my own children and grandchildren, and realized even I was rushing through everything in life. I was not living each moment with a God-given peace and gratitude for the life I'd been granted. It was a moment that marked me forever and forced me to whisper, "Make moments matter."

God is calling each of us to live on a mission, to intentionally share the gospel with those around us. What are we doing to make a difference in someone's life? Life is truly a vapor that is quickly gone. Treasure each moment, they matter. We must savor the gift of life God has given us.

"And of some have compassion,
making a difference."

— Jude 1:22

Day 185

Whose Side are You On?

Key Scripture: Joshua 5:13-15

This morning, I read of an encounter and simply cannot get it off my mind. Maybe we all need a fresh dose of the reality of God; but seeing how God's promise to the Israelites has now become real brings a warmth to my heart.

Every favorite song, every favorite passage of scripture, and every man or woman of God who is an influence on me is flooding my soul with comfort and joy. God miraculously brought His children across the Jordan and into the Promised Land, proving that He was giving them this land and that He would be with them. (Joshua 1:1-5).

The first obstacle in sight was Jericho, and God was with them. In the first verse of our key passage, Joshua had an encounter just outside Jericho. This man looked prepared for battle, so Joshua asked him whose side he was on. This was the wrong question to ask, for he told Joshua he was "the commander of the army of the Lord." (Joshua 5:14) and he was there to lead the army.

Who was this man? We probably each have thoughts about this. Maybe he was a ranking angel, or God, or perhaps the Son of God. In chapter 6 Joshua refers to Him as "The Lord."

Joshua recognized Him as deity and fell down and worshiped Him. John Calvin commented, "By asking, what command does my Lord give to His servant?" Joshua responds to Him, "a power and authority which belongs to God alone."

This encounter taught the Israelites and Joshua that although they would be fighting the battles ahead in Canaan, ultimately it would be God Himself who would be waging the war. The important question was not whether this stranger was on their side, but were they on His side in the conflicts.

In our daily battles and conflicts, what would our answer be? Where is God in these times? There is only one right answer: God is my commander in every battle. Believe it!

"And the LORD, He it is that doth go before thee;
He will be with thee, He will not fail thee,
neither forsake thee:
fear not, neither be dismayed."

— Deuteronomy 31:8

Day 186

Sometimes it Seems God Does Not Hear

Key Scripture: **Isaiah 59:1-2**

Why doesn't God answer our prayers? The answer to this is: He does. According to some, though, God seems to not answer particular prayers. Why is that?

I believe that many people, myself included, have a misunderstanding of what prayer truly is. Prayer is simply a conversation with God. By praying, we are talking with Him as He is helping to align us with what He is doing in our lives.

The question of why God doesn't answer prayers is usually brought up when we ask Him to do something specific. Prayer is not a 9-1-1 call or room service; that would be a one-sided conversation. Sure, we are to request things of God, but it goes deeper than that. It's like God is a battlefield commander who tells us to go here, stay put, attack, retreat, etc. He is in charge, not us, and He is setting His plan for us.

There are places in the Bible that talk about God not hearing people, as our key verse indi-cates. It also says after this verse that His people were living in unrepentant sin and were not concerned with God's plan. If this was the case, how could they expect God to hear their prayers? Other examples in the Bible when God will not hear our prayers are found in: 1 Peter 3:7; James 1:6; James 4:3; 1 John 5:14.

God is always up to something. For example, when Jesus prayed in Luke 22:42 about taking the cup from Him, it would seem that God did not answer Jesus' prayer. But remember, Jesus also said *"Thy will be done."* God's will and plan was to provide an escape for us from the penalty of sin. One day, we will see the "why" behind every seemingly unanswered prayer. Trust God.

One other reason why God would not hear our prayer and is probably the greatest is, we "Don't pray, we demand."

"If ye abide in me, and my words abide in you,
ye shall ask what ye will,
and it shall be done unto you."

— John 15:7

Day 187

When God Calls it Sin, What do We Call It?

Key Scripture: **Proverbs 28:13**

What should we do when we realize the things we're doing are sin? When God puts His finger on us and calls our actions "sin," this is something we certainly never want to hear. We would rather call it something else or try to excuse it and justify it ourselves. God forbid we forget that if God calls it sin, then it is sin and we cannot excuse or justify it.

Sin is Sin.

Many try to deceive God and think He will believe our pitiful excuses and turn His head and look the other way. Do we really believe God has done away with the concept of consequences for sin? (Psalm 32:5).

In most relationships, the tenseness we find as the root of the problems is a result of sin. We might try and point fingers and call it something else, but God still calls it sin. Remember, God is a forgiving God, so we must look at our lives and realize there are things that need forgiving.

This may be hard because pride will always come into play and try to convince us that others will look down on us if we confess our sin and admit our wrongdoings. Pride is a huge obstacle to overcome, but with God's help we can repent, turn from sin and turn toward a loving God who wants to forgive us and cleanse us.

Let's not argue with God when He shows us our sin. May we see our sin and act upon it by repenting and confessing with our whole heart.

"Hide thy face from my sins,
and blot out all mine iniquities.
Create in me a clean heart, O God;
and renew a right spirit within me."

— Psalm 51:9-10

Day 188

The Enemy's Plan to Disrupt Us

Key Scripture: 1 John 2:16

Today we must all be watchful and ask Christ to give us keen awareness of the enemy's plan and schemes against us. I certainly want to be able to recognize his traps and avoid them.

In Genesis 3, the story of Eve, along with our key verse, shows clearly how Satan goes after us. We can see his plan of attack upon our hearts. This is the same plan he used to tempt Jesus in Matthew 4:11. This fact tells me that the enemy may be powerful, but he is also predictable.

Let's look closer at his plan used on Eve and Jesus. Satan tempted Eve with fruit, which, *"was good for food."* (Genesis 3:6). Then he tempted Jesus with bread while He was fasting. (Matthew 4:3-4). We see here that Satan made them crave some sort of physical gratification to the point they became preoccupied with it.

So, we see Satan tempts us through our senses. God gave us these senses to enjoy within His boundaries. We must guard against venturing outside of God's intention for them, because Satan will attempt to have our desires met outside the will of God.

Next, we see that Satan tempted Eve by drawing her attention to what was *"pleasing to the eye."* (Genesis 3:6). He then tempted Jesus by telling Him that He could have all the. *"king-doms of the world for Himself."* (Matthew 4:8-10). Satan tempts us with the seemingly better things of the world, causing us to think we must have it. These things are temporary, because they are only material things.

Then, he tempted Eve and Jesus to elevate themselves in the eyes of the world—to become more like God and increase their worldly status. He wanted to make them boastful and proud, so he could choke the life out of them by using their own pride.

Let's not be tempted to become something the world calls worthy, or create a need within our flesh to have people notice who we are and what we do. Guard yourself and stay mindful of Satan's attempts to attack your senses as he tries to stop you from following the will of God.

He is out to destroy our trust and faith in Christ.

"Be sober, be vigilant;
because your adversary the devil, as a roaring lion,
walketh about, seeking whom he may devour."

— 1 Peter 5:8

Day 189

Love is Forgiveness

Key Scripture: **Matthew 6:15**

Any relationship without forgiveness given freely and received, will surely fail. One of the most important aspects of love is forgiveness. Without forgiveness, bitterness takes over.

Forgiveness is defined as: the intentional and voluntary process by which one who may feel victimized, undergoes a change in feelings and attitude regarding a given offense, and overcomes negative emotions such as resentment and vengeance. Forgiveness is a voluntary decision, not a feeling. Following our feelings makes forgiving most likely impossible.

God's ultimate gift to us was demonstrated through the gift of His own Son. He forgave our sins by giving us His Son.

Forgiveness cannot be granted without giving. We have to set aside our pride, hurt feelings and anger to offer forgiveness. This commitment in a relationship is a choice and a decision of love. When we decide to forgive we are showing our love, regardless of what was said or done.

Forgiving shows others God's love living in us. Remember the story in Luke 7:37 about the sinful woman with the alabaster box? She was forgiven, and Jesus told the religious leaders that those who have been forgiven much, love much. We have been forgiven much, so we are to love much by forgiving others.

"And be ye kind one to another,
tenderhearted, forgiving one another,
even as God for Christ's sake hath forgiven you."
— Ephesians 4:32

Day 190

Conviction

Key Scripture: **Genesis 6:3**

Jesus said the Holy Spirit would bring conviction, and He would convict the world of sin and the importance of living a Holy life. Also, He would remind everyone that we'll all face God's judgment.

The Spirit works to expose anything that displeases God. He brings these sins to light, particularly the sins, actions and attitudes we try to cover up. He will convict us about wrongful accusations and words we have spoken, and deal with us harshly when we fail to do the things we should.

Our flesh can run from conviction because for some reason we do not want to repent. It can be painful to deal with hidden secret sins, harmful hobbies, or damaging relationships. By ignoring the Spirit and His warnings, it can become harder to hear His voice and easier to justify our sins and go along with the crowd.

We must realize conviction is good, which means the Spirit is still striving in our lives. When we become preoccupied and the voice of the Spirit is dulled, it may become easy to ignore the Spirit and go our own way.

Conviction is indeed necessary in our lives and we must pause and remember the role of the Spirit, and let Him speak to us and challenge us to address sin and allow Him to lead our paths. Follow the Spirit and "deal with your sin."

"And Saul said unto Samuel,
I have sinned; for I have transgressed the commandment of the LORD,
and thy words;
because I feared the people,
and obeyed their voice."

— 1 Samuel 15:24

Day 191

Never Accuse a Righteous Man of God

Key Scripture: **Numbers 16:1-18 & 32**

What happens when a righteous man of God is falsely accused? In Numbers, we find that Moses and Aaron were accused of elevating themselves above the rest of the people. The story is told like this: After God punished Israel for their lack of faith, He promised to give them victory over the Canaanites. At this time, a Levite named Korah, along with 250 other leaders, were the ones who accused Moses and Aaron.

When Moses heard about this, he fell on his face. Along with this, they accused him of not leading them into the Promised Land, and not giving them their land as an inheritance.

Moses proposed a test the next day and God revealed His glory at the tabernacle and opened up the ground and swallowed up Korah and those close to him. Then God set fire to and consumed the 250 men who had been burning incense before God.

Moses, being a righteous man, simply obeyed God and never sought any glory for himself—only glory for God. These accusers forgot that God was the One who gave them the promise of the land flowing with milk and honey, not Moses. God punished these men for their disobedience. (Hebrews 12:5-11).

We must pay attention and know God's will. Here, God showed His approval and disapproval by signs, miracles, and plagues. Today, we have the completely revealed Word of God, and we can know how God thinks by reading His Word. Rebelling against God's chosen leader is not a wise choice at all. For Korah, it resulted in death.

Next time you feel a need to murmur or complain about how your church leaders are guiding your church under the direction of the will of God, think about Korah.

"Saying, Touch not mine anointed,
and do my prophets no harm."
— Psalm 105:15

Day 192

Serving God, Being a Lighthouse to Others

Key Scripture: **Matthew 5:16**

While walking our Christian life, we are to serve Christ by sharing our faith with others so that they, too, can have eternal life. Leading others to Christ is rewarding and pleases the Heavenly Hosts, because one destined for Hell is now transformed by God's glorious grace into the family of God.

We know that none of us deserve this new life, but we all certainly need it. We are Christ's disciples and are commanded to go into the highways and hedges to compel others to come to Him.

Sharing the gospel with others is not always easy, but it is needful. Where would we be headed today if someone had not shared the gospel with us?

While witnessing, it's important that we approach others with kindness and compassion so they can see the love of God in our lives. Even though they may not be interested in hearing your words, they will see the Spirit you represent.

How can we show others the love of God if we can't show the love we have for them, through God? Remember, when we are being a light to others, we approach them with the gentleness and understanding that God has shown us. They need to see Christ in us, and we will have all power in Heaven and earth to faithfully serve Christ to become a vessel used for His glory.

Lord, I ask that you keep us all sensitive to your leading regarding the needs of others, and we humbly ask that we be used as a willing vessel in leading others into the Kingdom of God.

"Let your light so shine before men,
that they may see your good works,
and glorify your Father which is in heaven."
— Matthew 5:16

Day 193

Our Guiding Light

Key Scripture: 1 John 1:5

I remember reading about how the children of Israel were led by God to the Promised Land. God did not give them a map to follow; instead, they were led by a cloud by day and a pillar of fire by night. It was comforting for them to know that God was with them every step of the way.

We, too, can have that comforting feeling of the Lord's presence through the Holy Spirit that indwells us as believers, to follow His will for our lives. We need the hand of God to guide us because there are so many false promises made by teachers of darkness, who prey upon the weak.

Hold fast to the Light of God that directs us through the dark tunnels and struggles we encounter in life. If we're misled, we will lose our focus and be tempted by the wiles of Satan, (Ephesians 6:11).

We might sometimes get off course, and find ourselves confused in darkness because we are not following the way to our true destination. In John 8:12, God promises that if we follow Him, we will never walk in darkness. It is of utmost importance that we stay focused on that clear path by trusting our guiding light, Jesus Christ.

If our light starts to dim, it's a warning that we have veered off course. Remember, we have the light of Jesus, meaning we have His presence with us every step we take, so we are to always walk in the light because He is our light.

"But if we walk in the light, as He is in the light,
we have fellowship one with another,
and the blood of Jesus Christ His Son cleanseth us from sin."

— 1 John 1:7

Day 194

Walk On

Key Scripture: **Colossians 2:6**

Many books have been published, many sermons have been preached, and lessons have been taught about the secrets of Christian living. I have my own say as to what the secret might be.

Life is like climbing a big hill and when you reach the top you find there is another hill ahead. There will be many hills to climb throughout our lives.

Some might say that's life, just one hill after another. This attitude mistakes the path we travel for the nature of the journey. The path has many hills but we make the journey by God's appointment. This gives the journey some meaning.

So, the answer to the secret of Christian living is not at all a secret It is as Paul wrote in our key verse. So, why do we walk? We walk because life is a long journey over many years and Jesus does not ask us to run the whole way. We are to keep walking; continuing on exactly as we started. (Colossians 2:7).

This means placing our lives in the hands of the Lord, and growing in Him. Walking implies a relationship. We do not walk alone, we walk with Christ at our side. We make the journey with Him, sharing the path we travel.

Yes, there are more hills ahead, but with the Lord Jesus Christ leading us through our journey, we will reach our destination: an eternal home with Him. So, keep on walking.

Lord, give us the faith in our journey to climb every hill and trust in Your abiding love to always lead us along the correct path.

"Ye shall walk in all the ways which the LORD your God hath commanded you,
that ye may live, and that it may be well with you,
and that ye may prolong your days in the land which ye shall possess."

— Deuteronomy 5:33

Day 195

Is Happiness Something All Christians Should Strive For?

Key Scripture: **Psalm 146:5**

I have not lost my faith and confidence that God has His hand over my life, and that He will cause all things to work together on my behalf. I know that if we really have a deep, anchored faith, then all is as it should be because it's in God's hands.

Is that not the truth of what happiness is? (See our key verse.) It is important to remember that a Christian's life should not be lived on the basis of feelings at all, but on the basis of faith.

What most people think of as happiness tends to be externally triggered and based on other people, things, places, and thoughts. But, what if happiness is really a deep foundation of trust in God? This is a choice we make over and over in our lives. We alone are not capable of making this choice without the Spirit of God leading us. (Proverbs 16:20).

We cannot think happiness only occurs when it's associated with good feelings. It's also not just a human emotion, but an established confidence in God and His love for us that brings a deep spiritual rest and certainty. (1 Thessalonians 5:16).

This does not mean we are to rejoice over bad circumstances that arise, instead we need to rejoice that God's hand is over us regardless of what happens. Have faith that we can lean on Him and He will hold us in His hand through any sorrow, pain, or trial.

Happiness should not be confused with pleasure, meaning enjoyment or satisfaction from following our selfish desires. It is through overcoming these passions and desires (sin in our flesh) that we find happiness deep in our spirit. (Matthew 6:19-20).

Knowing that something eternal and consistent is waiting for each of us after a life of faithfulness, no matter our circumstances, gives each of us deep internal joy and has nothing to do with feelings.

Additional reading: Psalm 1.

"To an inheritance incorruptible, and undefiled, and that fadeth not away, reserved in heaven for you."

— 1 Peter 1:4

Day 196

A Red Sea Experience

Key Scripture: **Exodus 12:31**

We all have people in our lives we choose to look up to, but sometimes God just wants us to rely on Him for our answers.

The children of Israel looked to Moses as their leader, and he, being used of God, certainly was a good one to look to. But, they complained, murmured, and were impatient because of their unbelief. They were fearful of the Egyptians who had kept them in bondage for so long, and their lives were in danger.

They complained to Moses, saying, "Why did you bring us out of Egypt? We were better off serving them, than we are dying in the desert." They felt stuck.

When they got to the Red Sea experience, they had to listen to God and He was able to show His glory in parting the Red Sea for them to cross. In so doing, He also destroyed their enemy. God simply wanted the Israelites to wait on Him, trust Him, and see His salvation.

We are no different. We become anxious, disappointed, discouraged, and fearful when our circumstances lead us toward troubled waters, but God in His infinite power wants to show His glory in our lives. Waiting on Him seems hard, and at times we try to work things out on our own, but the right thing is to allow God to open up the Red Sea so we can walk confidently on dry ground. In doing so, He may slay some of our enemies that had caused us to focus on ourselves rather than the Almighty God.

"The LORD is good unto them that wait for Him, to the soul that seeketh Him."

— Lamentations 3:25

Day 197

Do You Feel "Alone"?

Key Scripture: Luke 15:4

Feeling alone can be dangerous if it's not dealt with. I personally have gone through this and can first-hand say it is indeed a miserable, helpless feeling with seemingly no way out within myself.

Many people walking the streets have gone through or may be going through this now. When you are in this state, you may pretend you are fine when dealing with others, when in fact you are not. You might be smiling on the outside, but on the inside, you're screaming, "God, where are You?" In reality we should be saying, "God, where have I wandered off to?"

Our key verse is part of the parable of the lost sheep. Have you ever wondered how one sheep in a hundred could get lost? Was he disobedient, rebelling against the shepherd, and simply walked away? My thought on this is that he was eating from the fields, lost track of his surroundings and found himself hopelessly "alone."

Christians, we do the same thing. We get distracted and subtly slide away. We miss a few weeks from church, then make excuses as to why we are suddenly withdrawn.

This is exactly where Satan wants us, looking for a way out. He comes along, painting portraits in our minds of an easy way out. His lies start sounding like truth and we are now separated from friends who would gladly let us stand in faith with them. Most of all, we have turned a deaf ear to the voice of God.

This is a dangerous place to be, but as the shepherd sought his lost sheep, God does more to seek His wayward child. God's plan is good, and His ways are better than any we find in this world. Trust Him, follow Him, reach out to Him and know, faithful friends, you are never "Alone."

"Yea, though I walk through the valley of the shadow of death,
I will fear no evil: for thou art with me;
thy rod and thy staff they comfort me."

— Psalm 23:4

Day 198

Two Willing Hands and One Willing Heart

Key Scripture: **Exodus 31:1-6**

Bezaleel was a man specifically chosen by God to oversee much of the design of the beautiful tabernacle, and as our key verses states, he was an example we all should follow.

God called Moses to the top of a mountain and gave him detailed instructions about the place of worship, as well as directives on how people should live to glorify the One who would deliver them from bondage to freedom. These people needed a place to assure them of God's continued presence.

Bezaleel serves as an example for us today, not on our church building project, but our life-building projects. We must follow God's directions if we want to construct a fruitful life that honors Him. Even as Christians, we sometimes follow our feelings rather than God's clear instructions. We then wonder why our lives wind up in shambles.

Seeking to imitate this man chosen by God is important, but remember God's Biblical directions for living are not as precise as those required to build the tabernacle. Rather, scripture establishes the basic ethics for our lives. We are to put those ethics into practice each and every day. Our intentions should always be to honor God in all we do by following His guidance just like Bezaleel.

Lord, help us, not only in our desire to follow your directives, but also in our ability to discern Your will in the daily challenges of our lives.

"All scripture is given by inspiration of God, and is profitable for doctrine, for reproof, for correction, for instruction in righteousness."

— 2 Timothy 3:16

Day 199

Riches of Poverty

Key Scripture: **Matthew 5:3**

Christianity is sometimes seen as a conservative set of beliefs exposed by the world's views; a faith for those who are prosperous. But, Jesus tells us otherwise. He turns accepted ideas on their heads and says: how terrific it is for those who recognize their lack of spiritual and other resources, for God's resources will be poured into them.

This is not speaking ill toward wealth, nor glorifying poverty—it is simply recognizing that those who face spiritual bankruptcy are most likely to call for help. If we think we have no need for God's mercy, then we won't receive it.

He is not urging us to be miserable, He simply wants us to face the fact that if we are left on our own, we haven't a chance of becoming right in the eyes of God. He wants us to face our need of help and accept His promises through love.

In a strange and definite way, our areas of poverty are areas of greatest blessing. Our poverty may be financial, starving for human relationships, emotional illness, insecurity about our future or the pain of abandonment. These are all things we usually try to alleviate.

Let's not forget that God wants to bless us, not just in our times of success and accomplishments, but also in our poverty. He wants us to know He is there in the darkest times of uncertainty. Our poverty allows God to fill us with His riches; whereas, if we were self-satisfied in life, we might be tempted to turn our backs and not receive His riches.

Poverty may not be comfortable all the time, but it is the time and place where God enriches us with Himself, which is a treasure, because God is in it.

"Love not sleep, lest thou come to poverty;
open thine eyes, and thou shalt be satisfied with bread."

— Proverbs 20:13

Day 200

The Unrooted Will Fall Away

Key Scripture: **Luke 8:8 & 13**

In our key verse we find a reason why people fall away: because they have no root. Their religious experience is lived only when they are around other believers. They are happy to receive the blessings but not willing to go through any challenges. They follow others, never pray for themselves, and never learn to draw their life directly from God. They never produce spiritual fruit as those who have spiritual roots that produce lasting fruit do.

Many who start their spiritual journey knowing God, begin to receive His blessings with joy. Their hearts were filled with love, joy, and peace. But, when the time of testing comes, they feel as though being a Christian is more like a liability than an asset.

It is at this point we see many turn back, saying it's too hard. Times of testing will come, but they come by God's design, meaning we have to grow deep roots to pass the test.

We have probably heard a pastor say over and over that we need to spend more time in our personal devotions, reading, studying, and praying. This sounds redundant, but it's essential in developing strong, deep roots. By digging deep in God's Word, we come to know the foundational truths that can be a source of life in times of hardship.

Start praying fervently and studying the deep truths of the Word for yourself, so you do not depend on the strength of others.

"For if the firstfruit be holy, the lump is also holy, and if the root be holy, so are the branches."

— Romans 11:16

Day 201

Understanding Humility

Key Scripture: **Deuteronomy 8:3**

Some years back, I had a friend who confessed to me that she was discouraged with her employment. She worked hard to climb the ladder of success, but the powers above gave her little recognition or encouragement. Then, due to transitions in the company, she was demoted. After she poured out her feelings, I asked her if she knew what the opposite of pride is?

She quickly asked if I thought she was struggling with pride. I was not implying she was prideful, I was setting the stage to help her see her circumstance through a different lens.

I told her the opposite of pride is trust in God. Pride makes us believe it all depends on us. Trusting God requires us to place our dependence on Him. The path that leads us away from pride and to a place of truly trusting God is paved with humility.

Humility is costly, but worth the price we pay. I was telling her that God might be using these humbling circumstances to get her to a place of deep trust in Him. God knows what bigger things are ahead, and He must remove all hints of our pride.

Even if pride is only a tiny thorn in your heart, when you're given a bigger position with more recognition, that pride will grow into a dagger with the potential to destroy a close relationship with Christ. This is what I wanted my friend to see.

In the Old Testament, God used the manna to humble the Israelites, because He was preparing them for their journey through the desert to the Promised Land. (Deuteronomy 8:3). In this verse notice that God was their provider, i.e. God provided what they needed, not what they wanted. God's provisions protected their hearts because their desires had a potential to corrupt their hearts.

We all are either walking the pathway of pride by trusting ourselves or the pathway of humility by trusting God. God is not trying to break our hearts, rather He is making us ready for what He has for us in our future.

"But He giveth more grace.
Wherefore He saith, God resisteth the proud,
but giveth grace unto the humble."

— James 4:6

Day 202

Confusing Happiness with Joy

Key Scripture: **Philippians 4:4**

Many people today are living without the joy of the Lord in their lives because they confuse happiness with joy. One primary fact is that we must find joy, even during hard times. We cannot allow circumstances to dictate our mood. When we have faith and believe in God's promises, we should find joy in all situations.

Happiness is dependent on happenings. Circumstances in our life dictate whether or not we are happy. Joy, on the other hand, is a gift from God; a fruit of the Spirit that rises above whatever is happening in your life, like circumstances, challenges, and heartaches.

Joy comes from knowing who is in control and that He has a plan, which gives us hope and a future. (Jeremiah 29:11). If we draw our strength from the feeling we get when things go right, what happens when we face adversity? We would be powerless, and exposed as an easy target for Satan. The joy of the Lord is our strength.

Jesus was not happy going to the cross, but He did have joy in obedience. In Hebrews 12:2 God said: *"Who for the joy that was set before Him, endured the cross."* Jesus chose to go through suffering for us, rather than going to Heaven without us.

The apostle Paul wrote the book of Philippians which speaks a great deal about joy. Writing to the church at Philippi while he was imprisoned in a filthy, rat-infested Roman cell, Paul certainly was not happy, but he experienced the joy of the Lord and rose above his difficult circumstances. I pray we can also take advantage of our God-given joy.

"Hitherto have ye asked nothing in my name:
ask, and ye shall receive,
that your joy may be full."

— John 16:24

Day 203

Love is Not Envious

Key Scripture: **1 Corinthians 13:4**

Love is not envious. It celebrates the success of others with a smile of gladness because love soothes envy. Love does not depend on "the desire to get" for contentment, because contentment rests in Christ. To be content is to know that God *"rains on the just and on the unjust."* (Matthew 5:45).

There is no formula to figure out God's grace and blessings; they are at His discretion. Lavishing blessings from the Lord is not envious as love understands.

Christ establishes principles that, if obeyed, lead to blessings. (Psalm 119:1-2). God's truths can be applied and be benefited from by both unbelievers and believers. His ways work, and the wicked do succeed. Success in life is an option for anyone who adheres to the principles found in God's Word.

Ignore envy, it is a dead-end road and results in disappointment. Envy attracts the immature, the insecure, the greedy, and the faithless. Envy wants to get, while love wants to give. Love overcomes selfish desires by finding contentment in Christ for security, love, and affection. So, seek approval of our Almighty God in place of the acquisition of stuff.

Remember, a sure remedy for envy is giving. Giving admiration, compliments, and generosity; these deflate the opportunity for envy. Wish well to those who have done well and be grateful to God for their good fortune. Envy leads to a life of discontentment and sorrow, but love is Christ-centered, content, and joyful.

Envy has no place in a person who genuinely loves God and people.

"Godliness with contentment is great gain."

— 1 Timothy 6:6

Day 204

All Should Wish to be Barnabas
(Son of Encouragement)

Key Scripture: **Acts 4:36-37**

As children, we all could relate to someone in our lives who was an encourager. Around the age of thirteen, I loved the game of baseball and I had a coach who was that encourager in my life.

Having three older brothers, I was given many hand-me-downs, which included a ball glove. This glove looked like it came over on the Mayflower; but it was all I had to use.

One day at practice, my coach hit a hard line drive to me, and the ball went through the webbing of my glove and put a large goose egg on my forehead. After I shook off the incident, he walked me over to his car and pulled out a glove. He wrote my name on it and said, "This is yours." This act, along with many other acts of encouragement, has influenced my life even until today.

In the early Bible times, when people were in need it was not strange for someone to sell a piece of property and give to the needy. As our key passage said, Barnabas, meaning "son of encouragement," did that for the disciples.

This was not his only act of encouragement. In Act 9:27, he was instrumental in introducing Paul to the other disciples after he was converted. The disciples knew Saul, not Paul, so his reputation made them afraid. Again, Barnabas was used as an encourager. Paul might have failed to connect with the disciples had Barnabas not stepped in.

This world is full of hurting people who are afraid of the way their life is heading. Many are discouraged about circumstances they seem to have no control of. We, as Christians, need to be made aware that we can make a difference to someone who is in need of a Barnabas. We can be a comforter, a listener, a hand that can guide and help them to a place of rest, by leading them to the Lord Jesus Christ, our Comforter.

We needed a friend one day, and Christ met that need. Let's determine in our hearts to be sensitive to those in need and remember we never met a friend so faithful as Jesus. Let's serve Him by encouraging others as we express our faith and love for Him.

How can we say we love God and not make an effort to be a Barnabas?

"Wherefore comfort yourselves together and edify one another, even as also ye do."

— 1 Thessalonians 5:11

Day 205

I am Positive God Really Loves Me

Key Scripture: **Isaiah 54:10**

I'm sure at one time or another each of us has faced struggles that cause us to question just how much God loves us. If we were able to untangle the emotions wrapped around these questions, I believe doubt would come into play—not only doubting God's love but also our love for Him.

I wonder what our lives would be like if we really lived with the absolute assurance of God's love. I'm not talking about knowing He loves us, I'm talking about living as if we really believe it. I'm talking about training our hearts and our minds to process everything through the filter of absolute assurance of God's love without question.

I know at times in my own life I have faced heartbreaking situations, but I knew God could step in and change everything in an instant. When He didn't, it hurt deeply. Here is what God is continuing to teach me: I must process disappointments through the filter of His love, not through the tangled places in my heart that bring questions like; "If God loves me so much, why would He let this happen?" Processing through His love, the outcome is: "God loves me so much; therefore, I have to trust why He is allowing this to happen."

It's okay to feel hurt, lonely and sad at times, but these feelings shouldn't trigger us to doubt God's love. Instead, they should trigger us to look for God's protection and provision, as well as cause an opportunity to grow our love for Christ.

I know this can be hard, but if we really lived in absolute assurance of God's love, like our key verse says: "God's unfailing love for you will not be shaken."

"But thou, O LORD, art a God full of compassion,
and gracious, longsuffering,
and plenteous in mercy and truth."

— Psalm 86:15

Day 206

The Alabaster Box

Key Scripture: Luke 7:37-39

A few years ago, I was visiting my dear friends in Graniteville, South Carolina. I went to church with them on Sunday morning, and my friend Jackie sang a special about the alabaster box. It is a beautiful song and was presented wonderfully.

I enjoy looking at programs on TV showing properties being renovated. Sometimes I think they should be torn down because it would be much easier to just start over. But, witnessing the rebirth of something broken and unloved interests me.

In the scriptures, Simon felt this way about an uninvited guest who lived among the torn walls of failed relationships. Simon knew her reputation and questioned Jesus' discernment in allowing her to touch Him, because as our key verse said, "she was a sinner."

This brave woman ignored the stares and murmurs of those around her, and stood above her nervousness and shame to offer unto Jesus her most valuable asset, her alabaster box. She wondered if He would accept it and if He knew how she had earned it. She didn't comprehend that her most valued asset was not the box, it was the repentance that the contents in her alabaster box represented. She poured her pain and brokenness at Jesus' feet.

We all have things hidden in our hearts that we leave untouched because the cost of revealing them could be too high. The cost was high for this woman, but she was willing to make a spectacle of herself in order to receive what Jesus could offer: healing and restoration.

The tears flowing down her cheeks were her prayers of repentance. Jesus gathered the pieces of her broken heart and spoke the kindest, life-changing words she had ever heard: *"Your sins are forgiven… your faith has saved you, go in peace."* (Luke 7:48-50).

Our hurt boxes are transparent to God, and He gently exposes the places He wishes to restore. He is the God who sees us. Let us open our hearts and pour out our hurts at His feet as this woman did. He understands hurt; He paid a very high price at Calvary.

He knows the cost of our alabaster box; the reward is much greater.

"Repent ye therefore, and be converted,
that your sins may be blotted out,
when the times of refreshing shall come from the presence of the Lord."

— Acts 3:19

Day 207

Not Recommended for Hire

Key Scripture: **Ephesians 4:1**

Most of us have had to fill out an application for some kind of employment. We do this in good faith because we desire to work. I worked for a large construction company and many times we set up an office to interview people. I remember that as I asked a few questions and listened to the responses of the candidates, I had to place a judgment on some and honestly admit they were not recommended for hire. Placing judgment on someone I had just met was not an easy thing to do.

As Christians, we would never want this stamped upon an application we have submitted to anyone. Surely, we would want a resumé that points out our strong stand and perfect record of previous employment with very good references.

Let's suppose that Paul had to write a resumé about himself. What would it say? Bounced from church to church, run out of many towns, accused of starting riots, rarely supported by his own people, arrested, beaten and placed in prison several times? Ordinary people would think he must be a terrible person after reading this.

Truth is, most people would not know why Paul did what he did. This was not a job, it was a call from God to live and preach the Word of God to unbelievers through the known world. God anointed his ministry and he was persecuted for his stand with Christ. Most people would look at his resume' and say "Not for hire."

No matter what job we do, as Christians I would pray that you take a stand as Paul did for the cause of Christ. It may cost your popularity and moving up in the world, but you will have your dignity and the satisfaction that what you are doing is for the cause of Jesus Christ and His glory.

"Wherefore take unto you the whole armour of God,
that ye may be able to withstand in the evil day,
and having done all, to stand."

— Ephesians 6:13

Day 208

Look in the Mirror — It Starts With You

Key Scripture: 2 Corinthians 13:5

Have you ever known someone who is never wrong? They're always pointing their fingers at others, taking the heat off themselves so they aren't blamed? This is very annoying and makes me wonder if I have ever been that way. God help me if I have.

As humans, we are so quick to judge others and not accept responsibility for our own behavior. Have you ever done something wrong and said, "That wasn't really that bad" or "I really didn't mean it. I am not a bad person"?

ALERT—God doesn't look at it that way.

In Romans 2:11, God says He is no respecter of persons and in Act 10:34, He says He does not pick favorites. God treats His children the same, and never turns His back on any of us.

Our goal as Christians is to be a help to others, as an encourager, or by assisting in any way possible. In order to be a blessing to others, remember that Jesus taught us to get our own lives in order first. Then, we truly will be without blame, and be able to help others as Christ would want. We do this and we can be that encouraging help. "It all starts with you."

"I thought on my ways,
and turned my feet unto thy testimonies."

— Psalm 119:59

Day 209

When the Bonds of this World are Present

Key Scripture: **Acts 16:20-33**

Knowing the condition of this world and the lack of true faith of man, I fully understand how God wants us as Christians to be prepared to stand with our hearts and minds holding fast to our faith and trust in the Lord Jesus Christ.

In my reading today, I read about the imprisonment of Paul and Silas. They were beaten openly, locked in prison, and bound by chains. This reminded me of the many in this world, myself included, who are walking around looking defeated without the joy of the Lord. We are facing situations within ourselves, and are overburdened in the bondage of chains and really hurting.

Paul and Silas were beaten, bruised and hurting, and seemed to have no way out. They were like many of us, defeated and wanting to crawl into a hole and not be bothered by anyone. God does not want His children to live this way.

Instead, He wants us to find rest in Him. (Jeremiah 29:13).

In our passage we see that Paul and Silas were in a bad situation and found a way through the hurting and discouragement to praise God and pray. Sure, these were deep prayers, pleading to God fervently. This allows us to see what happens when we truly seek God—we will find Him and He will deliver us from bondage, discouragement and feelings of hopelessness.

I speak also to myself when I say that God does not want you or me to suffer. He wants to free us from the troubles of this world and put the joy of the Lord back into our lives.

Turn to God with your praises and prayers. Seek Him, and you will find Him when you search fervently with all your heart. There is a way out of bondage— it's Jesus Christ.

"Wherefore seeing we also are compassed about with so great a cloud of witnesses,
let us lay aside every weight,
and the sin which doth so easily beset us,
and let us run with patience the race that is set before us."

— Hebrews 12:1

Day 210

Who's Gonna Fill Their Shoes?

Key Scripture: 1 Peter 4:10

A classmate of mine just shared a video post of George Jones singing this song "Who's Gonna Fill Their Shoes?". I rarely listen to country music, but I did this evening and the Lord brought a question to mind about the men and women, faithful servants in our churches, who now have gone to be with the Lord. I had to ask myself: Who is gonna fill their shoes?

We hear statistics telling of churches closing and attendance reaching all-time lows. What is going to happen? Who are the new faithful willing to fill the shoes of those church leaders who have left this life?

I remember those who strived tirelessly to make a difference, encouraging others to do good. They led others to Christ and were true servants. In Judges 2:10, God tells us generations pass on and new leaders did not know the Lord nor what He had done for Israel. This goes for our churches today as well. False teachings come from those who no longer have the faithful men and women to guide them. They simply are not prepared.

I do thank God for the church I attend. Our pastor of 34 years passed. He was a man who had a great influence on my life. Now, his son has taken over and the church is stronger than ever, thriving and growing for the Lord.

Not every case goes bad, but my heart goes out to those who are struggling with no one to fill the shoes of the faithful men and women who stood for righteousness and truth, and gave their lives to serve in any capacity needed for the cause of Christ. There is a place to serve for everyone in the church. So, as leaders fall away, determine in your heart to let God use you to fill their shoes.

As believers go on to their reward, others must step up.

"And it came to pass, when they were gone over,
Elijah said unto Elisha,
'Ask what I shall do for thee, before I be taken away from thee.'
And Elisha said,
'I pray thee, let a double portion of thy spirit be upon me."

— 2 Kings 2:9

Day 211

Remember Lot's Wife

Key Scripture: **Luke 17:28-33**

In the 19th chapter of Genesis, God gives the details of the destruction of Sodom and Gomorrah. Lot was told to flee the city with his family and not look back.

At the time our key verse was written, Jesus was sharing with the disciples about His soon return. Also, how suddenly the world would end. He spoke of Noah and then of Lot and how they were pulled from this world just prior to destruction.

He reminded them that in the end there will be no warning and said to "Remember Lot's wife." She ended up as a monument on the plains because she looked back when God said not to. Her longing desires for the pleasures of the life in Sodom cost her dearly.

Surely this passage reminds us to keep our hearts and minds on the things of God, not earthly, temporal desires. God tells us that whoever tries to keep their life will lose it, and whoever loses their life will preserve it.

Lot's wife wanted to keep her old life in Sodom, so she lost it. This should be a warning to us today to not allow worldly things to distract us from God's will for our lives. We must not follow her example but rather be willing to lose our life for His sake.

This world is not our home. Remember Lot's wife!!!

"Set your affection on things above, not on things on the earth."
— Colossians 3:2

Day 212

Needing Victory?

Key Scripture: **Luke 22:39-40**

Jesus told His disciples that He would be handed over to be crucified, and they knew they would face new difficulties. He knew one would betray Him, so He led them to a secluded place and encouraged them to pray that they would not fall into temptation.

Instead of heeding Christ's words, they gave into the weakness of their flesh and chose to sleep. As a result, they were unprepared for the challenges that lay ahead. Jesus was ready and knew what He had to do, "Watch and Pray."

Jesus gave us a pattern to follow in our times of need. We are to always be watchful and pray in every situation we will face so we maintain a watchful attitude and create godly habits.

Secondly, Christ shows us in our passage to remember His words: *"the spirit indeed is willing, but the flesh is weak."* (Matthew 26:41). To be victorious, we need the power of the Spirit through prayer for guidance toward a victorious life.

Jesus did exactly that on this night and received victory over His flesh and overcame His temptations. His disciples, however, failed and experienced defeat.

Today, in our lives, I pray we remember to apply this Christ-given pattern to watch and pray. Be confident that God will give us the discernment and preparation we need to have a victorious life.

"For the LORD your God is He that goeth with you, to fight for you against your enemies, to save you."

— Deuteronomy 20:4

Day 213

God's Amazing Love

Key Scripture: **1 Corinthians 3:7**

We simply cannot buy God's love. As we see in our key verse, God brings the increase and we must put our faith in Him. As we do, God will increase our hearts toward Him by us being obedient and willing to follow Him in all things.

Worldly teachings will try to tell us that bad leadership is always the problem, and good leadership is always the answer. For believers, "Truth" is the answer. As believers, regarding leadership, we may do everything right, but still fail. The one who plants is no one special, nor is the one who waters, for God is the One who always brings growth.

When we put our trust in attempting to do everything right by the world's standards, we put our faith in what we do, how we do it, and how effectively we do it. The Lord cannot and will not bless what we do. He wants us to put our trust in Him.

It's great to study, to better yourself, and increase your knowledge, but it's more important to place your faith in the Lord. Unless He builds the house, those who labor are laboring in vain. Many times, when we face a setback we condemn ourselves and say, "I must be doing something wrong." Remember this, our increase does not hinge on us doing everything right; our increase depends on us placing all of our faith in the Lord.

Whether it is business, a relationship, or a financial challenge, it is by putting our faith in the Lord that He will bring the increase. As we do this, He will bring it to pass.

"Amazing love, how can it be?" I may never understand. May I always put my faith and trust in my Amazing Lord.

"The LORD is my rock, and my fortress, and my deliverer;
my God, my strength, in whom I will trust;
my buckler, and the horn of my salvation,
and my high tower."

— Psalm 18:2

Day 214

Denying Christ

Key Scripture: **Mark 14:66-67**
Additional reading: **2 Samuel 14:15; Psalm 113; Genesis 3:15-29**

Peter, a roughneck fisherman, was called by God to serve alongside Jesus and the other disciples. Peter is a perfect example of what could happen when a Christian has their back to a wall.

Pressure does strange things to people, as seen with Peter, a loyal, bold disciple. He exposed in his weakness as being weak enough to deny the Lord Jesus Christ. Just like fallen humanity, we are subject to do as Peter did in weakness. He swore he never knew Christ, but as the Lord prophesied earlier, this week state would fall on Peter and he would deny Him three times.

In agony, Peter invoked a curse on himself that caused him to swear. Realizing he had sinned by doing something he had promised he would not to, this big, tough fisherman broke down and wept bitterly.

We all are subject to temptation. We may sin when backed in a corner; we may sin because of a weakened state, and we may do wrong things because of circumstances that allow us to get caught up in inadvertent sin. In reality, we deny Christ, the One we promised to obey, love, honor and stand firm as soldiers of the cross.

Knowing we are capable of sinning, I would pray that we all could do as Peter did—repent quickly, with remorse, and ask forgiveness before the sin becomes unbearable, causing us to try to cover it up and not repent, thus becoming a defeated Christian.

Please understand, God is a God of second, third, fourth, and fifth chances, and we are without excuse for not repenting and asking for forgiveness. As the prodigal Son, God is ready to embrace each who need restoring. We are deceiving ourselves by not allowing the Lord Jesus Christ to bring all who fall into sin back into fellowship with Him.

"If we confess our sin,
He is faithful and just to forgive us our sins,
and to cleanse us from all unrighteousness."

— 1 John 1:9

Day 215

Calmness After the Storm

Key Scripture: **Mark 4:38-39**

Sitting here today, listening to the rain and thinking back on recent storms, I am reminded of this passage in Mark and the fear that gripped the disciples because of the great storm. We have an advantage they did not have; we know how the story ended.

What about the storms in our life that make us wonder if the Lord hears our cries? "Lord, carest Thou not that we are hurting? How am I supposed to live in the midst of this chaos?"

When the winds of broken relationships batter our hearts or the flooding waters of shattered expectations overwhelm our souls, when battering winds of broken dreams clutter our minds with thoughts that this will never end, Jesus rests peaceably on our behalf. Because waves batter and waters rise, fear easily overwhelms our souls. We are human and most likely our response will be as the disciples. Our minds won't be on Jesus, but on ourselves and our fear and doubt.

As I said earlier, we know the stories' ending; we have the Holy Spirit living within our hearts, ready to give comfort instead of fear because our loving, caring Savior possesses all power and authority on earth. Let's remember that every storm we go through is never outside God's control. All things fall under His watchful control.

Next, just as the physical storms never last forever, the storms in our lives won't either. His peace is your inheritance, even in the midst of tough waters.

Finally, every storm we go through deepens our faith. Our eyes may see only wreckage, but God sees His tireless work of redemption on our behalf through every storm we face. Jesus used the storm to call His disciples into a life of deeper trust. He calls us the same way.

'Til the storm passes over, and the thunder sounds no more; 'til the clouds roll forever from the sky; hold me fast, let me stand, in the hollow of Thy hand, keep me safe 'til the storm passes by."

"He that dwelleth in the secret place of the most High shall abide under the shadow of the Almighty."

— Psalm 91:1

Day 216

Day by Day

Key Scripture: Psalm 123:2

One of my most favorite hymns is "Day by Day." God has used this song with its heart-touched lyrics to strengthen me through many trials in my life and, believe me when I say, there have been many. God certainly has ways to send a song, a scripture verse, a soft voice, or even a friend to pray with encouraging words to get one through difficult times.

Never will we find a friend so faithful as our Lord Jesus Christ. With a grateful heart I say, "Thank You, Lord for being real in my life, seeing me through the most difficult times in my days and giving me the peace that I will one day share a Heavenly home in Your presence."

Lina Sandell wrote "Day by Day" in 1832, after she experienced a tragedy. When she was 25 years old, she accompanied her father, a pastor, on a journey by sea. Tragically, he fell overboard and drowned. She was devastated by the loss; however, instead of diminishing her faith, the event seemed to deepen it, turning her to God even more.

She had written hymns before this, but even more began to flow out of her heart afterwards. These hymns reflected her trust in Jesus and a deeper sense of His abiding presence in her life.

"Day by Day" told how she had learned to trust God at all times. She wrote, "Day by day and with each passing moment, strength I find, to meet my trials here, trusting in my Father's wise bestowment, I've no cause for worry or for fear."

Through everything she faced, she looked to God "whose heart is kind beyond all measure." He gave her "each day what He deemed best; lovingly, it's part of pain and pleasure, mingling toil with peace and rest."

In every situation, she realized that God was with her. She prayed, "Help me then in every tribulation to trust Thy promises, O Lord, that I lose not faith's sweet consolation offered me within Thy holy Word."

Remember through all your trials, God is with you today and every day; trust Him.

"Cast thy burden upon the LORD,
and He shall sustain thee:
He shall never suffer the righteous to be moved."
— Psalm 55:22

Spend Time in Silence Seeking God's Still Small Voice

Key Scripture: **1 Kings 19:11-13**

The prophet Elijah, through the Lord's authority and power, inspired repentance in the people of Israel. He called them to exercise God's judgment on idolaters by slaying 450 prophets of Baal and 400 prophets from the goddess of Asherah on Mount Carmel. This victory was preceded by the attack of threats on his life by the wicked Jezebel. Terrified, Elijah literally ran for his life.

The moment of his greatest victory came while undergoing his greatest temptation. He was devastated, discouraged, and depressed to the point of hopeless despair because of the threats made by Jezebel. He journeyed from Beersheba to Mount Horeb, a place where Moses first encountered God. He undoubtedly sought protection in this sacred place. For the next 40 days, we see that God was not through with Elijah, because God sent an angel to feed and encourage him.

Alone, Elijah sought refuge in a cave where God found him and began a casual conversation, "What are you doing here, Elijah?" Elijah poured out his heart, complaining about his desperate condition. God replied with a demonstration of acts for his discouragement: whirlwind, earthquake, and fire. These were all part of God's presence, but in a still small voice Elijah heard his Lord.

Perhaps some unrepentant sinners and wayward believers require demonstrations of devastating judgment to awaken their attention to God's presence. But, we who love Him are invited to a more intimate relationship that takes place in silence, listening to His still small voice.

Seek quiet moments with the Lord. I know personally that He still speaks that way. Take the time to listen and hear from our Lord.

"Therefore Eli said unto Samuel,
Go lie down; and it shall be,
if He call thee, that thou shalt say, Speak, LORD;
for thy servant heareth."

— 1 Samuel 3:9

Day 218

Depression or What is It?

Key Scripture: **Psalm 118:5**

Mental health authorities said that at any given time 17% of our population is struggling with some form of depression. They also say that two-thirds of these are women. This shows there is a lot of confusion in our world, and God is not the author of that.

I, along with many others I know, have experienced depression. If you have too, make some simple notes to help determine where you are and where you need to go for help. Ask yourself if you really are depressed or if you're only suffering from a momentary set back.

Early warning signs of depression are: withdrawal, difficulty in facing situations and people, or seeking some sort of escape. Take a look at how your habits have changed. Have things that were everyday routine now changed?

Next, ask yourself, "Did I cause the problem or is there something I know I should do to eliminate the situation?" Some things to look at are: Did I allow myself to get trapped? Am I doing something I shouldn't be doing, or is there something I am trying to cover up because I do not want to face the consequences if found out? Have I stopped talking to God, refused to talk to a preacher or counselor but realize I still need help?

Remember, God answers prayers in many different ways. Sometimes, He will encourage you to get help through someone else, but covering up the problem is not the answer; it will resurface. God is not the author of depression, though some of our depression comes from ignoring His direction for our lives.

God is the one who brings health, wholeness, and healing to our broken hearts, because He is the refuge for our troubled and hurting souls. Though depression is not a friend, it can bring us closer to Him, who is a friend closer than a brother, to walk with us through the gloom. This, my friend, is our best source of recovery from anything, not just depression.

Focusing on Christ will get you to the place where you need to be—"In His Presence."

"Thou wilt keep him in perfect peace,
whose mind is stayed on thee:
because he trusteth in thee."

— Isaiah 26:3

Day 219

Looking at Ourselves Through the Eyes of Jesus

Key Scripture: **Colossians 1:25-27**

We all had childhood idols. We wanted to be able to do the things they could do, and be just like them. I had several. I remeber: Timmy and his faithful dog, Lassie. Then there were Rusty and Rinnie, the Lone Ranger, Superman, and probably my favorite, Daniel Boone. I spent hours every day trying to throw a hatchet and split a pine tree like my idol.

I realize now that wanting to be someone I was not probably caused a roadblock to becoming who I am today. Sometimes, we look at ourselves according to how others see us. Being a hero is not bad, but when we want to be one for the sake of others, it can become a hindrance.

In fact, we need to look at ourselves the way God sees us. The Word of God is like a mirror, only when you look into it, you don't see "you" the way others do or even as you do; you see yourself the way God sees you. His Word will show you who you really are and exactly what is in your heart. Christ in you is your hope of glory.

I pray that God reveals to us all of His plans for our future. Without Him, we would be nothing. God desires we all come to repentance, trusting in His finished work on the cross. Believing He has come to seek and to save those lost and heading to a life of utter destruction. Trust Him today, ask His forgiveness, take the road of faith, and ask Him to abide in your heart and save you.

Childhood dreams can now become a Heavenly reality.

"I will praise thee; for I am fearfully and wonderfully made:
marvelous are thy works;
and that my soul knoweth right well."

— Psalm 139:14

Day 220

Love, Honor, Cherish

Key Scripture: **Mark 10:1-12**

One would think when being involved in a God-honoring church, marriages would be secure and not likely to fail. Not so, my friends, for Christians are not exempt from this tragedy. Even though God intended it to be for a lifetime, I would be hard pressed to find someone who is not affected by divorce in their family.

The church is just as affected as the secular world, and it is difficult at times to know what to do or what to say about divorce. Christ speaks such strong words against it, seeming to give no pardon and no excuse, and yet we know so many people who are children of divorce or those who have gotten a divorce. They're reasonable people with reasonable explanations, so this hits close to home because it affects us all.

Not really understanding, we ask, "When is it permitted? When is it okay?" As we try to seek answers, we wonder if there are any successful outcomes in divorce. Could it be that divorce freed someone from a destructive or dead marriage? This leaves us wondering why God allows it.

In our scripture today, we see that divorce never pleases God; it breaks His heart, because what God intended and gave to us as a gift and as a blessing is now broken. God's desire is that husband and wife would love, honor and cherish each other. If you are married, you should give thanks for the gift of your spouse and honor and cherish them. Pray that God binds you together, united as husband and wife.

Our God is a God of reconciliation. He reconciled us to the Father when we repented of our sins, He forgave us. As a God of reconciliation and knowing what it costs, He desires His people as one of reconciliation. He would have us to be reconciled in all relationships, even as we were reconciled to Him in Christ.

"Wherefore they are no more twain, but one flesh. What therefore God hath joined together, let not man put asunder."

— Matthew 19:6

Day 221

To Obey God Means We Know Him

Key Scripture: John 14:14-15

Christ told the disciples to pray "in My name." We are to stand before Him as followers in Christ's name. We are valued in the Lord's sight because of the value of the sacrifice He has made for us.

God no longer sees us as vile sinners but recognizes us as in the likeness of His Son, in whom we have placed our trust. To pray in Jesus' name means that we are to accept His character, manifest His spirit, and work His works.

In our key verse we see our Savior's promise is with condition, it says: *"If you love me, keep my commandments."* He has saved us not in sin, but from sin; and those who love Him will show their love through obedience.

True obedience comes from a heart transformed by God to walk in obedience because we love the One who transformed our hearts. He will identify Himself with our thoughts and our goals to bring together our hearts and minds in conjunction with His will.

So, by obeying His will, we will be consenting to our will; the two are now one. As we now are conformed to His will, we find doing His service to be delightful. Getting to this point in our life with Christ, we appreciate Him with a heart of gratitude and a life of continual obedience to Him.

"As obedient children,
not fashioning yourselves according
to the former lusts in your ignorance."

— 1 Peter 1:14

Day 222

Thou Art the Man/Woman

Key Scripture: **2 Samuel 12:7-14**

No matter who you are, we must see sin as it is. Too many people today have the mentality that they lead and answer only to themselves. In other words, a leader without a leader; one who controls without being controlled. Our scripture centers on King David, a divinely anointed king, who was loaded with God's liberality. He was a man but not without sin.

Like David, many who are in a position of leadership reprimand those under them and wind up committing much worse acts of immorality without anyone being bold enough to challenge them.

We see that the message of God through Nathan is instructive. It clearly shows that God is no respecter of persons and will not excuse any sin, even if it is committed by a leader. (Romans 2:1).

Leaders are held accountable for their actions, especially those among our churches. They must remember they are also accountable to God and avoid any acts of iniquity. This goes for every child of God—man, woman, or child. We must take responsibility for our actions and fear God, because to whom much is given, much shall be required.

If and when we fall into temptation, we must be humble enough to recognize our mistakes, and like David, follow the path of reconciliation and repent genuinely. The gate of mercy is still open for those with a contrite and humble spirit who wish to avoid the danger of having the Almighty hand of God showing His judgment on them.

"So then every one of us shall give account of himself to God."

— Romans 14:12

Day 223

God Equips the Called

Key Scripture: **Galatians 6:9-10**

I when I was growing up, we always lived in what I now think of as "back in the sticks," which meant we lived nowhere close to civilization. I wouldn't change it for anything.

God always had a plan and even though we are unaware of it. In His time, He will reveal it.

When I was about 16 years old, I came to know my Savior and His love, and He started showing me the beginning of my Christian experience with Him. Christ was real in my life, and He gradually started showing me His plan, step by step. He taught me to love others and this love that came from God filled my heart with the joy of His presence.

I was happy with the growing knowledge that I was fulfilling His will for my life. I could not see any fruit at first, but I did rejoice that He had me participating in His will, being a witness to others. (Mark 16:15).

If I could give any advice to others, it would be to always seek to reflect God with your behavior, love, and patience. We must be patient; results and changes are not to be expected all at once, but come over time. the fruit of your willingness to be used for Christ will come as God rewards, and you will start enjoying those rewards. (Isaiah 3:10).

The greatest reward is to be able to serve and be a useful tool in the hands of the Lord. Let us not grow weary in well-doing, because if we do not have the skills, God trains those whom He calls.

If you are truly called, be faithful and He will equip, train, and guide you in His path for your life.

"And let us not be weary in well doing:
for in due season we shall reap, if we faint not."
— Galatians 6:9

Day 224

God Will Lead Your Way

Key Scripture: **John 10:27**

How are you making decisions in life? Do you believe it's all up to you or do you rely on God to direct your steps? God has given us a free will to choose what to do and where to go, but He wants us to choose His ways. (Proverbs 3:5-6).

By choosing to follow God, you don't have to depend on your knowledge because He will lead you. By doing this, we will have the ability to hear the voice of God as our scripture verse has said.

Still, we have the choice to listen to God or go our own way. In order to distinguish the thoughts coming into our minds, we must cap-ture every thought to make it obedient to Christ. (2 Corinthians 10:5).

Just as Christ did in Luke 4:1-3 when Satan tempted Him in the wilderness and He turned to the truth of God. We must understand that our weapons are not of this world. Through studying God's Word, we can do as Christ did, and reject wrong thoughts from leading us astray.

Knowing and studying God's Word, we can become confident in hearing the voice of God. If we follow His lead, we will find the key to knowing in the Word of God. Understanding the scriptures equips us to hear His voice and distinguish between what is true and what is not.

"For the weapons of our warfare are not carnal,
but mighty through God to the pulling down of strong holds."
— 2 Corinthians 10:4

"Study to shew thyself approved unto God,
a workman that needeth not to be ashamed,
rightly dividing the Word of truth."
— 2 Timothy 2:15

Day 225

Setting Goals that Please God

Key Scripture: **Hebrews 10:36**

Ever feel that your current situation doesn't match the goals in your heart? Maybe things around you are hindering you from making the right move. I feel that way sometimes, because the situations around me make me want to just pick up and seek a new lifestyle or at least get a new start in a new environment.

I'm not sure this is the answer, since more often than not it does not work. Usually our current situations are the perfect environment for God to grow us the way we should grow. Imagine if a seed we planted got an attitude and left the dirt because it wanted a change. By leaving the dirt, the seed would never become what it was meant to be. Likewise, we sometimes must go through the less attractive situations to blossom into the person God wants us to be.

The promise in Hebrew 10:36 shows us there is something in store for us. Surely, we can seek Him in the midst of any situation and, as we do, become better prepared for His goal for us.

In Ephesians 2:10, God tells us we are created for His good works. We can trust Him with all our plans and desires (goals). We need to realize that our present situations are opportunities for growth and learning the lessons we need for the work God has prepared for us. Where we are today is equipping us for where we are going.

Be encouraged. Don't let today's situations trap you into longing for a new start somewhere else. Hold onto the promises of God's Word, and know He hasn't set you up to fail. He wants you to succeed in your goals to glorify Him, and He will see you through every move.

Lord, help me to see You in everything I do and to know I'm purposely planted to do Your will.

"For I know the thoughts that I think toward you, saith the LORD,
thoughts of peace, and not of evil,
to give you an expected end."

— Jeremiah 29:11

Day 226

Put Your Heart in God's Hands; What Can He Do?

Scripture: **Daniel 1:8**

World events never catch God by surprise. He has placed us precisely where we are for a purpose. Have you ever considered why we have been placed in this world at this time? Could we dare believe that the God of this universe, who has called us to Himself and equipped us with His Spirit, could work mightily through us?

Daniel didn't let the temptations of his day get in the way of his relationship with the Lord. He knew to be useful he must remain obedient in all things. Regardless of the king's commandment, he refused to compromise what he knew God required of him.

History repeats itself with examples of Christian men and women who believed God would use them to make a difference in His kingdom. God placed Esther in the king's court so that she could save the lives of her people. God placed Joseph as a powerful advisor to Pharaoh to save Jacob and his family from the famine.

We, too, are here for God's purpose and for His will. Wherever we are today, we must allow God to work in and through us to be used how He pleases. Be obedient.

God uses ordinary people to do extraordinary things. We are all ordinary!

"For as the heavens are higher than the earth,
so are My ways higher than your ways,
and My thoughts than your thoughts."

— Isaiah 55:9

Day 227

A Watered-Down Gospel

Key Scripture: **2 Timothy 2:3**

With all my heart I believe that the greatest thing in this world is to live life as a Christian. God takes a life that was empty, aimless, and worst of all, headed for a certain judgment, and turns it around and transforms it. He forgives all our sin, removes our guilt, and literally takes residence inside of us through the Holy Spirit.

He has directed our lives that were headed for hell to a heavenly home with Him. This is accomplished by the power of the gospel proclaimed and believed.

Some people believe in a watered-down version of salvation that promises forgiveness, but rarely mentions the need to repent of sin. Theirs is a gospel that promises peace but never warns of persecution, and one that says God wants all to be healthy and wealthy, and that we will always find the favor of God.

This is definitely not the gospel of my Bible. The Christian life is not a playground, but a battleground. Sure, we have a God that loves us and has a plan for our lives, but we also must remember Satan is real, opposes God's plan and wants to destroy our lives and kill us.

Some think that becoming a Christian is living a life of sickness, poverty, and always being miserable. Not so! A Christian life is about knowing God and walking in a life of faith with Him. Certainly, we will face difficulty. The Christian life is not always a bed of roses. But remember, as we seek to know and follow Him, we do have a promise of a happy and eternal life with Him in heaven.

"In hope of eternal life,
which God, that cannot lie,
promised before the world began."

— Titus 1:2

Day 228

Whatever it Takes

Key Scripture: **Philippians 3:11-13**

The song "Whatever it Takes" resonates with me. Be sure to give it a listen.

One thing about Christianity today is that it is more self-seeking than it has been in prior generations, and there's more commercialism and materialism.

Maybe people concentrate on "What can *I* get out of church?" or "What can *I* get out of God?" Thinking like this means people have accepted Christ but have not allowed Him to change their way of living.

The call of God today for His people is loving but urgent. He wants us to say to Him "I am an empty vessel, Lord. Please fill me and help me to walk in your steps, surrendered to your will, and worthy of your love, mercy, and grace. Whatever the cost, whatever it takes, God, I want to be faithful, fruitful and a blessing to everyone I meet, winning them for you."

I say, "Lord, lay some soul upon my heart, and love that soul through me; and may I ever do my part, to win that soul for Thee."

"And whatsoever ye do,
do it heartily, as to the Lord,
and not unto men."

— Colossians 3:23

Day 229

Moving Past Our Haunting Past

Key Scripture: **2 Corinthians 5:17**

We all have a past; some good and others not so good. Some are able to put their past behind them and move forward, but others can't seem to do this. I have been around people on both sides and I can testify that the ones who still hold onto their past are at times difficult to be around. While those who have disqualified their past and are able to move forward are pleasant to be around.

This is where our key verse comes into play. How do we step into our life as a "new creation" when everyone knows who we were before and knows so much about our past?

First, I believe we must know who we are and what God's Word says about us. Not knowing means we will listen to the voice of Satan. If we are rooted in God's truth and know what God says, when the enemy attacks us we will be able to stop him and remind him who we are.

Secondly, we must fully commit our life to Christ. By living our old life, we will never become fully who we are meant to be. Think about the apostle Paul. What if he had continued his old life of persecuting Christians after he became one himself?

We are impacted by others who have moved beyond their past. If we could think back about things in our own life that we have gone through, like failure, abuse, sinfulness, jealousy, and shame and then change each word that pertains by putting "redeemed from" in front of it. That is who you are in Christ—made new and washed clean.

Take this to heart if you are someone who is holding onto your past. Know that by doing this you are not only hurting yourself, but also those who love you as well.

"Brethren, I count not myself to have apprehended:
but this one thing I do, forgetting those things which are behind,
and reaching forth unto those things which are before.
I press toward the mark for the prize of the high calling of God in Christ Jesus."

— Philippians 3:13-14

Day 230

God, It's Your Fault

Key Scripture: **1 John 1:10-2:2**

Many people have different viewpoints on what sin is. We know that it suggests something bad and we never like to use it about ourselves. What the scripture calls sin, we call human frailty or bad tendencies or simply weakness. No matter how we sugar coat it; it is still "Sin."

Often, we choose to rename it and call it something a lot more pleasant. When addressing sin, we say we are too busy to do something about it. Others have poisonous beliefs that sin can be labeled as traits, unfortunate circumstances or just losing their temper. Still, all of these are sin.

The people who believe this way refuse to get a grip on the reality of the truth. They push their faults off to others and even blame God. They may say, "It's your fault, God, for putting me into this situation," which makes it impossible for them to obey God. They say, "You know my heart, God. I really want do right, but because of these circumstances, I can't. So, it is really your fault, God."

Romans 8:35 says, *"Who shall separate us from the love of Christ?"* It goes on to list the possibilities. In our key passage, it says if we say we sin not, we are a liar. Remember 1 Corinthians 10:13 about Christians in difficult situations, and Job and all his circumstances.

Now, to be honest, we must admit we fall because we do not choose to meet the circumstances with His strength. Instead, we run away from them. We do not like them and we don't want to live with them, yet we choose to blame them all on God. Because of this, there are so many unhappy Christians walking around out of fellowship with God.

There is never a need to sin. But if we do, we have a perfect defense available to us—an Advocate—our Heavenly Father, who will gladly receive you back into fellowship with Him. Be quick to reach out to our loving God and avoid miserable days of blaming Him. Realize He is faithful and just, and wants us to be cleansed for His glory and honor.

"Now then we are ambassadors for Christ,
as though God did beseech you by us:
we pray you in Christ's stead,
be ye reconciled to God."

— 2 Corinthians 5:20

Day 231

Being Perfect is Not What God Asks

Key Scripture: **Colossians 2:13-14**

We all have moments in life that, if we are honest about our true feelings, make us afraid. Whether it be raising children, marriage or starting a career; they are all to be taken seriously.

Thinking about this, we need to realize that children don't need perfect parents, nor does a wife need a perfect husband or a husband a perfect wife. What they all need is someone who loves them unconditionally, someone who is faithful and someone who gives all they can in what they do.

Think about this: if we were perfect, we wouldn't need Jesus. The reason Jesus came was because we are not able to achieve perfection.

When I read the key verse, I feel such deep gratitude. Christ's finished work on the cross has cancelled the record of our debt. He bore the penalty of the punishment we deserved. Because of His love, not for who we are or what we have done, God looks at us and sees Jesus.

His death on my behalf allows me to live with freedom and joy. This means I'm free from having to live life chasing after pleasing other people, being perfect or managing my reputation. We will never be perfect in parenting, marriage, or working a job. That is not the goal. We simply need to be honest enough to admit our mistakes and imperfections, and most importantly, our need for Jesus each and every day.

Lord, give us strength when we are overwhelmed, clarity of mind to know what to do, and grace to face the difficulties that each day holds. Thank you, Lord, that you are perfect and give us the truth that we can rest in you every day.

"He hath shewed thee, O man, what is good;
and what doth the LORD require of thee,
but to do justly, and to love mercy,
and walk humbly with thy God?"

— Micah 6:8

Day 232

Breaking a Stone-Hardened Heart

Key Scripture: **Ezekiel 11:19**

"And I will give them one heart, and put a new spirit within you, and I will take the stony heart out of their flesh, and will give them an heart of flesh."

One of the most dramatic stories in the scriptures is the story about the conversion of Saul. A religious man who kept the Jewish law, Saul thought Jesus was a mere man who sought to disrupt the Jewish traditions by teaching a new and blasphemous doctrine. Saul zealously sought the followers of Jesus to have them either imprisoned or killed.

In Acts 9:1-19 we see where Saul came face to face with God through a blinding light and heard the voice of Jesus ask, *"Saul, Saul, why persecutest thou me?"* From this point on, Saul began a new journey of faith in God through Jesus Christ.

Of all the stories of the Old and New Testament, from the parting of the Red Sea to the raising of Lazarus from the dead, the conversion of Paul may be the most miraculous. With Paul, God changed a human heart; just as He had promised in Ezekiel. God promised through the prophet that He would take away the heart of stone from the hard-hearted Israelites and replace it with a heart of flesh, tender and God-fearing.

It is discouraging to see the hate and violence among people today. They do not show any reverence to God and His teachings. Many who once regularly attended a God-fearing church no longer darken the doors.

People seem so hard-hearted; but we serve a God who can change a heart. God can turn hearts of stone into loving hearts of flesh. As Ananias was a great help to Paul, we can also be ready to help others we know who need their stone-hardened hearts changed. Let's commit to faithfully praying for those we know who need a new heart, and be willing and ready to assist them in their change.

"And I will give them an heart to know me,
that I am the LORD:
and they shall be my people,
and I will be their God:
for they shall return unto me with their whole heart."

— Jeremiah 24:7

God Will Never Steer You Wrong; Listen For His Direction

Key Scripture: **Proverbs 3:5-6**

Have you ever been in an unfamiliar place and your GPS tells you to turn and it is into a church parking lot when you weren't headed to a church? Or, it tells you that you've arrived and there is no house? We no longer depend on maps or written directions, and for the most part our GPS is a handy tool we rely on every day.

It really would be nice to have a guide that knows every road and turning point we need to take to reach all of our destinations. In all reality, we do have that guide—our Lord Jesus Christ.

Our GPS will tell us when we get off course and tell us to make a U-turn to get us back on course. The Lord does this as well. He keeps us on the paths we must travel. In fact, He's with us always and as we stay faithful and listen, He gives us step-by-step directions.

We have His Holy Spirit, and His Word, to guide us in His plan for our lives. So, let's determine to always listen, follow His Word, and seek His will for our lives each and every day. Stay focused on God's plan and never waver in the ways of the flesh.

"In all thy ways acknowledge Him,
and He shall direct thy paths."

— Proverbs 3:6

Day 234

The Wrong Way to Be Right

Key Scripture: **James 4:10**

It really hurts when we find out we're wrong about something, but more than that, it hurts that others know we are wrong. For example, when we know without a shadow of doubt that we are right we want to rally around anyone who could confirm just how right we are so our righteousness is validated.

Because of this, when we are absolutely positive we are right, we dig our heels in the ground and stand firm. Is this right? When this happens, we must look at our key verse, and while it is an answer we certainly would not expect, it makes sense. *"Humble yourselves in the sight of the Lord; and He shall lift you up."*

We spend so much time digging in our heels and rallying our troupes that we are anything but humble. Let the words of this verse sink in. Read them over and over in context. James writes from the point of view of an everyday life with Jesus, to people dealing with everyday conflicts and interpersonal struggles. We are a prideful people and pride has no place in a spiritual resolution.

I'm sure we all struggle with living this verse, but try and wrap your mind around it and its context, then apply it by being humble before God. He will work all things out as we stay faithful. Remember: "The way up is down," meaning we must humble ourselves before the Lord and He will lift us up.

Lord, help us to lay before you our struggles, give us clarity and humility to see that we can be right in a way that pleases You and not our own selfish desires.

Give us the compassion to understand the viewpoints of others and always work through conflicts in ways that please you.

"To do justice and judgment is more acceptable to the LORD than sacrifice."
— Proverbs 21:3

Day 235

A Step in the Wrong Direction

Key Scripture: **Luke 24:13-14**

The key verse speaks about the two disciples on the road to Emmaus. They had been to Jerusalem to witness Jesus' crucifixion and were experiencing much grief and pain. They were not going to hang out in Jerusalem, and they wanted to leave town right away.

As was true for these first century disciples, it is also true for us today: every step going away from the cross is a step in the wrong direction. When we are hurting, feeling down, or when we have failed spiritually, this is most definitely *not* the time to walk from the cross. This is the time we should run to it.

Satan's strategy is to whisper something in your ear like: "You are spiritually okay, you read the Bible all the time, you do so many things and go to church when you can, so you don't need to pray, you are good and solid." What Satan is really saying is to stay away from the cross when we should be listening to the Holy Spirit telling us we need to run to the cross.

Remember what Christ has done for you. Seek forgiveness and repent of any and all sin that is keeping you from the cross. Anything other than stepping toward the cross is a step in the wrong direction.

"Trust in the LORD with all thine heart;
and lean not unto thine own understanding.
In all thy ways acknowledge Him,
and He shall direct thy paths."

— Proverbs 3:5-6

Day 236

Don't Miss Out on Life's Ride Due to Fear

Key Scripture: **Joshua 1:9**

I remember as a kid, I would never ride those seemingly dangerous rides at the fair. They made me feel like if I rode them something terrible would happen. So, I went through my childhood years not experiencing many rides.

My family and friends always said that I was missing out. Truthfully, fear has always been a problem in my life. Being afraid of the unknown always kept me safe, so I avoided risks.

Later in life, my wife's daughter came to visit and wanted to go to the fair. I had no idea she loved danger and wanted to ride every ride, but she did not want to ride alone. I was her arm to lean on, even though I disliked the situation.

Now that I'm much older know that I have the Lord Jesus Christ who has promised to be with me wherever I go, I find great courage to do things I normally would not do on my own.

God has told us to be strong and courageous and not to be afraid.

He originally spoke these words to Joshua, who was given the task to lead the children of Israel into the Promised Land. What if Joshua allowed the unknown to keep him from saying yes to God, or his insecurities kept him within his own comfort zone? Joshua would have missed his calling and God's blessings on his life.

We need to learn to trust God's Word, be courageous and follow His leading into new paths He has laid out for us. We need to step out of our comfort zone, and say "yes" to God and "no" to fear when He opens new opportunities for us to serve Him.

So, the biggest thing in your life may be just ahead. Let's determine to hang onto God and His presence and experience an abundant life with Him.

"I will instruct thee and teach thee in the way which thou shalt go:
I will guide thee with mine eye."

— Psalm 32:8

Day 237

Wake Up and Smell the Coffee

Key Scripture: **Deuteronomy 8:8; Matthew 4:4**

The title today is a heart-felt thought about people in general who aren't taking life, and more important the giver of life, seriously. Our key verse says that man shall not live by bread alone. This means we need something else. Unfortunately, so many people are literally walking around giving no regard to the latter part of this verse; *"but every word that proceeds out of the mouth of God."*

Where are we missing the boat? To wake up and smell the coffee simply means that we must understand that the Bible is the living Word of the living God. How can we survive without it?

God spoke the world into existence by the power of His spoken word. (Hebrews 11:3). He then breathed life into the first man and woman; living souls, that could not live without God. Tempted by Satan, they tried to live apart from our sacred Creator by neglecting God's Word, and lost sight of Him.

The death spiral began, but God provided a covering for their shame by giving a sacrifice so they could be restored into fellowship with Him in His presence, by faith, and according to His Word. The same goes for each of us. We can come to know the Lord through the saving knowledge of the gospel. (2 Corinthians 5:17).

Still, we are tempted to live without His Word. Big Mistake! Our physical body may be able to survive on physical food alone, and our brain will continue to function, and our heart will continue to pump blood—but we won't really be alive unto God.

Our souls cannot live without spiritual bread, without *"every word that comes from the mouth of God."* We must wake up and smell the coffee. Our spirit cannot thrive without Scripture. It is the soul-satisfying food our heart should delight in. (Psalm 119:19 & 77)

We must never think that we need only to survive our time of suffering without the Living Word. Always seek to thrive by living an abundant life within the Living Word.

"Let thy tender mercies come unto me, that I may live:
for thy law is my delight."
— Psalm 119:77

Day 238

Sin—Nip it in the Bud

Key Scripture: **Judges 2:1**

None of us like to acknowledge our sin, but some will try and hide it or just ignore it. Truth is, we all struggle with sin because we are each born with a sin nature. Eventually, we have to confront it or we will be consumed by it.

I do pray that this is not the case, and that we acknowledge our sin and say today that "enough is enough." We must address our sin and say that we want God's best more than we want the temporary pleasures outside His will. When we sin, we desire something that goes against God's instructions. Our hearts become defiant and in disobedience we sin. This is what the enemy had in mind all along; to steal, kill and destroy. (John 10:10).

Sin may seem appealing and alluring, but make no mistake; it will eventually end in weeping. We see what God did for His people in our key verse and surrounding verses. He was always faithful to His promises, but the children of Israel did not stay faithful to Him.

Remember the cycle of sin starts with misplaced desires, and this is where our passage gets personal for me. I have a choice to make today: Am I entertaining my misled desires or am I carefully placing them into God's hands and asking for my heart to be aligned with His? This is where sin is stopped in its tracks—nipped in the bud.

When we humbly bow our heads, surrender our hearts before God and say; "I only want what You want. I dedicate my desires to You, Lord, and I ask that You totally remove any desire in me that could be defiance, disobedience, and destruction."

Nip it in the bud!

"Search me, O God, and know my heart;
try me, and know my thoughts:
And see if there be any wicked way in me,
and lead me in the way everlasting."

— Psalm 139:23-24

Day 239

Seeing as if it Were the Face of God

Key Scripture: **Genesis 32:30** (Also read the entire story, verses 22-30)

In our world today, we have many ways and devices that allow us to stay in contact with one another instantly. And yet we travel long distances to have face to face contact, longing for the time we can express ourselves in person with one another. In our human thinking, face to face interaction is important. What if we could have a face to face encounter with God Himself?

We find in the Scriptures that Jacob speaks of having a face to face encounter with the Lord after he wrestled all night with an angel of the Lord, who spoke to him on God's behalf and with God's authority. He was completely changed after this and received a new name, Israel. With this new identity, and a God-given name, new opportunities opened up for him.

This encounter left Israel limp, but he walked away with God's blessing. Then, he sought to reconcile the differences with his brother Esau. Israel was changed as he told Esau later, *"To see your face is like seeing the face of God, now that you have received me favorably."* (Genesis 33:10). Picture this remarkable truth, as bitterness and jealousy melted away because of the change in Israel's life after his encounter with God.

Looking around in your own circle, you can see that bitterness, strife, and jealousy are certainly there. We may look differently at a brother or sister because of some past feelings that may be eating away at our heart and mind. If only we could have an encounter with God to wipe away those bitter feelings.

Israel was able to look at his brother differently because of his cleansed heart. God wants us to have that same freedom; don't let it slip away.

"Follow peace with all men, and holiness, without which no man shall see the Lord."

— Hebrews 12:14

Day 240

Where do We Turn when We Find Ourselves Competing Loyalty with Friends and Family?

Key Scripture: **1 Samuel 20**

One major problem with loyalty is that everyone has their own definition of what loyalty means. So, at some point we will find ourselves in that painful position where being loyal to one person makes it feel like being a betrayer to another.

In our key passage we see the scripture helps relieve that burden and gives us the guideline to use when we have to choose. Simply, to be loyal is to honor our commitment, even if it's more beneficial for us to break it. An honorable person *"sweareth to his own hurt, and changeth not."* (Psalm 15:4).

Unfortunately, many believe that loyalty is an unwavering commitment to someone's personal agenda. When loyalty is viewed this way, the guidelines vary, and confusion and strife follow.

Saul's misperception of loyalty created a horrible situation for his son Jonathan. Jonathan swore an oath to his friend David. Unfortunately, Saul feels threatened by David and is extremely upset that Jonathan will not help him find and kill David. Jonathan is faced with the painful situation of competing loyalties.

Jonathan deeply loved his father and David, but he knew his primary loyalty was to God. He couldn't assist his father, who had a personal vendetta motivated by insecurity and pride. On the other hand, David had done nothing to deserve death. The choice was clear.

When we feel trapped by competing loyalties, the only way to make the right choice is to remember that our primary loyalty is to God, and that our hearts are to be *"fully committed to the LORD our God, to live by His decrees and obey His commands."* (1 Kings 8:61).

What's your definition of loyalty? Have you felt trapped in a competing loyalty situation? Remember to ask yourself what Jesus would do.

"Let every soul be subject unto the higher powers.
For there is no power but of God:
the powers that be are ordained of God."

— Romans 13:1

Day 241

Do We Obey the Lord?

Key Scripture: **Numbers 20:8-11**

Moses, a very notable patriarch in the Bible, was used mightily by God to free the Israelites from Egyptian bondage and lead His children to the Promised Land.

While doing my reading this morning, God again spoke to me about this passage in Numbers, so I will try to share my heart. God told Moses to speak to the rock to bring water, instead he struck the rock with his staff because there were so many miracles that God used Moses to perform by using his staff.

Even just a few chapters before, God told him to strike the rock. But this time, God told him to just speak to the rock. Because he didn't, Moses was not able to enter into the Promised Land.

Before we can make a move to do something, we must already have decided in our heart. Thinking deeply about Moses, I try to understand why he only partially obeyed God. Maybe it was because of anger at the moaning Israelites and constantly listening to complaints, or maybe it was just disobedience to the direction of God.

Looking at my own life and also the lives others, I realize we don't take every word from God seriously. We seem to always want to add our own twist to what God wants. Friends, this is nothing more than an outright sin against God. How can we live a life pleasing to God if we cannot obey His voice?

So many today are playing this "living under the grace of God" and "whatever we do God will forgive and forget because He is a gracious God" game. We misuse God's grace. This is a worldly cop-out taught and practiced by many. Like Moses, we will miss the promises of God for our lives if we take this path.

We must examine our hearts and never rely on thinking that we can and will be forgiven if we follow our heart's desires and not every word that comes from the mouth of God. Staying faithful does not mean just being faithful sometimes. It means always keeping our hearts and minds focused on Him.

I am reminded of a wonderful song that has doctrinal truths and something we all should hold true in our hearts, "I Call Him Lord." Give it a listen.

"The heart is deceitful above all things,
and desperately wicked:
who can know it?"

— Jeremiah 17:9

Day 242

Where is Our Hope When Life Hurts?

Key Scripture: **Romans 15:13**

Life can change in the blink of an eye and deliver blows we could never expect. I, myself, have struggled through hard times, seen the death of my parents that left a void, I lost a wife through death. These losses leave one grieving and filled with heartache. The loss of family members leaves only memories to try and hold onto.

I am thankful for God's Word and especially promises like our key verse, Romans 15:13. Hope is mentioned twice in this verse. In one Bible dictionary, hope is defined as: "trustful expectation," particularly with reference to the fulfillment of God's promises.

Biblical hope is the expectation of a favorable outcome under God's guidance. A dictionary definition of hope is: "a feeling of what we hope to happen will happen."

The first time hope is mentioned in this verse refers to God as the origin of hope. We anticipate favorable outcome because of the person of Christ. We will face disappointments and life-altering circumstances, but can have hope because of who God is: powerful, wise, sovereign and good.

The second mention of hope in this verse refers to us as the recipients. God pours hope into us as we choose to believe He is who He says He is, and that He always keeps His promises. When we do this, God will give us a rock-solid anticipation of a favorable outcome under His guidance.

The more we meditate on this verse, the more God will heal our hurting hearts. We can hang onto hope, knowing that someday Jesus will return and set everything right. Someday, He will wipe away every tear from our eyes. (Revelation 21:4). In the meantime, we can live in hope because the source of hope lives in us.

"And now, LORD, what wait I for?
My hope is in thee."

— Psalm 39:7

What was Intended for Evil God Meant for Good

Key Scripture: **Genesis 50:16-21**

From the very beginning, we saw that Joseph was set apart for a special purpose. As a young boy, God spoke to Joseph through a dream about his future. From there, Joseph's life spiraled through years of delays and detours before reaching his final destination.

Joseph was betrayed by his brothers, placed in a pit, sold into slavery and sentenced to prison. However, during the delays and detours of Joseph's life, scripture reminds us that God was with him the entire way.

We see in our key scripture that Joseph and his brothers were reconciled. The story of Joseph's life is filled with life application topics. For me, the older I get, the more I know that lack of patience is one of my weaknesses. Joseph waited over 13 years to receive the promise from God. This reminds me of promises God gave me years ago, and I realize that He has to prepare me before I will see the reality of these promises in my life.

In Joseph's story, we see that forgiveness and reconciliation stand out as an important application God wants us to see. Betrayal hurts, hearing lies with your name attached is not an ideal situation for anyone; being falsely accused is not easy to deal with. Joseph endured all of these and more.

How we respond to these situations in our lives is important, and being able to forgive and reconcile relationships certainly pleases the heart of God. Remember Romans 8:28, and say with assurance that God has a purpose for us, no matter what people may do in hopes to hurt us. Know that He can use that very situation for your good and ultimately for His glory.

Lord, help us to patiently wait on You in all our situations that intend harm, and realize You have a Divine purpose for each of us. All we need to do is stand and see Your salvation in our lives.

*"To every thing there is a season,
and a time to every purpose under the heaven."*

— Ecclesiastes 3:1

Day 244

God Will Reward Blind Obedience

Key Scripture: **John 9:3**

When you think about something you did or something someone else has done to you, do you ever think there might be a reason God allows us to go through suffering connected to these things? Do you think there might be something you did in your past that prevents you from living a life of purpose that glorifies God?

In John 9, we read about the blind man in Jerusalem. He'd been blind from birth. The disciples asked if he was blind because of his own sins or his parents' sins. The way Jesus answered them is our key verse: this happened so the power of God could be seen in him.

The story continues as Jesus spat on the dirt, made mud and rubbed the blind man's eyes. He then instructed him to go to the pool of Siloam. Notice that the man was not healed immediately, it wasn't until he obeyed the instructions of Christ that he was able to see. He followed the command of Jesus to "go," and without hes-

itation, he went. His blind obedience to Christ resulted in him being healed.

Unlike this blind man, we often find ourselves questioning God's call and talking ourselves out of obedience rather than blindly trusting and obeying His commands. When we walk forward in faith, even if we really don't feel ready to push through our doubts and fears, true healing and purpose can begin to take shape in our hearts and lives.

This means we can experience pain and struggles in our lives, but regardless of our circumstances or limitations, we can take a leap of faith with blind obedience and trust God even when we don't know what lies ahead. We then can experience true spiritual healing, and discover God's purpose for our lives.

Lord, help us to serve as proof of the goodness of God. Fill us with courage and motivation to trust and obey you, then share with others what You have done in and through us. Make our lives count for You.

"And if it seem evil unto you to serve the LORD,
choose you this day whom ye will serve...;
But as for me and my house,
we will serve the LORD."

— Joshua 24:15

Day 245

God is Always There in Your Hardest Days

Key Scripture: **Psalm 139:10**

Can you remember when you received some devastating news and could not understand what was really happening? Did you find yourself wondering what in the world are were going to do? Did you ask the most heart-felt question: Where was God in all this?

This does indeed happen to many of us, but please note that through the tears, questions, and loneliness placing your eyes on yourself is never enough. We need to remember that Christ upon His resurrection left with us the Holy Spirit who leads us to open our hearts to God, commit our darkened hours to His care, for His glory in our suffering. (Romans 8:26b).

As our key verse states, His hand shall lead us. This is a promise to us as Christians and gives us hope during dark times. He will lead us through places we never want to go; He will hold us in the places that seem beyond our reach, but not His.

Through any dark times in our lives, we must never forget that the Lord knows and cares about everything we face. Through the hardest days and darkest moments, the Lord will meet us and hold on; He will never let go.

"My soul followeth hard after thee:
thy right hand upholdeth me."

— Psalm 63:8

Day 246

Turn to Me

Key Scripture: **Deuteronomy 11:22-23**

Can you wrap your mind around that statement: "Turn to me?" Have you ever felt that life has dealt you a bad hand and no matter where or which way you turn you simply feel stuck? Life is sure tough and we want to see a light at the end of the tunnel, but what we feel is hopelessly stuck, not able to see the end. We often start to wonder if we ever will.

I do remember one particularly hard season in my life. I closed my tear-filled eyes and asked. "Am I going to be stuck in this season of darkness the rest of my life?"

Then from the darkness these words came boldly into my heart and mind: "Turn to me." This sounded great, but turning to God in my state of mind felt like hugging air.

Gradually I turned to our faithful God, and when my mind cleared, the key scripture verses spoke to my heart.

Though our circumstances may not change today, our outlook sure can. We never have to run, because we can turn to Him. By doing this, we will see light in our dark times and hope is restored in our hearts that were once filled with doubt.

"Fear thou not, for I am with thee:
be not dismayed; for I am thy God:
I will strengthen thee; yea, I will help thee;
yea, I will uphold thee with the right hand of my righteousness."

— Isaiah 41:10

Day 247

Just Can't Wrap My Head Around That

Key Scripture: **Proverbs 3:5-6**

I have a pastor friend in Baxley, Georgia, who I want to dedicate this post to. The title of this post is a favorite saying that I so remember him for. Love you, Brother Shaun, and pray for you daily.

As a teen, I started attending church with some of my high school peers. God had a plan and it started there. Listening to the pastor for several weeks, I soon found things he said that bothered me. They included: "God sent His Son to earth as a sacrifice for the world's sin, even mine." This was hard for me to wrap my head around.

The other thing was "if I put my faith in the finished work of Christ, Him shedding His blood for me on the cross, and ask Christ to come into my heart and save me, He would." I just could not wrap my head around that.

After a few weeks of listening and being under the conviction of the Holy Spirit, God brought me to the point of trusting in Him as my Savior. In other words, He allowed me to wrap my head around His truths.

Now, 54 years later, there are things I just can't wrap my head around again, like individuals claiming to be a child of God but still doing as they please without regard to what the scriptures say. They never seek repentance when they sin. They attend church when it is convenient. I just can't wrap my head around this.

Another thing is about our churches. We see so many false doctrines, false teachers, social clubs or groups catering to the world and not calling out to a Holy God for direction, guidance and understanding what the will of God is for His church and His people. I just can't wrap my head around this either.

Where is our heart today? I trust you are seeking the truth, and a church that teaches truth that is being led by a pastor that stands for the truth. God keep us in your perfect will.

I do thank God for being real in my life and I always want to be sensitive to His leading in all things.

"The ungodly are not so: but are like the chaff which the wind driveth away.
Therefore the ungodly shall not stand in the judgment,
nor sinners in the congregation of the righteous.
For the LORD knoweth the way of the righteous;
but the way of the ungodly shall perish."

— Psalm 1:4-6

Day 248

God Gave Us a Choice Not to Eat the Forbidden Fruit

Key Scripture: **Genesis 2:3**

God caused the Tree of Knowledge to grow in paradise, and He made a covenant with Adam and Eve to refrain from eating from it. So, they had a choice between receiving the eternal blessings that come through obedience and worship to a gracious God or the consequences from disobedience and idolatry against a just God.

Instead of embracing their destiny to rule creation in joy, freedom, and life, they sadly chose their own path to pain, enslavement, and death. God gave them an invitation to fully satisfy their desires, yet they ignored it and chose dissatisfaction and a diminishing life instead.

All problems in humanity can be traced back to this simple truth, as Paul explains in Romans 1:18-22. However, in the seemingly hopeless point in Adam and Eve's story, we catch our first glimpse of the Gospel. (Genesis 3:15). God set forth a plan to help those who have been tempted. Hebrews 2:18:

"For in that he himself hath suffered being tempted, he is able to succour them that are tempted."

Adam gave us death, which reigns over humanity, and now Jesus offers us eternal life and an abundance of grace. (Romans 5:14). But remember, the forbidden fruit shows us that we as humans can choose to respond to God's goodness by turning to Christ from our sin instead of following our fallen nature to rebel against God and choose sin. In fact, the riches of God's grace is simply meant to lead us to repentance.

What choice will you make? Will you seek fulfillment of God who promises His love, joy, power, and truth, or will you seek your fulfillment elsewhere, which only promises unhappiness, disappointment, and ultimately death?

I pray you choose the right path and experience the promise of everlasting life through our Lord and Savior, Jesus Christ.

"Therefore to him that knoweth to do good,
and doeth it not,
to him it is sin."

— James 4:17

Day 249

Life Changes are Not Easy

Key Scripture: **Malachi 3:6a**

Change is difficult, and many times it's hard to accept. I well remember a few years back when my late wife was diagnosed with pancreatic cancer. She went through surgery and had a hospital stay of about six weeks. They told us they got everything and she didn't need chemo.

In less than a year, they had to do some x-rays and found the cancer was back. Her doctor told her she had one to six months to live. What a blow!

We tried with all that was in us to carry on, but it was extremely hard. One day, I was out doing a job with my son, and while driving from one place to another, I picked up my phone and dialed her number and we talked. Upon hanging up, I stared at the phone, because I realized that soon if I dialed that number, no one would answer.

Whether we like it or not, the living of our lives involves change. Life is change, and the longer we live, the more certain we see that the only thing constant in this life is change.

As our key verse states, God never changes. Also, Psalm 102:27:

"But thou art the same, and thy years shall have no end."

I'm so glad that we have a God that never changes. No matter what changes in our lives, He is and will always be the same.

Not only does God stay the same, but so do His loving plans for us, for they are based on His Word. (Psalm 33:11; Isaiah 40:8). As change comes our way, we can find comfort that He and His Word, along with His loving intentions for us, never waiver.

There are many things in life we cannot control, but we can depend on God always being our refuge in times of trouble and certainly in times of change.

"Thy faithfulness is unto all generations:
thou hast established the earth,
and it abideth."

— Psalm 119:90

Day 250

Knowing The Will of God; In His Steps

Key Scripture: **Psalm 37:23**

"The steps of a good man are ordered by the LORD: and he delighteth in his way."

In the life of a Christian there is nothing more gratifying than to be living in the will of God. It is good to know that God actually delights in leading us along the way. *"In all thy ways acknowledge Him, and He will direct thy paths."* (Proverbs 3:6).

We need to seek His leading in everything, knowing full well it may not be an easy path. Christ suffered for us as seen in 1 Peter 2:21. Even if the path seems difficult at times, it is always a good path because it is His choice and it honors Him. (Psalm 23:3).

He, indeed, is our good Shepherd. And if by chance we lose our way for a time, He will bring us back in fellowship with Him. (Jeremiah 10:23). The problem with this is that many are not quick to realize when they have drifted off the path. We recognize far later than we should

that we have strayed from His path, allowing sin to get hold of our life.

We should check our relationship with Christ each day, and not question His Word. (Psalm 119:133). Then we will certainly hear His promise as in Isaiah 30:21:

"And thine ears shall hear the word behind thee saying, This is the way, walk ye in it, when ye turn to the right hand, and when ye turn to the left."

It may not be an audible voice, but we can hear His voice, because we are His sheep and we know him. (John 10:27). Then we can without question say as Abraham, an ancient servant testified: "...I being in the way, the LORD led me..." (Genesis 24:27).

Being in the will of God is always a good place to be; then we can say, "He leadeth me, He leadeth me, Oh blessed thought."

"For even hereunto were ye called: because Christ also suffered for us, leaving us an example, that ye should follow His steps."

— 1 Peter 2:21

Day 251

Power of a Grateful Heart

Key Scripture: **Psalm 100:4-5**

A very simple truth that we all must believe is that gratitude kills attitude. Thinking grateful thoughts, having an outlook of gratitude and verbalizing that outlook removes all negative emotions that can wreck and ruin your heart. Scripture is clear that our heart should first and foremost be full of praise toward our amazing Lord.

We evidently do not believe this because it is far too easy for us to give in to complaining, self-pity, discouragement, and bitterness. Gratitude takes our eyes off ourselves and puts them back on the Lord. It helps us realize who is in control and where our help comes from. By forgetting this, we open ourselves up to feelings of fear, worry, and other things that cause problems for us.

Gratitude invites God's presence and makes the enemy flee. The Bible says that the Lord actually inhabits the praises of His people. (Psalm 22:3).

Gratitude leaves no room for complaining. We often fall into this temptation more than we would like. Complaining is all about us and is selfish because we just do not get our way.

Gratitude, most certainly, is not about us, it is about our Savior, who unselfishly died for us. Be a child of God that realizes everything God has given us, and thank Him for it. That gratitude will for sure kill any bad attitude and fill us with a life of peace, strength, comfort, and hope.

"Every good gift and every perfect gift is from above,
and cometh down from the Father of lights,
with whom is no variableness,
neither shadow of turning."

— James 1:17

Day 252

Be Sure Your Sin Will Find You Out

Key Scripture: **Galatians: 6:7-8**

We should always be motivated to live holy, obedient lives, avoiding sin and disobedience at all times, so that we never dishonor, shame and hurt our Savior.

The Bible warns us repeatedly about how our sins will come back to bite us. What we think we are doing in private will eventually come out in public. The consequences of our sins or if we persist in known sin, will reap the judgment of God's hand, as our key verse states. (Numbers 32:23) *"…and be sure your sin will find you out."*

I remember a story that was brought out in newspapers as an example that caused public disgrace. A man who called for an escort service to send him a woman for the evening, answered the knock on the door and it was his daughter.

People just do not go out and commit flagrant and gross sins unless they have first planned to commit them, flirting with temptation, which in itself is a sin.

Our primary motivation should be our love and respect for Christ. Be aware of the fact that if we sin, we take the risk we will be publicly exposed. Doing the right thing is to deal with your inner sin with the Lord now, not hear about the consequences publicity.

God gives us all grace to live a godly life. This does not mean sinless perfection, for we are all sinners. Dare not to despise God's grace and forfeit what He so freely offers us. So, don't blow it.

If you are one who can plan to sin or even sin willfully without conviction, my belief is that you need a salvation experience with Jesus Christ.

"If we confess our sins,
He is faithful and just to forgive us our sins,
and to cleanse us from all unrighteousness."

— 1 John 1:9

Day 253

We Cannot Please Everyone All the Time

Key Scripture: **Galatians 1:10**

Do you ever struggle with trying to please people? We try to be a "yes" person, even when we don't have the capability or the desire to do what others are asking of us. We can't figure out how to manage the fear of disappointing others.

We need to have the mindset to draw healthy boundaries in our relationships. The problem is we live allowing other people's opinions to define who we are; therefore, trying to control their perception of us. We feel good about ourselves when others think favorably about what we do.

Think about the tragic reality of this. We're busy being too concerned about gaining the approval of others and it's giving us a heart divided with God. Our key verse explains this.

It is impossible to please all the people all the time. There is something inside us that will always want others to believe the best about us. People-pleasing will tell us that drawing boundaries means we have failed. In reality, we have the beautiful Biblical revelation that only God can meet everyone's needs. (Philippians 4:19).

We all want to be loved by others. But, we do not want the fear that another person's love for us is based on always making them happy. Love should be what draws us together, not what tears us apart. God's love isn't based on us, it is simply placed on us, and it's the place from which we should live, "loved."

Lord, when we're tempted to look at others for validation and acceptance, please remind us to look to you instead.

"Servants, obey in all things your masters according to the flesh:
not with eyeservice, as men-pleasers;
but in singleness of heart, fearing God;
And whatsoever ye do, do it heartily,
as to the Lord, and not unto men."

— Colossians 3:22-23

Day 254

Is Your Life Like a Hallmark Movie?

Key Scripture; **John 15:9 & 11**

I will make a confession here, I have watched some Hallmark movies in the past. Now, please understand that I am not criticizing anyone who watches these movies. They are made to give people a hopeful feeling, dreaming their lives could be just like those and have happy endings. Every time these movies end, it's a happy day.

They are peaceful, friendly, and calming. They are pleasant and kind, and focus on family and friends doing good things. These are wholesome and non-violent movies, and the stories revolve around love and happiness.

We all love and desire happy endings for ourselves and the people we know, but that is not always reality. Relationships fail, friendships end, divorce happens, loved ones pass away, and true love is hard to find. Our real lives can go forth with disappointment and heartache.

Although earthly relationships can add to happiness, that should never be what determines our happiness If happiness depends on our earthly love and perfect relationships, we will always feel disappointed, unhappy, and lacking joy.

In our key verse, we see that Jesus calls us to realize how much we are loved, just as the Father loved His Son. In verse eleven, Jesus explains why it is so important to recognize, embrace, and abide in His love for us. God's joy is the real love we all long for, but too often we look in the wrong places for it.

It would be nice if life were like a Hallmark movie and every relationship had a happy ending. But, it is possible to feel happy no matter what happens in our lives or relationships because true joy comes from God, who is the Hallmark of Christianity.

"...happy is that people,
whose God is the LORD."

— Psalm 144:15b

Day 255

Do We Have the Fear of the Lord?

Key Scripture: **Proverbs 14:26**

When we submit to God, we do not have to be afraid of anything because He becomes our *"refuge and strength."* (Psalm 46:1). Fearing God does not mean being afraid He's going to hurt us, because He is a great wonderful God. The fear of the Lord is about honor and respect; meaning, we follow His directions and recognize His authority in all things.

Looking around us, it is easy to see there is not a lot of respect for authority these days because we've developed a mentality that says, 'nobody is going to tell me what to do.' Looking at the Bible, it says, in the reverent and worship fear of the Lord there is strong confidence.

This means we are to be respectful and obedient, doing what God says we should do, allowing our trust and confidence to continue to grow. Our outlook about others will change because we learn that we are accountable to God, so we recognize that others are just as important to God as we are.

Solomon wrote, *"Let us hear the conclusion of the whole matter: Fear God, and keep His commandments: for this is the whole duty of man"* (Ecclesiastes 12:13). Moses told the children of Israel, *"what doth the LORD thy God require of thee, but to fear the LORD thy God, to walk in all His ways, and to love Him, and serve the LORD thy God with all thy heart and with all thy soul."* (Deuteronomy 10:12). Having the fear of the Lord is not difficult; make sure He is your refuge and your strength.

"The fear of the LORD is the beginning of wisdom:
and the knowledge of the holy is understanding."

— Proverbs 9:10

Sin Plugs Up the Ears of God

Key Scripture: **Isaiah 59:1-2**

We all need to understand that sin hinders our prayers. Our key scripture surely drives home this fact as does Psalm 66:18, where God says without question, *"If I regard iniquity in my heart, the LORD will not hear me."* The big question is: "Why does God not hear me?"

In the days of Isaiah, the Israelites had a long history of God helping them by answering their prayers. Now, trouble is at hand and God did not seem to care. Why wouldn't He listen? Why didn't He answer? God gave Isaiah a clear convincing answer. The fault was not in God, but His people. Their sins hindered God from hearing their prayers.

Their wickedness caused Him to hide His face from them and close His ears to their cries. In Psalm 66:18, we can interpret this as: God will not hear my prayer if I commit sin. This passage doesn't condemn our sin; but our attitude toward sin.

An example of this idea is how many Christians have gotten a divorce, which is contrary to God's Word. How many have rationalized their behavior and never repented and would do the same thing again? You could substitute any sin and it would be the same.

God wants us to have the same attitude about sin as He does. If you will not hear and heed His Word, don't expect Him to listen to what you have to say.

"If we confess our sins, He is faithful and just to forgive us our sins, and to cleanse us from all unrighteousness"— 1 John 1:9.

"Whosoever abideth in Him sinneth not:
whosoever sinneth hath not seen Him, neither known Him."

1 John 3:6

Day 257

Seek God in Everything

Key Scripture: **Judges 20 & 21**

God truly has a sense of humor. Some Bible stories are really hard to believe, but they are part of God's Word. One such story is the civil war between 11 tribes of Israel and the tribe of Benjamin.

Every passage in the Bible teaches us lessons and this one is no different. Here, God commanded the 11 tribes to go up against Benjamin and they did, but they had issues about doing so. They prayed and fasted, making sure it was what God wanted. Seeking God first was no mistake. God's Word is sure. He commanded Israel to war against Benjamin.

In Judges 20:46, the Bible says that twenty-five thousand men of Benjamin fell that day. After the battle, Israel realized that there were no men for the women. In Judges 21:7, they had sworn to not give the Benjamin men wives.

Israel did not seek God in this matter. The Benjamin men were told to go down to Shiloh and kidnap one of the dancing virgins to wife. (Judges 21:21).

So the lesson we see here is that while Israel was going against Benjamin, they prayerfully sought God. But, when a new problem arose they forgot about God and did things their way.

We must seek God's will in everything we do, not just for the big battles. (Matthew 6:33). God is willing to guide us in every aspect of our lives, including: seeking a spouse, finances, life's decisions, and whatever else comes up.

Let God lead, and seek Him in all things. Allow Him to work with you in all choices you make. He knows us and by following His path we can never go wrong.

Lord, help us to trust You in everything in our daily life. Guide our footsteps through all of life's challenges.

*"Commit thy works unto the LORD,
and thy thoughts shall be established."*

— Proverbs 16:3

Never Alone, There's Power in Our Prayers

Key Scripture: **Psalm 34:4-6**

Throughout the scriptures, God makes it clear that our prayers are important to Him. He loves our communication with Him, just as we would our closest friend. He promises to be there for us whenever we call. (Jeremiah 29:13).

God wants us to tell Him our burdens and give Him all our cares so He can bring hope to our hearts, peace to our souls, and strength to our lives. (1 Peter 5:7). If you are at times not able to find the words, are too burdened, and just don't know what to pray, the Holy Spirit speaks on your behalf. (Romans 8:26).

God really wants us to talk with Him about all things: our victories, failures, fears and everything in between. It is comforting to know we have a direct line to God, day or night. We can tell Him our feelings, our deep hurts, our pain and anger, and our disappointments.

Telling Him we love Him, need Him, and are grateful for all He gives helps to show our appreciation. Prayer moves God. When He moves in your life, you feel His presence, experience His peace, and draw from His strength in ways you never thought possible.

"Let us therefore come boldly unto the throne of grace,
that we may obtain mercy and find grace to help in time of need."

— Hebrews 4:16

Day 259

Is Your Heart Hardened?

Key Scripture: **Exodus 5**

The scripture says, if you can hear God's voice, do not harden your heart, for God desires us to keep a tender heart. Billy Graham once said in one of his sermons that Christ can re-sensitize your conscience. Christ will and can do just that; He can soften a hardened heart.

Hardening of one's heart can happen to anyone. If you are not a Christian and reject the Gospel, every time you hear God's offer of forgiveness and reject it, your heart will harden a little more.

Remember the Christian faith is always real. Many false teachers and preachers are out there spreading false doctrines, saying they have the truth. Listen to God's voice; He alone will lead you to truth. Pharaoh made the decision to harden his heart and God strengthened that decision. If your heart gets hard, then you have chosen to allow it to do so yourself.

The easiest place to harden your heart is while in the church. You get complacent and never allow God's Word to speak directly to you. You look at others and not yourself. The same sun that softens the wax hardens the clay. If you are facing opposition all around you, it doesn't mean that you're doing the wrong thing; it probably means you are doing the right thing. Christians are always in a spiritual battle with Satan and our flesh. God will bring our gods down to show us that there is no other god but Him.

There are several ways to know that your heart has hardened: you stop caring about your spiritual growth, you stop caring about others, you stop caring about lost souls, you no longer see how important worship is in your life, and you seem to always have a critical spirit.

Let God re-sensitize your conscience and keep your heart tender.

"A new heart also will I give you,
and a new spirit will I put within you:
and I will take away the stony heart out of your flesh,
and I will give you an heart of flesh."

— Ezekiel 36:26

Day 260

Bending God's Ear

Key Scripture: **Psalm 145:18**

When we near a river or lake where there are stones or pebbles along the shore, no matter your age, it is always tempting to pick up a handful and toss them in the water. As they hit the water they disappear from sight and head straight to the bottom. They hit the water, sink and we never doubt they wind up on the bottom.

The faith we use in prayer works the same way. We pray daily, recognizing who our sovereign God is, and we pray with a heart of thanksgiving. In addition, we pray for help, for loved ones, for big and even little things. As Christians, it is our duty to always pray with a thankful heart as long as we live, so that we have a life aligned with scripture and from our hearts.

To strengthen our prayers, we can even use the Lord's Prayer, a model prayer given to His disciples. (Luke 11:2-4). Whether a person is new to the Christian faith with little experience in praying or a seasoned believer with many years of praying, a prayer sent forth in truth within the belief in Christ does reach the Lord.

Sometimes our prayers can seem to hit the ceiling and fall back to the floor. But, Jesus Himself told us to keep praying. Don't give up. God is listening because He cares and acts on our behalf for His glory. Keep praying.

"And He spake a parable unto them to this end,
that men ought always to pray, and not to faint."

— Luke 18:1

Day 261

The Lord is There

Key Scripture: **Ezekiel 48:35**

The prophet Ezekiel saw the fall of Jerusalem, and was among those taken captive to Babylon. Along with the city, the armies destroyed the temple, as God removed this physical symbol of His presence among them. The Israelites believed their situation was hopeless, and the destruction permanent.

God spoke words of encouragement and hope to Ezekiel as He described the new temple and the New Jerusalem. The name of the new city would be "Jehovah Shammah," translating to the Lord is there. This was meaningful to the Israelites because Jerusalem was destroyed due to their disobedience.

This place was more than their home; it was where God dwelt with them in the temple as they interacted with Him through the priest and the sacrificial system. The temple was destroyed, meaning that God's presence left their midst.

The New Jerusalem, called "the Lord is there" reveals God's persistent and abiding love. The Lord had not abandoned them. He was still with them in their future. He will redeem what they lost. His presence will once again be in their midst.

We need to be reminded that God is with us, still taking our up and down lives, offering us a way of reconciliation to bring our hearts into subjection, mercifully restoring us to be used for His glory. He has already prepared for us a New Jerusalem where we will dwell with Him someday. Whatever is coming, "The Lord is There."

"And if I go and prepare a place for you,
I will come again, and receive you unto myself, that where I am,
there ye may be also."

— John 14:3

Day 262

Living in Utopia

Key Scripture: **Psalm 18:30**

Some time back, I saw an inspirational movie called *Seven Days in Utopia.* The movie was about a golfer who lost his game and ran away. He landed in a small town in the middle of nowhere called Utopia, a town of 375 people. Robert Duvall, the main character, told the young golfer, Luke Chisholm, if he gave him one week in Utopia he would fix his game.

Wouldn't it be nice if someone promised to fix our problems in one week?

I looked up the definition of Utopia, and surprisingly the definition gave me new insight about the movie. Here is the meaning: An imagined place or state of things in which everything is perfect.

In Revelation 21:5, God's Word says:

"And He that sat upon the throne said, Behold, I make all things new. And He said unto me, Write: for these words are true and faithful."

Just where else can you imagine that all things are perfect? Only in the perfect will of Jesus Christ can one even think they could find a perfect setting together with our faithful Savior. (Hebrews 5:9).

Christ is the perfect sacrifice, placed here for us, that our eternal security is settled in our lives as a believer. We have ahead of us a lifetime designed for us by a perfect Heavenly Father who gave himself that we can obtain that perfect place prepared for us by Him.

"Thou wilt keep him in perfect peace,
whose mind is stayed on thee:
because he trusteth in thee."

— Isaiah 26:3

Day 263

Is Your Life Going God's Way?

Key Scriptures: **Matthew 6:21-34; Romans 12:1-2**

There are two great indicators that show us where our priorities lie: our schedule and our budget. Money and time are both finite resources, so where we spend them says a lot about what matters to us. In setting a budget, we are deciding what matters to our family by designating our money accordingly.

This is why Jesus tells us to pay attention where we spend our money; *"For where your treasure is, there will your heart be also."* (Matthew 6:21).

God gives us everything we need to do what He's put in our hearts to do. When we say we can't afford it, then we are really saying that we have not prioritized that. If we align our budget with His plan, we'll always find we have enough. (Matthew 6:31-34).

The same is true of our time. God wants us to budget or prioritize our time to include eternal matters. (Matthew 11:28-30).

If you fill a bowl with sand, then try to cram in a few big rocks, it won't fit. But if you put the big rocks in first, then pour the sand on top, the sand will fill in the cracks and suddenly, everything fits. Romans 12:1-2 says we should take everything we have or do and place it before God as an offering. Don't become so well adjusted to your culture that you fit into it without even thinking.

When we align our priorities with Gods, our lives will look different, and are heading the way it should, toward Him.

"For my thoughts are not your thoughts,
neither are your ways my ways, saith the LORD.
For as the heavens are higher than the earth,
so are my ways higher than your ways,
and my thoughts than your thoughts."

— Isaiah 55:8-9

Day 264

Does It Really Matter If I Read God's Word?

Key Scripture: **Isaiah 55:11**

Do you sometimes feel overwhelmed with temporal things and literally do not feel like reading your Bible?

In these times it is easy to simply want God to shower us with wisdom, filled with answers and solutions for what's breaking our hearts. We must learn a great truth; by spending time in God's Word, this offers us so much more than quick fixes. The Bible doesn't just give us instructions for today; it also plants wisdom in our hearts for the future. There is a powerful truth in Isaiah 55:10-11 and Psalm 19:7-10.

Water was needed for the Israelites as they depended on it for survival. The Israelites' need to depend on God for their physical needs was a continual reminder of their need to depend on Him for their spiritual needs as well.

Recently I have asked God to strengthen my desire to read, study and listen to His Word, even if I am tired and really do not feel like it at all. I am truly amazed with the power of the Holy Spirit in my life as I study the scriptures. Does it really matter if I read God's Word? For me, yes it does. Remember that storing scripture deep in our hearts prepares us for difficult moments; realizing that believing these promises strengthens our trust in a Faithful God.

So let's open God's Word today whether we feel like it or not. Maybe for just a few verses, just determine that you will read the scriptures. More than just reading His Words, we must choose to receive them. Even more importantly, we must live them.

The more we apply God's teaching to our lives, the more it becomes part of us. There are 1.439 chapters in the Bible. Set a plan to do so many each day, because it really does matter that we read God's Word.

"Study to shew thyself approved unto God,
a workman that needeth not to be ashamed,
rightly dividing the Word of truth."

— 2 Timothy 2:15

Day 265

Do You Live What You Believe?

Key Scripture: **1 Timothy 3:1-13**

Every decision we make reveals every standard we set for our lives. Giving in to our own desires, buying things we can't afford, thinking that we are better than others, all these reveal our character. How we act will be determined by whether we are allowing the values of the world or God's Holy Word to set the standard of our lives.

When our standards are dictated by people rather than God, we are automatically limited. We have to be careful not to draw conclusions about our values from what others are saying about us. Being a Christian is about how we live out our faith and oftentimes, the right choice is not going to be the most popular one.

In our scripture passage, Paul is giving us guidelines to live by because they are consistent with what God says is true and right. God is more concerned with who we are than what we do. We are not given a list of duties to carry out, but qualities to live out.

Living a Godly life starts in the heart; a heart surrendered will certainly make God's priorities our priorities. When we see others the way Christ sees others, then we are less likely to treat them wrong. What and how we treat others matters; our testimony reflects what we believe. How can we be a witness for Christ if we do not live what we believe?

Guard your testimony with all diligence; this one thing if you lose, may take a lifetime to regain.

"I have chosen the way of truth;
thy judgments have I laid before me."

— Psalm 119:30

Knowing God's Plan and Living Your Own Plan

Key Scripture: **1 Kings 22:1-53; Psalm 138:1-8; Proverbs 17:17-18**

Do we really want to know God's will? We may say we do, but the reality is that many people don't. Why? Because it interferes with our wants and desires, in other words, "Our own will," and this becomes a problem. We have to choose between doing what we know is the will of God and not what we want to do, deliberately going against what we know is His will.

We tend to not seek God's will as we should. We try to pretend we are clueless so everything will be alright, thinking that it is alright to live our lives the best we can, and not get God too involved in our personal life. Having this mindset will help us feel we will not have to put ourselves into deliberately disobeying what we know is the will of God.

Do you realize if you are a child of God and are trying to do something that is against God's plan, you will either fail or become really miserable? (Jeremiah 29:12-13). How can we know what God's plan is for us? Sit down with God, determine the goals you desire for your life. Pray and seek His answers through His Word and ask, are your goals in-line with God's goals for you? Much of God's work in our lives seems to develop without a purpose.

The will of God for our lives comes not by chance, but by determining in our hearts to intentionally seek it through prayer, faith, and trusting that God alone will direct our steps. We must leave our own desires behind and press forth to what God's plan is for each of us.

Lord, your ways are always better than mine. Help me to take my eyes off me and to see things through your eyes. Help me to take only the steps you desire.

"The steps of a good man are ordered by the LORD:
and He delighteth in his way.
Though he fall, he shall not be utterly cast down:
for the LORD upholdeth him with His hand."

— Psalm 37:23-24

Day 267

Never Alone; God Hears Our Cry

Key Scripture: **Psalm 31:17**

Difficult things we face in life often come with what we feel are unbearable and very hard to cope with. One such thing we face in life is loss. Because God made us with feelings, other difficult emotions we may experience when grieving or facing emotional circumstances are hopeless, helpless, confused, fearful, anxious, and even angry. Recognizing these emotions and releasing them in ways that will be healthy is extremely important toward the healing process. Ignoring these emotions will only delay or may even cripple the healing.

Heartache and pain are some of the feelings we face; you may think of others not mentioned. The fact is, they are real and we need to express them in some way. Maybe all you want to do is cry; that is thought by some to be a sign of weakness, but not so. Jesus Himself wept when He faced tragedy (John 11:35).

Sure, it is good to be strong while going through difficult times, but it is important to acknowledge the emotions that pain, suffering, and loss can bring. How can your heart truly heal if you don't acknowledge that you're hurting? Take the first step, get alone with God; tell Him just how you are hurting. Cry if you want, "God Help Me!!" Pouring your heart out to Him will help the hurt and give a feeling of cleansing to the soul.

In Psalm 56:8, David tossed and turned all night, crying to God and God heard Him. It is great to know that our tears are important to God. Tears are a language that God understands.

"And it shall come to pass, that before they call, I will answer;
and while they are yet speaking, I will hear."

— Isaiah 65:24

Day 268

No! Never Alone

Key Scripture: Hebrews 13:5

Facing tragedy in life's storms of any kind can be extremely difficult; but in the midst of heartache and pain, we can find the hope and courage to go on. With God's help, a family member, friend, and God's Word, we receive the necessary strength to overcome.

If you have ever experienced or been affected by a crisis, you may feel you've been abandoned by God. You may feel as if your whole life has been turned upside down, wondering how or if you can ever survive. These times make you feel very alone.

Understand wherever you are, God is. Through any circumstance you are facing, God is there, willing to help pick up the pieces as necessary, or even make a way to escape the circumstance. He loves you beyond understanding, holding you up, making a way where there seems to be no way. (Psalm 46:1).

In Psalm 139:7-10, you will find comfort and support, and assurance when you are feeling God has forgotten you. In Psalm 23: "His rod and staff will lead and comfort, and He will never leave you." In addition to needing God's presence in your life, you also need others. Share with your family or friends your feelings, and by sharing one another's burdens, along with sharing your burdens with God, the feeling of being alone will soon be no more.

A favorite hymn starts out saying: "No never alone, No never alone; He promised never to leave me, never to leave me alone."

"Fear thou not; for I am with thee: be not dismayed;
for I am thy God: I will strengthen thee;
yea, I will help thee;
yea, I will uphold thee with the right hand of my righteousness."

— Isaiah 41:10

Day 269

Developing The Fire Inside Us

Key Scripture: **2 Timothy 1**

Many times I have been around and even started campfires, whether just setting up camp alongside a river while fishing, or building a campfire at our hunting club for many to enjoy. Doing so you need to have on hand some good kindling material that help in igniting the wood, setting it up in such a way that the proper airflow will help the fire to keep burning. To help in starting the fire, it helps if there is a fuel source to give it a quick start.

In our Christian life, God gives each one gifts which take attention to maintain as we do a fire. The gifts from God are ignited when we believe and faithfully use them for His purpose. Because God desires us to "fan (the gifts) into flame," He has given to us the tools, instructions, and ability to seek His Spirit to guide and develop those gifts through His power, love, and strength. 2 Timothy 1:6-7:

"Wherefore I put thee in remembrance that thou stir up the gift of God, which is in thee by the putting on of my hands. For God hath not given us the spirit of fear; but of power, and of love, and of a sound mind."

God desires our love, and when we're able to show love as He does, our passion reveals our gifts. When our gifts are revealed, our faithful discipline along with the proper maintenance of those gifts, God will use for His glory by allowing us to use them in His perfect will. By submitting to His will and purpose, He gives us the power to develop and use those gifts in ways unimaginable.

Unlike a campfire that can be contained, the fire God ignites when those gifts are known and used will never be contained. He puts a boldness and desire in our hearts to use His gifts. We will want to serve Him by reaching out to everyone we meet, wanting them to experience His wonderful grace. God will help fan our flame into a roaring bonfire, spreading light into this darkened world.

"Ye are the light of the world.
A city that is set on a hill cannot be hid.
Neither do men light a candle, and put it under a bushel,
but on a candlestick, and it giveth light unto all that are in the house."

— Matthew 5:14-15

Day 270

Step by Step

Key Scripture: Psalm 119:104-105; Psalm 37:7 & 18

At times in our lives we try to forget about past problems we have gone through. How exactly do we handle difficult circumstances? We go through marital problems, financial problems, or maybe health problems. These problems, whatever they may be, never surfaced in one day, but usually took many days. Therefore, fixing the problems will take many days of commitment.

God desires to solve any difficulties that arise by us turning to Him, seeking wisdom, and following His path. As our scripture states, He is a lamp unto our paths, meaning that our path is illuminated only a little so we can take one step at a time following Him.

When we seek God's help in solving our problems, we may hope that He answers our prayers immediately and completely. Sometimes He may give us instant results, but usually He answers them one step at a time through preparation and process, resulting in long term solutions.

As the lamp illuminates the next few steps we take, the light is given to us by the Word of God which ends up lighting the path we should take toward God. We must trust that God knows and sees the full path, but all we need to see are the next few steps to follow. It takes trust and faith to take one step in front of another toward the path that God has for us. *"Lean not to your own understanding, in all thy ways acknowledge Him."* (Proverbs 3:6). Then your 'step by step' will be illuminated and directed toward the path chosen for you to follow.

Lord, help us to abide in You, knowing that You will lead us safely down the path that You designed for us.

"A man's heart deviseth his way; but the LORD directeth his steps."

— Proverbs 16:9

Day 271

My Cup Runneth Over

Key Scripture: **Psalm 23:5**

I am sure many of us remember our parents or grandparents sitting around the table with their cup and saucers, sipping their morning coffee. My parents did this, and as they poured their coffee, they always ran the cup over so some would overflow into the saucer. The coffee in the saucer cooled much quicker and they would take the cup, set it aside and sip the cooled coffee.

Many analogies can be made from this picture, but for me I read the key verse and think of just how blessed I am because of God's unmerited favor that none of us deserve. God's grace is real and let's never take that for granted.

Psalm 23:5 is one of my favorite verses and it causes me to think of drinking from a saucer as an experience of abundance and a reason for gratitude.

Today, in a world filled with so much negativity, it's easy to forget just how often our cups run over with blessings we should be grateful for. I heard a song last evening called "Drinking from My Saucer," while attending a camp meeting and was moved by its blessed words. Be sure to check it out.

With a grateful heart I say: Thank you Lord for the blessings placed on me.

"A good man out of the good treasure of his heart bringeth forth that which is good; and an evil man out of the evil treasure of his heart bringeth forth that which is evil: for of the abundance of the heart his mouth speaketh."

— Luke 6:45

Day 272

A Lesson from Anathoth

Key Scripture: **Jeremiah 2**

While reading through the book of Jeremiah, I have searched out more information on the significance of the city of Anathoth. I believe that Jeremiah was reminding us that we never outgrow God.

It's tough to work at something and when it is taken away you are left frustrated, however, this frustration can turn into a blessing. In Anathoth, the hometown of Jeremiah, he could look to the east and see grain fields flourishing. But, just beyond he saw a bleak, barren wilderness, a land not sown with seed. The Lord used a similar image by telling the Israelites how they started out in a wilderness following after Him through a land not sown (Jeremiah 2:2), but they turned from His ways.

We must remember that sometimes our best efforts will not hold water. In Anathoth, there were no springs or flowing water. So in order to have water they dug cisterns, a deep hole with plastered walls to hold water. (Jeremiah 2:13). The Israelites left the lush Nile delta to follow God through the desert where they depended on rain which meant life or death. They abandoned God to serve the worthless idols that supposedly gave rain. They traded the best for the worst.

We must learn a lesson from Anathoth. We feel tempted to view God as good for salvation but lacking for what we need in real life. Picture God as a set of jumper cables, like we use to jump start our vehicle, and now the cables are no longer needed. We didn't start out to follow God only to abandon Him when we grew up.

God will always be our Father; we never outgrow this relationship. Jeremiah teaches us that our own efforts cannot hold water, pointing out that we are to trust the Lord alone for all our needs. How many cisterns have we dug, just to watch our effort leak out through the cracks? As we start following God, let's delight in doing His will today.

"As our lives feel empty, we should see it as a sign that we are trying to find satisfaction in something other than God." — Wayne Stiles

"Great is our LORD, and of great power:
His understanding is infinite."

— Psalm 147:5

Day 273

Hold Fast to What God Gives Us — G L O S S

Key Scripture: **2 Corinthians 8:1-6; Psalm 139:15a**

I remember years ago, my wife and I worked in a church outside of Chattanooga, Tennessee. There was a special push in the neighborhood to reach the young people. We walked just outside the church and found a young teenager sitting alone. We went over to try to see if we could be of assistance to her and found out quickly that this girl had an attitude that God needed to change.

We asked if anything was wrong and her reply was, "Oh, this is all fake. This whole weekend is all about being somebody you are not, and just being friendly to one another. When we get back to school, these girls won't even speak to us. That's why I'll never come back here." After telling us this, she accidentally turned her bag over and her cell phone, along with a tube of lip gloss fell out.

I asked, "If I took your phone and walked away, what would you do?"

She said, "I would take it back from you."

"What about the lip gloss? If another girl came by and took it, what would you do?"

She replied, "I would take it back too."

I told her she was right to do so, because they belonged to her and so does your faith in God. You have to defend it as you would these items. You cannot go through life letting others walk off with what belongs to you and God.

In a world where people sometimes disappoint us, it's easy to give away pieces of our faith and of ourselves. We do this every time we look at someone and feel inferior. It is so simple, but sometimes hard to grasp the truth found in our key verse that tells us He created us and knew us from the beginning.

God loves the child He created, which these letters represent: GLOSS, or God Loves Our Secret Selves. God has poured beauty into the very parts we often feel are less than when we compare them to others. We all need to accept these truths: I am loved. I am okay. I am treasured.

"But God commendeth His love toward us,
in that, while we were yet sinners,
Christ died for us."

— Romans 5:8

Day 274

Can We Start Over?

Key Scripture: Jonah 3:1-2

Jonah was in the belly of the whale because he was running from God and what God wanted him to do. Sure, while there he probably thought God would never use him again, and certainly God was not obligated to do so. But, as the story goes, we know God ordered the whale to spit him out onto dry land.

Then, the Lord spoke to Jonah a second time and told him to go to the city of Nineveh and deliver His message. God loved Jonah and gave him a second chance in life.

A second chance was also given to Adam and Eve. God warned them to not eat of the forbidden fruit, but they did anyway, and sin entered their lives. God could have simply started over, but instead He chose to offer them a way out and allow them to come back into fellowship with Him.

God gave David a second chance after he committed adultery and then murder. When the prophet Nathan confronted him, David repented and asked God's forgiveness, which resulted in his second chance.

Finally, Simon Peter failed miserably, denying the Lord three times. Yet, after Christ arose, He sent a message out telling His disciples, Peter included, that He was going ahead to Galilee and He would see them there. God included Peter, and he was used mightily in the ministry.

God can change our outcome even when we fail miserably. So, remember that our situation is never without hope to be used of God.

"Therefore if any man be in Christ, he is a new creature: old things are passed away; behold, all things are become new."

— 2 Corinthians 5:17

Day 275

Our God Helps Us Begin Again

Key Scripture: **2 Corinthians 5:17**

Unplanned mishaps in our lives can make us feel devastated and give us a sense of hopelessness. They can place us in a deep well of discouragement that we never expected. Tragedies in life make us feel stuck or too messed up to begin again.

Let's be reminded of our key verse, 2 Corinthians 5:17. In this verse, Paul is reminding us that we never have to feel like we are stuck in our mistakes, because we have been made new in Christ. Paul was reminding us that these Corinthian Christians struggled with the truth of freedom in Christ because of the powerful pagan influences in Corinth.

This should remind us that even today when we place our hope in Christ, we are made new.

Our relationship with Christ will not enable us to change our past, but it will make our future new in Him. Christ says that the mistakes in your life do not define you, He does. Failures in the past are overshadowed by our hope in the future. We can start over.

So, the next time a mishap surfaces in your life, remember you have Jesus Christ to give you the hope that never again do you have to be stuck in discouragement. We can open our eyes each morning knowing that we can always embrace the hope of our future, remembering all things are become new in Christ.

"Remember ye not the former things,
neither consider the things of old.
Behold, I will do a new thing:
now it shall spring forth; shall ye not know it?
I will even make a way in the wilderness and rivers in the desert."

— Isaiah 43:18-19

Day 276

Is Your Balm Gone?

Key Scripture: **Jeremiah 8:22**

"Is there no balm in Gilead; is there no physician there? Why then is not the health of the daughter of my people recovered?"

Gilead, an ancient city in Israel known for its great aromatic tree extract (balm), is used for healing and soothing abilities. This is probably equivalent to a modern medicine that is used for healing. The question in our key verse: "Is there no balm in Gilead?" This meant that they had the healing balm but were still sick.

God's question was not to imply that the balm or physicians were not there, because both were, but the sick were not cured. The Lord was their God, but they were oppressed as though God was not present. Something was wrong with their relationship. They were seeking idols rather than God.

The same principle is running rampant in our churches today. Christ's blood has been shed, forgiveness is available, and many have heard the Gospel but do not believe and are sadly bearing their own sins and headed for hell. They are dying without receiving Christ's forgiveness.

The power of God is available to believers, but they suffer by choosing not to repent and seek forgiveness to overcome their failures. There is balm and there are physicians in Gilead. We should do as they did not, come to Christ with open hearts, removing all the obstacles that may be keeping us from having a true abundant relationship with Him.

Question: Why are we choosing to live with sin controlling our lives and without Christ? Doing this means we're destined for an eternity without Him!

"The righteous cry, and the LORD heareth,
and delivereth them out of all their troubles."

— Psalm 34:17

Day 277

We Are To Enjoy Peace Like A River

Key Scripture: **Isaiah 66:12**

"For thus saith the LORD, Behold, I will extend peace to her like a river, and the glory of the Gentiles like a flowing stream."

In this post I will try to show the difference between water and a river. Water is referred to as a spiritual supply that meets our needs. A river is an abundant, continuously flowing collection of water. Try thinking of a place where you have an endless and abundant supply of every single thing you need in life, whether it be spiritual or natural. That is just a glimpse of what Eden was to Adam. This is only a peek at what Christ is.

The river of God or the Holy Spirit has many streams and rivers for our needs. One mentioned in our key verse is peace like a river. God does not give this peace in a bottle or cup, instead it is as a river that flows endlessly and continuously and cannot be exhausted.

If the world could create such a thing as a medication or chip to be inserted to grant inner peace, people would pay millions for it. No generation has ever seen such confusion, unrest, fears, anxieties, and lack of peace as ours has today. Remember, as Christians we are not of this world; we are a people created unto His good works.

Jesus says, *"My peace I give unto you, not as the world gives."* There is a river of peace waiting for His children in the form of God's Holy Spirit; trust Him and rest in His presence.

A secret to experience this flow of peace is to rest in God as He fights our battles.

"And the peace of God, which passeth all understanding, shall keep your hearts and minds through Christ Jesus."

— Philippians 4:7

Day 278

Kicking Against the Pricks (Conversion of Paul)

Key Scripture: **Acts 9:1-9**

"It's hard for you to kick against the pricks," as a Greek proverb says, but it is also familiar to the Jews and anyone who has made a living in agriculture. An ox goad was a stick with a pointed piece of iron on its tip that was used to prod the oxen when plowing.

The farmer would prick the ox with this piece of iron to steer it in the right direction. Sometimes, the oxen would rebel and kick out at the prick. This would result in the prick being driven deeper into the animal's flesh. In essence, the more the ox rebelled, the more it suffered.

Saul's life was a constant resistance to the Gospel and to God's plan revealed in Christ in the fulfillment of God's law. Saul thought he was the chief defender. On the road to Damascus, Saul became Paul because of the glorious conversion that God placed upon him.

Jesus' words to Saul on that road were: *"It is hard for you to kick against the pricks."* Jesus took control of Paul and let him know his rebellion against God was a losing battle. His efforts were as senseless as an ox kicking "against the pricks."

Saul's passion was to fight against Christianity. He was not heading in the direction God wanted for him, so Christ forced him to go in the right direction.

Do you know someone rebellious to the ways of God, who is trying to go their own way? Maybe they need to be warned, because certainly, God will not always strive with their rebellion.

When we rebel against Christianity, we are rebelling against Jesus Himself.

"And the LORD said,
My spirit shall not always strive with man,
for that he also is flesh…"

— Genesis 6:3

Day 279

What Does it Really Mean to Follow God?

Key Scripture: **Mark 8:33-34**

A modern day Christian (one who thinks they are) most likely dresses up once or maybe twice a year and expects a pat on the back when they attend a church service. Maybe they will even give a little something to a worthy cause. This is far from the early Christians' outlook on following God though. Their lives were devoted in their service to God — there was no question of half-heartedness.

In our key verse there are three significant things needed to follow God. First, we must deny self. The word deny means we must separate ourselves by following Jesus, forgetting our own fleshly desires and interests. God is calling us to a life that puts away self to seek Him and serve others. (Matthew 22:36-40). Additional verses to look at: (1 Peter 2:21; 1 John 2:3-4; Ephesians 5:1-2; 1 Peter 1:14-16; Matthew 6:33.)

Second, remember when Christ called His first disciples? He told them to: *"Take up their crosses and follow Him."* They never gave Him any excuses—they put the calling first and left their lives behind, giving their allegiance to Jesus Christ.

Finally, we see the key passage said essentially, *"I want you to follow me,"* which meant fulfilling their mission to lead others to Him. When we make a commitment to Christ, it is not for self, but to make God's purpose our purpose and His will our will. If we love God, we will love others and bring them to a relationship with Christ.

Our personal relationship with Christ means we are to deny self, take up our cross, and follow Him. This is a commandment, not a request.

"Be ye followers of me,
even as I also am of Christ."

— 1 Corinthians 11:1

Day 280

Mocking God

Key Scripture: **Proverbs 14:9**

Fools never apologize for their foolishness. Even when they make an attempt to do better, usually when being pressured, they will always add the word "but." As in, "But I did not mean to hurt anyone" or "But I'm trying to do my best," or "But people just don't understand me."

Fools believe that admission of sin or guilt is a sign of weakness. They want to perceive themselves as strong and confident. They believe that weak people worry about offending others or making wrong decisions. These fools just don't get it.

The strong are strong, not because they won't admit their failures, but because they are willing to bear the responsibilities for their mistakes. The strong man will say, "I blew it." Then he moves on, having learned from his failures. This is the mark of an upright person. They accept responsibility and then they enjoy the acceptance of others who respect their truthfulness.

The tragedy for the fool is not that he doesn't win the acceptance of others, but that he placed himself under the wrath of God. It is God who calls for a guilt offering;. It is God who must be appeased. It is God the fool is mocking, and God will not be mocked.

Know that we do not have to bring guilt offerings for our sins and we do not have to do favors to win our way back to God. But, we must come in repentance, giving God the honor due, by turning to the Guilt Offering He has provided, the Lord Jesus Christ.

"Be not deceived: God is not mocked:
for whatsoever a man soweth, that shall he also reap."

— Galatians 6:7

Day 281

Need Victory Over The Flesh?

Key Scripture: **Luke 4:3-12**

Many of us probably remember an actor from years back named Flip Wilson. He was a comedian and made this statement often: "The devil made me do it!" This statement was one trying to explain away a sin or failure. This statement, whether in jest or not, is actually like someone said, "We start the fire, and the devil supplies the gasoline." Building the fire is our choice.

In our key scripture, we see that Satan was trying to entice Jesus. Jesus never allowed the fire to start, so then Satan never had the opportunity to add gas to the fire. Jesus was tested, fought the battle, handled temptation, won the victory, and moved ahead by the power of the Holy Spirit to teach truth and display His authority.

Jesus rebuked Satan in every temptation, showing that we, too, can resist Satan by turning to the power of Christ and the scriptures. So, the next time we are tested, what can we do?

- Trust that God is faithful. 1 Corinthians 10:13.
- Take up the whole armor of God. Ephesians 6:13-17.
- Know you never stand alone. Hebrews 4:16.

Victory in our lives comes many times because we know what our purpose is. We can accomplish amazing goals with persistence by standing with Christ in the power of the Holy Spirit. Many people drift through life with little to show they even existed or had a purpose. Question: Do we know our purpose?

- Joshua knew his. Joshua 24:15.
- Mary the mother of Jesus knew hers. Luke 1:38.
- Paul knew his. Philippians 1:21.

If we are not sure of our purpose, we need to ask God. Focus on living for Christ and staying planted in Him will give us that purpose. Remember, with God's help we can handle temptation and stay on His desired path for us.

"This I say then, Walk in the Spirit,
and ye shall not fulfil the lust of the flesh."
— Galatians 5:16

Day 282

Exercising Faith in Dark Times

Key Scripture: **Psalm 31:21**

In Psalm 31, we see David trusting fully in God as his refuge and source of hope, even in the darkest times. Verse 1, God is his refuge; verse 2, his rescuer: and verse 3, his rock and fortress.

Often, we think that our ability to obtain the goodness of God is conditional. When the weight of this world presses in along with fear, anxiety seems to be overwhelming. We struggle as these feelings consume us, making it difficult to see how the love of God can reach us in that dark place.

Yet, it is at these times we can find that God's love is real, present, and waiting on us. As in the time of David, the same is true today. However dark things may be, God's love will always be able to teach us. (Romans 8:38-39).

You may feel that your life is perfect. You have a successful career, wonderful family, great church, and you're looked up to by many. The exterior looks great, but internally, your life is a disastrous mess, just like David, you're a city under siege.

Do you have secret doubts, fears, and insecurities that you're holding within and have never told a soul?

Do you live in a place of constant anxiety and doubt that has left you unable to move forward in faith and trust in God? God is simply waiting with open arms to enter into rest with you, if you open your heart to Him.

If you are under attack, reach out to God's calming presence in the midst of all your storms.

Lord, remind us today that your love reaches us in our deepest place of need, lighting our darkness, and replacing fear with hope, trust, and love.

"Fear thou not; for I am with thee: be not dismayed;
for I am thy God: I will strengthen thee;
yea, I will help thee; yea,
I will uphold thee with the right hand of my righteousness."

— Isaiah 41:10

Day 283

Fading Inner Beauty

Key Scripture: 1 Peter 3:3-4

In our world today we see more and more focus put on the painted elegance of actors and actresses in movies, on billboards and everywhere else. No wonder our youth are getting lost in their quest for physical beauty. This can leave us with a feeling of hopelessness and worthlessness, and it can seem impossible to obtain the beauty this world covets.

However, true and unfading beauty is much more than what's on the exterior. As in our key scripture, we see the Bible tells us our beauty is not measured by the clothes we wear or how we look. Instead, we have inner beauty, which is based on who we are — not what we look like.

In 1 Samuel 16:7, the prophet Samuel is told to go meet Jessie's sons and that the Lord has appointed one of them to be the new king of Israel. Samuel sees Eliab, one of Jessie's sons, and believes he must be the one the Lord has chosen to be king. The Lord tells Samuel not to be swayed by his looks, because the Lord looks at the heart. As our looks change, our hearts remain the measurement of unfading beauty.

Knowing that our beauty is not an outward trait, we can have confidence in Christ. (Philippians 1:6). Too often, we let our perception of beauty cloud our confidence and confuse our identity while seeking Christ's image. Having confidence in and through Christ is not about how we look or feel. Rather, it's about knowing our Creator and that what He has created is good enough. Our inner beauty is based on our hearts.

In our Christian journey, we are designed to become more like Christ. When we do, our inner beauty increases.

"But the LORD said unto Samuel,
Look not on his countenance; or on the height of his stature:
because I have refused him: for the LORD seeth not as man seeth;
for man looketh on the outward appearance,
but the LORD looketh on the heart."

— 1 Samuel 16:7

Day 284

You Feel Unlovable?

Key Scripture: **Psalm 139:13-14**

Have you ever been given something by a loved one or a special friend that you could never part with? That special item means the world to you and every time you look at it, you are reminded of the person who gave it to you.

In a much deeper way, as seen in our key scripture, you are precious and lasting. God took immeasurable care in the planning and creating of you. I can imagine the delight He had when He finished His purpose in creating you. God loves you simply because He made you.

Maybe you are stumbling over past mistakes, failures and sins, and feeling undeserved and undesirable. When we feel unlovable, we can learn from David, who said, *"I'm fearfully and wonderfully made."* The phrase before this was: *"I praise you."* The first part of this verse makes the second true, because we start with praising the Creator—the One who gets all glory.

The phrase I'm fearfully and wonderfully made, in all reality is bragging on the Creator for His handiwork. In praising God, loving ourselves becomes an act of worship toward our Creator. On days you feel you are unlovable, embrace the fact that you're loved.

Lord, I may feel I'm unworthy of love, but I thank You for Your deep love for me. Because You created me, I worship You by loving who You made me to be.

"The LORD is nigh unto them that are of a broken heart;
and saveth such as be of a contrite spirit."

— Psalm 34:18

Day 285

Briars and Thorns

Key Scripture: **Ezekiel 2:6-7**

In my daily reading, I see again and again verses that contain the phrase: *"Do not be afraid."* I'm not certain at times what I want this to mean, but I want it to mean, "There is nothing to be afraid of." Nothing is too ugly, nothing is too powerful and nothing is too dangerous to actually destroy me. Dreams are exactly that.

I have been protected and surrounded by beautiful things my entire life, but I am aware there is much unthinkable ugliness, power, and danger out there—things our human heart cannot endure. We are not immune to the evil around us; however, we can trust in God's almighty hand.

God tells Ezekiel that there are going to be briars and thorns and they are going to make

him feel vulnerable, but he tells Ezekiel not to be afraid. When God says do not be afraid, I believe He means, "There is nothing to be afraid of."

There are 365 times in God's Word where we are told to "fear not." That is one for every day of the year. Even though there are many things to be afraid of, and it's not easy out there, God is more powerful than any of those other things. He says, "I am with you," and that is the strongest and most valuable protection you can ever have.

Do not be afraid. We have Someone inside us, Someone who has covered the earth with His grace and love; Someone who has always been and will forever be.

"For God hath not given us the spirit of fear;
but of power, and of love, and of a sound mind."

— 2 Timothy 1:7

Day 286

One Lost Sheep

Key Scripture: **Luke 15:4**

I remember an incredibly difficult period in my life when I was a teen. I pulled away from everyone and wanted to be left alone. Before I knew it, I was feeling more alone than I had at any time in my life. I remember asking, "Where are you God?" The question I should have asked was: "God, where have I wandered off to?"

The parable in Luke 15 is about the shepherd with the 100 sheep. The shepherd loses one, and he leaves the 99 behind until he finds the one lost sheep.

Have you ever wondered how that one sheep got lost? Was he mistreated or was he willfully disobedient? I believe he started wandering aimlessly, eating grass and never noticing where he was. Before he knew it, he was alone.

This is much the same way we get lost. We find ourselves a little discouraged or distracted, and we subtly slide away. We start missing a church service here and there, miss reading God's Word, and then we make excuses to not serve God and start looking for ways to avoid anything to do with God. One day we wake up and ask, "How did I get here?" This is a dangerous place to be.

Maybe you have found yourself completely alone or you've wandered off course. In the midst of the wilderness, the Shepherd pursues us, calls out to us, brings us back into the fold and lovingly takes the lead in our journey. He never intended for us to walk through this life alone.

"I am the good Shepherd,
and know my sheep,
and am known of mine."

— John 10:14

Day 287

Making God Our Portion

Key Scripture: **Psalm 73:26**

It's a frightening feeling when your hearbeat suddenly goes out of control, which comes with great pain. I now have only 50% of my heart working as it should, which is plenty if I learn how to handle certain situations. God is good and I am thankful I am still here.

Frightening experiences can draw us deeper into God's Word. Sometimes, we want comfort, and other times we want answers. I am thankful for our key scripture verse.

We all learn our greatest lessons by trusting God through difficult times. In 1 Samuel 1, we find Hanna who knew what it meant to live for God as her portion. (1 Samuel 1:5). However, something was missing in her life and Samuel described her as downhearted.

She took the put downs from Peninnah for two years, then finally had enough. She went straight to the Source of all comfort by putting her hope in God. (Samuel 1:11). Hannah's decision changed her entire outlook. Instead of being downhearted, she became hopeful. Her discouraging thoughts turned to triumph.

This should encourage us to go straight to God in prayer, so His comforting presence will be our portion when enough is enough. I am learning, as Hannah did, that God is my Source and He is enough. When we fully grasp what it means to let God be our portion, we will live a fulfilled life that He created for us.

"The LORD is my portion, saith my soul;
therefore will I hope in Him."

— Lamentations 3:24

Day 288

All Is Vanity and Vexation of Spirit

Key Scripture: **Ecclesiastes 1:14**

"I have seen all the works that are done under the sun; and behold, all is vanity and vexation of spirit."

In my reading today, I turned to the book of Ecclesiastes and I wondered why Solomon would pen these words repeatedly: vanity and vexation of spirit. He, like most of us, really was afraid to consider exactly the impact life is making.

Solomon had acquired great wisdom, and found it was a vexation of spirit. Wisdom will never fill the emptiness of one's heart. He tried mirth and folly, yet his spirit was vexed. He tried to sooth the vexation with wine, but it did not work then as it does not work today. He built great houses, gardens, and orchards as many do today, and they didn't fill his void nor will it fill ours today.

He realized that the rich and mighty end up in the same place as the poor and humble, the grave. (Luke 12:20; Ecclesiastes 2:16.) After care-ful examination of life and all its complexities, Solomon came to a wise conclusion: Our main duty in life is to fear God and keep His commandments. Because we all, rich or poor, wise or unwise, will stand before God to answer for our deeds done in this life. (Ecclesiastes 12:13-14).

Today, we are up against tough times with our economy, government, and our sin-filled world. We, too, can come to the conclusion that all is vanity and vexation of spirit. Those of us who have the peace of God have the opportunity to share this with others, so they will also know that Christ is the only answer.

Our prestige and possessions are nice, but we can't take them with us into eternity. What we can take with us is the value of a pure heart that has been washed by the blood of Jesus. Faith without works is dead. It is as useless as a screen door on a submarine.

"Turn away mine eyes from beholding vanity; and quicken thou me in thy way."

— Psalm 119:37

Day 289

He Restoreth My Soul

Key Scripture: **Psalm 23**

Our scripture today is a familiar one that is used in different settings, and if taken verse by verse it really is deep and meaningful. One small phrase in verse three says: *"He restoreth my soul."* If only we could grasp the depth and meaning of this verse, it would change our lives.

In Ezekiel 34, there is another passage about the shepherd, known in this passage as the Good Shepherd as in John 10. In Ezekiel we see the Lord condemning the shepherds of Israel. They were condemned because they were not bringing back the sheep that had strayed.

In Ezekiel 34:16 the Lord said He would be the Good Shepherd and would bring the sheep back that have strayed. He also restores our souls by feeding our hunger and quenching our thirst for His righteousness. It is the Good Shepherd who restores our souls, binds up our wounds, heals our sicknesses, and gives us strength in place of weakness.

I was just recently told a story about a man who lived next to a sheep farmer. One morning he looked out across the pasture and saw a sheep lying on its back with its legs straight up in the air. He called the farmer, then he rushed over to the sheep and met the farmer there.

They found the sheep still breathing and the farmer explained that sometimes sheep lose their balance and fall over, then all fluids drain away from their lower body parts and they aren't able to get up. The farmer started massaging the sheep's legs, chest and body, trying to get the fluids and feeling back.

Soon he reached under the sheep, lifted him up and set him on his feet again. The sheep's body was restored and he was able to join the other sheep. This is exactly what our Good Shepherd does for His children as He restores us back into fellowship with Him.

We try to restore ourselves and fail over and over. The sooner we learn that we can rely totally on our Good Shepherd, the sooner the procedure of restoring our souls will go as He planned.

"Surely He hath borne our griefs and carried our sorrows…"
— Isaiah 53:4

Straddling the Fence

Key Scripture: **2 Kings 17:39-41**

Scriptures show us how it was in the days of Israel, and we see today many are re-living this history. They know there is a God, they believe in Him — at least with their speech — but hypocritically worship and live for other gods. In this case, their gods could be a possession, a job, or something they do; anything that gets more attention than God Himself.

God commands that we put Him first. (Deuteronomy 6:5; Mark 12:30). We believe if we do this others will think of us as outcasts and will laugh and make fun of us. The lost respect for Christianity comes with this kind of thinking by those who claim to be a Christian. (Matthew 6:31-33). We are in the world and do need things it offers; however, we must not make what it temporarily offers our primary concern. To do so is not putting God first. (Matthew 12:30; Luke 11:23).

Stop straddling the fence, trying to be on both sides — Gods' and the worlds'. God will provide and take care of each of His children, if we simply trust and obey Him. Determine to make the right choice today. (Joshua 24:15).

"No man can serve two masters;
for either he will hate the one, and love the other,
or else he will hold to the one, and despise the other.
Ye cannot serve God and mammon."
— Matthew 6:24

Tender Heart and Strong Voice

Key Scripture: **Psalm 150:2**

Have you ever posted something on Facebook and someone replied who disagrees with your message? In some ways it hurts and in others it ruffs up a righteous dander because you know full well that what was written came directly from God's Word. You know your words were certainly from inspiration.

Listen to this strong word of caution. We live in a world of different cultures and divisions regarding spiritual, political, and policy matters, so our reaction should be directed by God. He desires us to learn to be tenderhearted. A tender heart is a listening heart.

I'm learning to listen, and it's hard. We always want to put our two cents in so badly, but God is teaching me to open my ears, shut my mouth, and seek to understand — even if I disagree.

Having a tender heart also means we must have a feeling heart. Truthfully, I am afraid of my emotions. My passion for things runs ahead of my wisdom, but having a heart for God requires passion and with this we will experience joy and sorrow.

Working for God means entering into others' sufferings and being able to bring the love of Christ to them. God does want us to feel, but God wants our feelings to follow Him.

Having a tender heart means we must have a meditating heart. God wants us to search and meditate on the scriptures, because this is where He shows us our sin that leads to repentance. This results in a righteous heart.

Our walk becomes blameless as we listen to God. We listen, then we feel. We feel, and then we do what is right. It is then that we can confidently speak with a strong voice. That, my friend, is the path of a tender heart.

Lord, make my heart tender through listening, feeling, and doing what is right. Then and only then, help me to have a strong voice for you.

"My voice shalt thou hear in the morning, O LORD;
in the morning will I direct my prayer unto thee,
and will look up."

— Psalm 5:3

Day 292

Got Itching Ears?

Key Scripture: 2 Timothy 4:3

Our key verse is a warning to the church about how one day men will not stand for sound doctrine. Instead, they will gather around a number of teachers who will say what their itching ears want to hear. Itching ears is a figure of speech that refers to people's desires, selfish needs, or wants.

These impel a person to believe whatever they want rather than the actual truth. They decide what is right or wrong and they seek out others to support them. Paul's warning is that the church will one day turn away from those having itching ears.

Evidence today of these people includes the popularity of messages that people are not required to change, as if repentance is not required, and that people are basically good. They are taught that God is too loving to judge anyone, and that the cross, with its blood, is not necessary. They believe that God wants His children to be healthy, wealthy and content in this world.

As people turn their backs on sin and condemnation, they disregard their need of repentance and forgiveness. The church today needs to re-examine the teachings it endorses. These questions need to be addressed and answered by Biblical truths:

- Are our teachings truly from God or simply itches we want to scratch?

- Are we standing on solid Biblical ground, or have we allowed the world to influence our thinking?

- Have we guarded ourselves from the schemes of Satan? Ephesians 6:11

- Are we keeping ourselves "blameless for the coming of our Lord Jesus Christ?" 1 Thessalonians 5:23

The truth is, God is not concerned with scratching our itches, but in transforming us into the image of His Son. (2 Corinthians 4:4)

"And be not conformed to this world:
but be ye transformed by the renewing of your mind,
that ye may prove what is that good, and acceptable,
and perfect will of God."

— Romans 12:2

Day 293

Time is Ticking

Key Scripture: Psalm 39:4

Reflecting on the past years, I can't help but wonder if I've done my best, been faithful as I should have been, and used my time for the Lord wisely? Sadly, I must plead guilty on all three counts. Now facing the latter years of my life, I've learned that with life we cannot bottle time. We must determine not to waste time wondering what is next.

If you are still breathing and have a good mind, there is still something here for you to do. (Jeremiah 29:11). But what? We must pray and seek God's purpose for our lives moving forward. Get curious and seek God's answer.

In the not so far away future, I have an appointment with my Eternal Savior and won-der just what I'll do at that moment. Really and truly what I want to hear is, *"Well done, my good and faithful servant."* (Matthew 25:21.) Will you hear those words? We must stay about our Father's business and allow Him to use each of us for His glory.

We are commanded to go into all the world and preach the gospel. (Matthew 28:16-29.) Time will not wait while we are deciding what to do. We may trip sometimes, but let's start walking. Some may say to "take it easy" or "eat, drink, and be merry," yet God says that is not the way we should be living our lives. We must find a clear purpose and stay faithful to the task God has for us.

"Who hath saved us, and called us with an holy calling,
not according to our works, but according to His own purpose and grace,
which was given to us in Christ Jesus before the world began."

— 2 Timothy1:9

Day 294

Power of a Grateful Heart

Key Scripture: **Psalm 100:4-5**

A very simple truth that we all must believe is that gratitude kills attitude. Thinking grateful thoughts, having an outlook of gratitude and verbalizing them removes all negative emotions that can wreck and ruin your heart.

Scripture is clear that our heart should first and foremost be full of praise toward our amazing Lord. We evidently do not believe this because it is far too easy for us to give in to complaining, self-pity, discouragement, and bitterness.

Gratitude takes your eyes off yourself and puts them back on the Lord. This helps us to realize who is in control and where our help comes from. By forgetting this we open ourselves up to feelings of fear, worry, and anything else which causes problems for ourselves and others. Gratitude invites God's presence and makes the enemy flee. The Bible says that the Lord actually inhabits the praises of His people. (Psalm 22:3).

Gratitude leaves no room for complaining. We often fall into this temptation more than we would like. Complaining is all about us and is plain selfish, because we just do not get our way.

Gratitude most certainly is not about us. It is about our Savior who unselfishly died for us. Be a child of God who realizes all God has given us, and thank Him for it. That gratitude will for sure kill any bad attitude and fill us with a life of peace, strength, comfort, and hope.

"Every good gift and every perfect gift is from above,
and cometh down from the Father of lights,
with whom is no variableness,
neither shadow of turning."

— James 1:17

Day 295

Is Trusting Your Heart Trustworthy?

Key Scripture: **Psalm 73:26**

Trust your heart. This is the advice we often receive, whether seeking true love in a relationship or making weighty decisions, as well as when we are struggling with a big emotion. The problem with this advice is that our hearts are not always trustworthy.

Our hearts may respond to short-term emotion and fail to weigh the long-term effect. This may give us permission to do what we want, but fail to consider the hearts of others around us. Then again, our hearts might even lie to us to get us what we want.

In today's verse, the psalmist recognizes he is both weak and strong. In his own power he is a mess; yet he is not alone. He is united to a powerful God and all the goodness this relationship brings to him.

As believers, our hearts are attached to our relationship with an omnipresent, all-knowing, all-powerful Heavenly Father. That means our hearts are attached to truth, wisdom, strength, healing, and so much more. It demands that the messages filtering through our hearts must first pass through our faith.

It's okay to acknowledge our hearts might not be trustworthy at the moment. That isn't weak, that's strong. It's confessing we need more than emotion to direct our path. It's saying we choose a stronger foundation than a temporal emotion or temporary situation.

When we put our trust in God rather than in our fickle hearts, He anchors it. Trust does not fix a momentary circumstance, but it grounds us to an eternal, unmovable source of strength.

Trust our hearts? No, not until all is filtered through our faith in our Holy Omnipotent God.

"The heart is deceitful above all things,
and desperately wicked:
who can know it?"

— Jeremiah 17:9

Day 296

Ever Felt You Were Just Not Good Enough?

Key Scripture: 2 Corinthians 12:9

As a child did you ever feel you just weren't good enough to be the best at anything you really wanted? Were you the one who always settled for being in the audience and not on stage? Many people have this same outlook on their self-perspective.

Moses had a good case of the "not good enoughs." God spoke through a burning bush to call Moses to lead His people out of Egyptian bondage. That is when he had a one-sided argument with God, trying to convince God he was the wrong man for the job.

Moses questioned God about his fear that the Israelites would not believe he was sent from God and would not follow him. God told him to tell them "the God of their fathers has sent me to you."

Moses asked, *"What if they ask your name"?*

God replied, *"Tell them I Am Who I Am; I Am has sent me to you."*

I'll go out on a limb and say that you, too, have likely struggled with feelings of inferiority, insecurities, and inadequacy. But, here is what we need to remember: Whatever positive characteristics we feel we are not, God is. He is the God who fills in the gaps of these characteristics.

When we say, "I'm not strong enough," God says, "I Am."
When we say, "I'm not smart enough," God says, "I Am."
When we say, "I'm not good enough," God says, "I AM."

Once we get free of the lies that we are not good enough and take hold of the truth that we're more than enough because of the presence of Christ and His power in us, then the fear and insecurities will be conquered, and we'll be on our way to experiencing the confidence to do everything God calls us to do.

That's what happens when we allow God to fill in our gaps. He turns what we perceive as our greatest weakness into our greatest strength.

"I can do all things through Christ which strengtheneth me."
— Philippians 4:13

Day 297

Do You Have a Good Father?

Key Scripture: **Matthew 7:11**

For many years I defined my understanding of God's interest in me based upon my father's interest in me. I knew my dad loved me but his upbringing was one that did not openly show love.

Thankfully, we know that God's love is unhindered by any human background or upbringing. Every day is a new understanding of God as a perfect Heavenly Father. What we missed as a child, we can certainly gain while understanding more about our Heavenly Father.

- Our Father cares for and provides our every need. (Matthew 6:25-34.)

- Our Father is merciful toward us. In Luke 6:36 God shows His loving kindness instead of anger when we make wrong choices.

- Our Father hears our prayers and will answer them. In Matthew 18:20 God shows His heart when He says "where two or more agree upon something in prayer, He hears and answers."

- Our Father protects us. In Psalm 91:11, God says He will send angels to guard over us in all our ways.

- Our Father watches and waits for us when we turn away from Him. In Luke 15:20 the prodigal son's father waited and longed for his son's return and when he did, the father ran and embraced him, showing his love toward him. This story modeled our Heavenly Father's love and compassion for our return when we too go our own way.

No matter what our situation with our earthly father, we can say with full assurance that we have a good Heavenly Father who loves us unconditionally. He is all-in, and we will never outgrow His care and provision.

"But now, O LORD, thou art our father;
we are the clay, and thou our potter,
and we all are the work of thy hand."

— Isaiah 64:8

Day 298

God Desires Us to Be an Instrument

Key Scripture: **Acts 1:9-19**

It's been a long time, but back in the '70s I was a student at Tennessee Temple College. There were many hard days, but also some very rewarding days. I loved going to student recitals and special services where the many choirs participated. Even now, I can shut my eyes and open my heart and ears and still hear those wonderful sounds.

One of the most memorable moments was seeing and hearing Dr. Charles Wiegle give his testimony at the ripe old age of 95. He was a Bible student in his early '20s when God called him to preach. After he told his wife the wonderful news, she packed up and left him, then filed for a divorce.

He was so devastated and down on himself that he went out to an old dock leading out into the river because he wanted to end his life. But, God intervened and instead of ending his life, he found a new outlook because God gave him the words of the song: "No One Ever Cared for Me Like Jesus." He was a great man, used by God in the field of music and had a rewarding life.

Remember the story about someone demonstrating about using an instrument for God. He took a cheap starter violin and played it beautifully. No one thought that sound could come from this cheap instrument.

Then, he picked up an instrument that cost him dearly and began to play. It made the most horrible screeching sound. He then explained that it does not matter how costly something is, it depends on what we do with what we have. We are all called to be some kind of instrument for the Lord, and we all have the ability to make some kind of sound with our lives.

Remember Saul before he became known as Paul? He persecuted and tried to destroy Christianity. When God saved him, others were still afraid of him because of his reputation.

Jesus told them Paul was His chosen instrument. Anyone chosen by God can make a beautiful sound with their life as long as they are obedient to Christ, because then that life will make a beautiful loving tune.

"Neither yield ye your members as instruments of unrighteousness unto sin:
but yield yourselves unto God,
as those that are alive from the dead,
and your members as instruments of righteousness unto God."

— Romans 6:13

Day 299

Broken Promises

Key Scripture: **Nehemiah 5:13**

We live in world full of broken promises. It's sad that promises mean so little to people today.

A couple stands before an altar repeating vows and promise to be faithful as long as they both shall live. But eventually one or the other goes back on that promise. Politicians promise the moon, but when they're elected they forget about their promises.

In our churches we see people making promises to God and the church to always be there and support the activities, only to see them not show up or sit back and forget their promises.

What can we do to better keep our word? One thing is to always think before you speak. Never promise to be somewhere or do something if there is a chance you can't keep that promise.

We can get over-involved and under-committed. This means we stop wanting to do everything that comes up, causing us to not be able to meet our commitments. We bite off more than we can chew. So, try under-promising and over-achieving instead. Commit to something small, but always keep your word.

In the end, your integrity matters. If you fail to keep your word, others will see you as someone who is unreliable. Worst yet, as a Christian, our faithfulness is a reflection of God's faithfulness. God never lets us down. How does our faithfulness (or lack thereof) reflect upon our faithful God?

Lord, help us to always say what we mean and mean what we say; be honest and keep our promises.

"Better is it that thou shouldest not vow,
than that thou shouldest vow and not pay."

— Ecclesiastes 5:5

Day 300

God's Way to Forgiveness

Key Scripture: **Colossians 3:13**

Remember when as children we held grudges against a brother, a sister, or maybe a friend? Looking at those times now, I know I never should have been critical or held grudges. As our scripture says, life is about relationships.

As humans, we are not perfect. Even people we know who are closest to us are one day going to hurt us. How will we respond when we get hurt?

Referring to the first part of our scripture, we must understand that the godliest people we know are not perfect. They will say or do something that offends us. If and when that happens, we are to be gracious and loving as we explain to that person why we're offended.

God expects us to forgive one another as our scripture says. That is very straight-forward and while some people might think it is not good advice— it is a command.

The last part of our scripture gives us the perfect answer: as the Lord has forgiven us, we are to forgive others. Christ died for our sins, forgiving every offense we have committed against God and everyone else. Whatever we have done or whatever our motivation was, He has forgiven us. He expects us to do the same.

We as humans find this hard to do, but it is something we must do. We want to experience God's forgiveness in its fullness so we must forgive as He forgives. Only then will we experience and enjoy relationships without being hindered by the hard feelings or grudges that we tend to hold onto. That is why God wants us to forgive others,—not just for their benefit, but also for the peace it brings to us.

"For if ye forgive men their trespasses,
your Heavenly Father will also forgive you;
But if ye forgive not men their trespasses,
neither will your Father forgive your trespasses."
— Matthew 6:14-15

Day 301

Put Your Heart in God's Hands—What Can He Do?

Key Scripture: **Daniel 1:8**

World events never catch God by surprise. He has placed us precisely where we are for a purpose. Have you ever considered why you have been placed in this world at this time? Could we dare believe that the God of this universe, who has called you to Himself and equipped you with His Spirit, could work mightily through you?

Daniel didn't let the temptations of his day get in his way of his relationship with the Lord. He knew to be useful he must remain obedient in all things. Regardless of the king's commandment, he refused to compromise what he knew God required of him.

History repeats itself with examples of Christian men and women who believed God would use them to make a difference in His kingdom. God placed Esther in the king's court so that she could save the lives of her people. God placed Joseph as a powerful advisor to Pharaoh to save Jacob and his family from the famine.

We too are here for God's purpose and for His will. Wherever we are today we must allow God to work in and through us to be used how He pleases. Be obedient.

God uses ordinary people to do extraordinary things. We are all ordinary!!!

"For where your treasure is,
there will your heart be also."

— Matthew 6:21

Is My Life Making a Difference?

Key Scripture: **Jude 22**

I learn more each day I am a mere vessel praying that in some way I am used by God. In reflecting on the key scripture chosen for this post, I look back a few years when I made this my new life verse.

Back then, I heard a sermon by Dr. Lee Roberson on compassion. He was a great man and this was an important message. We all need to have a compassionate heart for others. Scripture teaches this and certainly we should all show compassion. The last part of this verse says we are to make a difference. This surely does not mean to be a bad influence, but a difference that pleases God.

Knowing God uses anyone who is a willing vessel, we must realize the key to being used is to be willing to follow God's leadership. We are His children, to be used for His purpose. No matter when or where we are, each of us can be used of God for "making a difference."

A dear friend told me recently that when they go out to eat and the waitress or waiter comes to take their order, they always tell them they are about to pray and ask God's blessing on their food. Then they ask the one taking their order if there is something particular in their life they are in need of prayer for. Usually they get a prayer request and the waiter or waitress always seemed to appreciatie their compassion.

Many things God asks us to do will be simple, but the reality is we serve an incredible, compassionate God who wants to use each of us to make a difference. My challenge today is that we all open our hearts and think of something He wants us to do. When you've done that, mark it down and pray that He will use you to make a difference in someone's life, by simply being obedient.

Be in the business of doing and making a difference, not just entertaining the idea, but making it happen.

"But ye are a chosen generation,
a royal priesthood, an holy nation, a peculiar people;
that ye should shew forth the praises of Him who hath called you out of darkness
into His marvellous light."

— 1 Peter 2:9

Day 303

Our Enemies' Plan For Christians

Key Scripture: **1 John 2:16**

The Lord has opened my prayer life in the past year, and certainly I pray this heart of prayer never grows cold.

Sometimes I pray regularly that God will always make me aware when Satan is out to damage my life in any way he can. His plan for each of us is to steal, kill, and destroy. Remember in Genesis chapter 3, how Satan tempted Eve?

Our key scripture verse outlines his plan and attack on our hearts; the same way he used to tempt Jesus in Matthew 4:1-11. We can see that he is powerful, but predictable.

Satan tempts us with whatever physical senses we are preoccupied by; be it taste, smell, sound, touch, or sight. God gave us our senses with boundaries and said they are good. But they sometimes venture outside God's intention for us, and cause us to attempt to get our needs met outside the will of God.

Eve was tempted (Genesis 3:6) with something *"pleasing to the eyes,"* and Satan told Jesus (Matthew 4:8-10) that the kingdom of the world could be His.

Satan flashes the newest, biggest, and seemingly best things of this world before us, trying to lure us into thinking we must have it. He wants us to think these material and fleshly things will make us feel fulfilled and happy. But, these things are only temporary and will get old.

Satan also tempts us to try to elevate ourselves above others. This is only the world telling us we are worthy and creates a need in us to have people notice us, which only strokes our pride.

There is a huge difference between the responses of Eve and Jesus. Eve allowed Satan to weave a tangled web of justification, while Jesus quoted at every temptation, *"It is written,"* just as we should. We must shut Satan down with the truth of God.

We can train ourselves to recognize Satan's strategies, and then stand on the promises of God, putting him in his place. When we are filled with the goodness of God, there is no room for Satan.

"Submit yourselves therefore to God.
Resist the devil,
and he will flee from you."

— James 4:7

Day 304

God Will Lead Your Way

Key Scripture: **John 10:27**

How are you making decisions in life? Do you believe it's all up to you or do you rely on God to direct your steps?

God has given us a free will to choose what to do and where to go, but He wants us to choose His ways. (Proverbs 3:5-6). So by choosing to follow God, you don't have to depend on your knowledge because He will lead you. By doing this, we will have the ability to hear the voice of God as our key scripture verse says.

We still have the choice to listen to God or go in our own direction. In order to distinguish whether the thoughts coming into our minds are our own or God's, we must capture every thought to make it obedient to Christ. (2 Cor-

inthians 10:5). As Christ also did in Luke 4:1-3 when Satan tempted Him in the wilderness, He turned to the truth of God in responding.

Understand, our weapons against Satan are not of this world. Through studying God's Word, we can do as Christ did, and reject wrong thoughts from leading us astray.

Knowing and studying God's Word, we can become confident in hearing the voice of God so we can follow His leading. The key is to know the Word of God. Understanding the scriptures equips us to hear His voice and distinguish between what is true and what is not.

"Study to shew thyself approved unto God, a workman that needeth not to be ashamed, rightly dividing the Word of truth."

— 2 Corinthians 10:4, 2 Timothy 2:15

Day 305

Waiting On God

Key Scripture: **Psalm 27:13-14**

One of the toughest things to do in life is "wait" on something we want to happen. We live in an impatient society, and as individuals we can be selfish. Waiting requires surrender of a precious commodity — time. We all think our time is valuable and belongs to us.

Time is important, but we have to understand that God's timetable is not ours. So, our impatience causes us to try to rationalize with God. We tell Him how badly we need an answer, or how He did this for someone else so why do we have to wait? We can even start telling God that waiting is not acceptable.

Waiting on an answer to a specific prayer can be painful because sometimes waiting turns into a disaster and things don't go our way. Waiting is not for weak spiritual Christians, it is for the strong at heart. Obeying God in waiting requires true faith. It's handing over our time in waiting for God, and trusting and believing God's plan is the best.

Doing this is deferring what is good for what is best. God doesn't ask us to wait to torment us; He sees what we can't and in His infinitely perfect nature He wants to give us more than we can ask for or think of. Taking things into our own hands will cause heartache and disappointment.

So, remember this one thing: those who wait on God will experience joy that far surpasses any temporary pleasure you may receive by not waiting on Him. Wait on God!!!

"But they that wait upon the LORD shall renew their strength; ..."
— Isaiah 40:31

Day 306

Do I Have a Bitter Spirit?

Key Scripture: **Ephesians 4:31**

Most people don't recognize they have a bitter spirit. In many cases, their perspective is they are completely justified in being bitter. They'll say, "It just isn't fair."

Make no mistake, bitterness is a sin. (James 3:14-16). It is one that has broken up marriages, friendships, and has hindered many people from finding peace and rest in their Christian life.

In Hebrews 12:14-16; we find a verse that helps us understand the dangers behind bitterness. Bitterness is a root that grows into division, accusation and hatred. Over time, bitterness can overwhelm our hearts, consuming any care, love and gentleness that existed. This will show in our actions. (Proverbs 12:23).

It is only after we acknowledge the sinful tendencies that are a part of our bitter nature that we will begin to take up the battle against bitterness. Until this happens, those who justify or make excuses for their grudges, animosities, envy or the chip they carry on their shoulders will never become free from their bitterness.

The bitter person is only feeding their flesh and giving in to their self-desire to protect their honor above all else. (Philippians 2:21). We must become reliant upon the Holy Spirit to show us the truth about ourselves. When we cry out in need, the Holy Spirit will be there to reveal to us it is not others who need changing but ourselves.

When we realize this, the healing process will begin and the Holy Spirit will give us the power to overcome our bitterness. Find the root of the problem and arm yourself with the mind of Christ and do God's will. (1 Peter 4:1-2). We must choose to do the right thing (goodness) over bitterness and sin. (1 Corinthians 13:4-8).

We must acknowledge bitterness for what it is and then make a firm decision to hate it with a perfect hatred.

"Doth a fountain send forth at the same place sweet water and bitter?"

— James 3:11

Day 307

Forgiving Yourself

Key Scripture: 1 John 1:5-10

Forgiving someone else can sometimes be very difficult, but how are we supposed to forgive ourselves?

Forgiveness is always a choice, whether we are forgiving someone else or in need of forgiveness ourselves. On the path of healing, forgiveness remains the same: confess, repent, and believe.

We can keep our sin secret, or we can bring it to Jesus and others. We can take steps to prevent these things from happening again, do as Christ did, and believe what He said: "It is finished." Then again, we could do nothing and wake up miserable each morning and punish ourselves for sins Jesus has already paid for.

Every day, we make the choice about whether we will live in the light or in darkness.

(1 John 1:5-7). Satan wants us to believe the lie that we don't deserve forgiveness so we deceive ourselves.

We will never feel worthy of forgiveness or be able to work hard enough to feel worthy. To think we can is prideful. By God's grace, we are saved, and by the same we are forgiven day by day.

After repenting of our sin and receiving forgiveness from Christ, the key to forgiving ourselves is to simply agree with God that we are forgiven. God's grace is greater than our greatest sin.

Jesus Christ sacrificed His life for our sins. We are most definitely free to move past our past and into Jesus' light.

"In whom we have redemption through His blood,
the forgiveness of sins,
according to the riches of His grace."

— Ephesians 1:7

Day 308

Seventy Times Seven

Key Scripture: **Ephesians 4:32**

Throughout His life on earth, over and over Jesus gave us examples of how to forgive. He taught us to turn the other cheek, as He forgave those who hung Him on the cross, He always loved His enemies.

Giving forgiveness can be difficult for some, but He gives us strength to continually forgive and show His love, no matter the circumstances. Sometimes, we have to forgive someone more than once, maybe even daily. We are able to forgive because God enables us to do so because He forgave us.

Harboring unforgiveness in our hearts keeps us from God's plan and purpose. It's like a poison that seeps into our thoughts, attitude, and desires, and will affect our life tremendously if it's not dealt with.

People try to punish the other person by not forgiving them, but the truth is bitterness hurts everyone around us, especially the one not able to forgive. This keeps us from hearing God's voice and direction.

Forgiveness cannot come through our own strength. Only with God can we forgive and show the fullness of His love. An earthly focus holds onto bitterness and grudges so it may fuel our own revenge or cover up pain. But, with a Godly focus, we can forgive because we are already forgiven.

God helps us to focus because He wants us to show grace in and through our lives to others, as He has shown His grace to us.

"Then came Peter to Him, and said,
Lord, how oft shall my brother sin against me, and I forgive him?
Till seven times?
Jesus saith unto him, I say not, Until seven times,
but, Until seventy times seven."
— Matthew 18:21-22

Day 309

Samson Faced Opposition While Fulfilling God's Call

Key Scripture: **2 Corinthians 10:4-5**

In the story about Samson, we find he faced all kinds of resistance as he sought to fulfill God's calling. He was opposed by the Philistines, by his fellow countrymen, and even Delilah, his beloved wife. In addition, Samson was his own worst enemy.

In this same way, we are to seek to honor God by obeying His leadership in our lives because we are going to face opposition. (John 15:20). One chapter later God says more of the same. (John 16:33).

Jesus warns not that we might face opposition, but as we try to fulfill our calling, we *will* face it. Thankfully, we are not alone. We need to continually lean on Christ, as it says in the great commission: He will be with us unto the ends of the age.

So, seeking to fulfill God's purpose for your life, rely on His strength, wisdom, and abiding presence to overcome obstacles. With His help, we can walk in the strength of God who helped Samson.

You can win the battles God has called you to win.

"Cast not away therefore your confidence,
which hath great recompence of reward."

— Hebrews 10:35

Day 310

Subtle Sins Obscure Our Clarity of Doing Right

Key Scripture: **Matthew 7:3-5**

In our key scripture, Jesus compares sin to specks and logs in our eyes. These words paint a picture of sin's ability to distort, confuse, and blind us.

We want to make decisions in line with the Spirit's leading and His will, but subtle sin allowed into our lives impairs our vision. We think these subtle sins are "not so bad" and write them off as a mistake or something normal. We accept them and never deal with them.

The tempter has laid a trap of deception so the path of subtle sin obscures our vision as to what sin really is. We think because the sky didn't fall these sins are something normal and we don't have to worry because the "bigger" sins are the only ones God really cares about.

In James 4:17 we see that if we know to do good, and do it not then it is sin. Murder, pride, greed, and stealing is sin. If we avoid sin only to keep us out of trouble, we are missing some essential truth. To make light of any sin is to make light of the suffering of our Lord in His death on the cross. We are to treat sin with all seriousness, and do whatever we can to root it out of our hearts and lives. (Matthew 5:29-30).

We need to wage war against sin and realize that sin is sin and repentance is needed, and comes through the conviction of our hearts to believe in the wrongness of sin and the loveliness of Christ.

Sin does impair clarity in making decisions. It removes God from our thinking and how we live, and replaces it with us; our thinking with us in mind, making selfish choices and not including God.

Clarity will come when we learn to live in the center of God's will. Certainly it is God's will to not make peace with our sins, but to help us glorify God in doing and living in righteousness.

"Take us the foxes, the little foxes, that spoil the vines:
for our vines have tender grapes."

— Song of Solomon 2:15

Day 311

Living The Life God Has Given You

Key Scripture: **2 Peter 1:3**

Do we at times wrestle with feelings of envy toward others in our circle of friends? Does the ugliness of that green-eyed greed settle within your heart, causing you to focus on what's lacking in your life, rather than on the blessings that you have? You, like myself, need to stop envying the lives God gave others and be satisfied with the life He has given us.

In light of our key scripture verse, we could think about the empty blank in this statement: While I might not have _____, I do have what it takes to live a life of godliness.

As a Christian, we have turned our lives over to God; therefore, we all have the Lord and His strength to carry us through. His unfailing love toward each of us is vast, without respect of persons, and never-ending.

We look around at our circle of friends, and make assessments and compare our lives to others. We may not have the financial stability or had the ideal upbringing, or maybe our health is not the greatest, or we don't have a family without problems, but we do have all we need to live a life of godliness as we grow in the knowledge of God.

So, the next time you find yourself getting an envious spirit within, focus on the Mind of God, and thank Him for the blessings, no matter how simple. These are what God has gifted to you.

We have to choose to be content rather than waste devilish energy wishing we resided in someone else's circumstances. Let's spend our time pursuing godliness as we deepen our walk with Christ. Maybe we don't have what someone else has, but we do have Christ.

"But godliness with contentment is great gain."
— 1 Timothy 6:6

Day 312

If God Really Loved Me...

Key Scripture: **Isaiah 54:10**

My mind wonders what would happen in our lives if we really lived in the absolute assurance of God's love. Meaning as Christians, we know God loves us.

The knowing is not what I mean. What I mean is living as if we really believe God loves us. I'm talking about walking confidently in the certainty of God's love, even when our "want to" isn't working.

I know in my own life, I have faced heart-breaking situations where I know God could step in and change everything in an instant. When He doesn't, it hurts. But here is what God wants to teach us: we must process disappointments through the filter of His love, not through the tangled places in our hearts.

When we look through the tangled places of our hearts, we will often ask, "If God loves me so much, why would He let this happen?" It's okay to sometimes feel hurt, lonely, and sad, but these feelings should not be a trigger to doubt God's love for us. Hold on to the scripture verse in Isaiah and whatever we are facing today, rest assured, God really does love us.

Dear Lord, thank you for being the great God that you are. I trust your plan for me and believe you allow things to happen for a reason. Things may get difficult, but I'd rather be close to You through a thousand difficult moments, than apart from You in a thousand good ones. I love You, Lord. Amen.

"For God so loved the world,
that He gave His only begotten Son,
that whosoever believeth in Him should not perish,
but have everlasting life."

— John 3:16

Day 313

Samson Fulfilled God's Purpose Through God's Strength

Key Scripture: **Philippians 4:1**

The story of Samson illustrates how God's strength enabled him to live God's purpose. Through this story, God shows us that He desires to enable the same for us.

Samson did only what God gave him strength to do. Without that strength, he could do nothing, but with it he was unstoppable.

God gives us divine power, and He calls us by His glory and goodness to live a godly life. (2 Peter 1:3). God has a plan for us to help build His kingdom. How different would our lives, our families, and our churches be if we walked with a greater sense of mission, along with a steadfast trust in God's strength to help us fulfill our purpose?

We need to encounter God's strength to walk through hardships. When we discover God's purpose for us, we can tap into God's strength freely, given us by Jesus Christ.

A word of caution, when things are going great in your walk with Christ, there will always be someone or something standing in opposition against your faithful stand for Christ. Stand strong.

"Be strong and of a good courage,
fear not, nor be afraid of them:
for the LORD thy God,
He it is that doth go with thee;
He will not fail thee,
nor forsake thee."

— Deuteronomy 31:6

Day 314

Walk the Talk, and Talk the Walk

Key Scripture: **Colossians 2:6**

If we say we have received Christ into our hearts, our new lives must display Christ Jesus by our walk of faith in Him. Walking implies action. Our new life is not to be hidden in a closet, but revealed in our walk.

Being in Christ, we must act as Christ: in His hope, in His love, in His joy; and as reflection of His image so that others see Jesus Christ in us. Walking signifies progress, "So Walk In Him."

A continual abiding in Christ is what is needed, not just having a devotion time and then disregarding Christ the rest of the day. Our walk should be always treading in His steps. Walking in Christ should become a habit.

This is why when we speak of a man's walk and conversation, we mean the constant theme of Christ in his life. Being hot and cold regarding your walk with Christ is not a constant lifestyle. We must hold onto Christ, follow His steps, and never let Him go.

Therefore, as you have received Christ as Savior, remember at that hour how grateful, joyful, guilt-free, and thankful you were. Preserve these feelings and never let them depart. Maintain your eagerness to walk as Christ, holding onto your strong faith and trust, which is the source of your walk. Do this and your joy may remain full for the rest of your days.

"But they that wait upon the LORD shall renew their strength;
they shall mount up with wings as eagles;
they shall run, and not be weary,
and they shall walk, and not faint."

— Isaiah 40:31

Day 315

God Gives His Best
to Those Who Leave the Choice to Him

Key Scripture: Psalm 123:2

To follow Christ is to choose Him and His ways with our free will.

It's true that from the beginning, God has given mankind the power of choice (free will). To say that God is all about choice or that He respects our choice is only partially true. He gives us the ability to choose or reject His ways, but we know His desire.

The tree of knowledge of good and evil represented a choice of life and death; to follow God or not. He gave us a free will, but He does not approve of sinful choices. He is very gracious and merciful when we sin and gives us the opportunity to seek forgiveness. It definitely is not His will for us to sin.

Shouldn't we as believers want God's desire, rather than the bare minimum of doing what we can easily get by with? God gives us a choice to be a racist or not, to love or hate, to be greedy or generous, to preserve life or to kill. What God allows is not always the same as His will.

Because of our fallen world and sinful nature, our free will is in conflict with His will. God gives the best to those that leave the choice to Him. He always wants to be our choice. We don't worship our free will; we follow Him, His will, and His ways.

"The LORD is good to all;
and His tender mercies are over all His works."

— Psalm 145:9

Day 316

God's Purpose for Samson and for You

Key Scripture: **Judges Chapters 13-16**

Samson was handpicked by God to liberate God's people. He grew up knowing God's will for his life. An angel visited his parents and fully explained the purpose placed upon Samson's life and they made certain to raise him with God's purpose as the major factor in his life.

God gave Sampson supernatural strength and everything he needed to deliver Israel from the oppression of the Philistines. God also has chosen you, and has given you a purpose before you were born.

When God created Heaven and earth, He knew that one day you would find yourself right where you are at this moment. Being created in the image of God, and made for a purpose, the most important thing you can do is to seek God's guidance concerning what your mission should be. Then, God Himself will best fulfill this purpose through the leading of His Spirit.

"See then that ye walk circumspectly,
not as fools, but as wise,
Redeeming the time, because the days are evil.
Wherefore be ye not unwise,
but understanding what the will of the Lord is."

— Ephesians 5:15-17

Day 317

We are Alive in Christ

Key Scripture: **Ephesians 2:1-10**

Being alive in Christ does not mean that you are happy all the time. It does not mean that our lives are all put together as portrayed in a Hollywood movie. In fact, being alive in Christ means the opposite.

Our key scripture today states that even though we were dead in our sins, God made us alive together in Christ. It is in imperfection that grace appears. God is at work in our daily routine of existence.

Remember, Christ came to this world to live an ordinary life, miraculously connected to God the Father. We become alive in Christ when we are baptized into His life. (Galatians 3:27).

As we said earlier, being alive does not mean we will be in a constant state of smiles and joy, but it does mean our foundation is so strong that when storms come, we can live through them. Even when we were dead in our sins, God gave us life through Christ. So, know that in Christ, our feet are planted firmly on an unshakable foundation of God's unconditional love for you and me.

Lord, help us to always remember that we are alive in Christ.

"For as in Adam all die,
even so in Christ shall all be made alive."

— 1 Corinthians 15:22

Day 318

Lord, Stir Our Hearts

Key Scripture: **Ezra 1:1-5**

God stirs up His people along with unbelievers for a reason, as we see in our key scripture. Here, God wanted Israel released from captivity in Babylon to go back to the Promised Land to rebuild the house of the Lord.

The meaning of the words "stirred up" means to "arouse, wake as if from sleep." Oh, that God would stir our hearts to live our lives in faithful service to Him.

The Lord stirs our hearts to do what is right in His eyes because the natural man does not understand the things of the Spirit of God. (1 Corinthians 2:14). *"No man can come to Me, except the Father which hath sent Me draw him..."* (John 6:44). Unless God "stirs up" our hearts first, none of us would do anything good. (Romans 3:10-18).

We need to pray that God will stir our hearts for Him, and that the church will turn back to Him, reaching lost souls here and around the world.

Things looked bleak for Israel, as they were in captivity in a foreign land until He stirred the heart of King Cyrus. That's when everything changed.

Knowing God stirs hearts gives us hope for our country, our churches, our homes, and lost loved ones. Let's pray that He will indeed "stir our hearts" today so that we can pray and follow God's will.

"For it is God which worketh in you both to will and to do of His good pleasure."
— Philippians 2:13

Day 319

Do We Serve God or Does God Serve Us?

Key Scripture: **Luke 4:8; Mark 10:45**

It is interesting to think Biblically of the question above. We are inclined to think that God serving us as totally wrong. But, what does the scripture teach? The scriptures teach; *"You shall worship the Lord your God and Him only shall you serve."* (Luke 4:8).

However, there is another side of the question that is not considered enough: not letting God serve us. Mark tells us *"the Son of Man did not come to be served, but to serve."* God is not looking for people to work for Him, as much as He is looking for people who will let Him work for them and through them.

In the parable of the Expectant Steward waiting for the return of the Master, he was told to sit down and he would be served and attended to by the Master. It was the Master's pleasure to serve the servant.

The parable teaches that it is God's glory to serve sinners. God's heart overflows with love and kindness to His children, and He enjoys dispensing that love to them because it brings glory to His name. God is never more glorified than when He is saving and giving grace to sinners. (Psalm 145:9).

Sometimes, our pride will not allow us to even think that God is being exceedingly good to us. We can resent the idea that we need such mercy and grace. As a Christian, we are to be servants of God, and we are also to accept that God desires to serve us and shower us with His love, mercy, and grace resting in Him.

There are three kinds of relationships:

- Selfish + Selfish = a brutal relationship

- Selfish + Servant = an abusive relationship

- Servant + Servant = a beautiful relationship

"For even the Son of man came not to be ministered unto,
but to minister,
and to give His life a ransom for many."

— Mark 10:45

Day 320

When You Feel Like Quitting, Press On

Key Scripture: **Hebrews 10:35-36**

I'm sure many of us have felt the strain of waiting on an answer or the anticipation of a certain project to come to an end. I know that for myself I have missed out on needed blessings because I've just thrown in the towel and given up instead of being persistent and finishing. If only I had pushed on a little more and kept my nose to the grindstone, things would have been different.

Remember the story of Joshua? His instructions were simple: to march around Jericho for seven days and on the seventh day, march seven times around the city. Day after day, the Israelites marched with no change, and no stone fell from the wall. What if they had given up? God wants us to be steadfast, unmovable, always abounding in His work. (1 Corinthians 15:58).

Whenever God gives us a promise, He keeps it. However, our minds work differently. We trust in what we can see and we lose sight of God's promises and want to interject our own desires instead of waiting on God. Because we can't see any changes, we get tired of waiting and our patience wears thin. This is when we want

to give up, when all along we should trust God's timing and not let our feelings get in the way of God's plan.

Just because we can't see God's hand working in our midst, does not mean He's not busy. In John 5:17, God said He is always working. In our key scripture, God said to hold fast with confidence and we will be rewarded. I wonder how many blessings from God I have missed because I have chosen to give up and not wait on what is promised from Him?

We are not promised a specific time that things will come to pass, but we are promised they will happen. This means quitting is not an option. Standing on a promise from God is definitely the solution every Christian should endeavor to make and place their trust and confidence in.

Waiting for God's hand and guidance will allow us to determine in our hearts to always push through and collect those missed blessings He has for us. This pleases the heart of God. Tomorrow could be the day in God's timetable that we get our answer.

"And let us not be weary in well doing:
for in due season we shall reap, if we faint not."

— Galatians 6:9

Day 321

We Plead to God Because of Our Relationship

Key Scripture: **Isaiah 64:8**

As Isaiah appeals to the covenant relationship he has with God: "O Lord you are our Father," we have the same relationship with God through our Lord Jesus Christ. He is our Father.

This means we can plead to God without hesitation by saying: "Lord, I am an unclean, unrighteous, unstable person, but hear my petition today because you're my Father." Christ is the only sinless person to offer up prayers to God, so our prayers hinge on the mercy of God. Because God is our Father we can petition to Him through Jesus Christ.

In our key scripture we see Isaiah praying, *"we are the clay, and You are the potter."* He is inviting God to make whatever He wants of his life. Here is my life and I totally surrender all for you. Make of me anything you choose.

Pleading with God is not about you getting God in line with what you want. It's about getting us in line with what He wants. "You are the potter; I am the clay; I want you to shape my life into anything you want. Do anything in and through me that pleases you. Your ways are always perfect."

"Have Thine own way, Lord, Have Thine own way; Thou art the potter, I am the clay. Mold me and make me after Thy will while I am waiting, yielded and still."

"O house of Israel, cannot I do with you as this potter?
Saith the LORD. Behold, as the clay is in the potter's hand,
so are ye in mine hand,
O house of Israel."

— Jeremiah 18:6

Day 322

Pleading with God...Does It Work?

Key Scripture: **Isaiah 1; James 5:16**

A great Bible teacher, Oswald Chambers, emphasized the importance of praying for someone else. He said, "Intercession is putting yourself in God's place; it is having His mind and perspective." It's praying for others in light of what we know about God and His love for us.

Have you ever pleaded with God in prayer? Does this really work? How often do we hear of doctors telling loved ones they have no explanation as to the change in the patient's condition? "The disease is no longer there" or "surgery is no longer needed" are just a few phrases that come to mind. In these cases, I'm sure that multiple people were offering up intercessory prayer for those friends and loved ones.

The dictionary definition of pleading is to present your case like a lawyer in court. When you and I plead to God in prayer, we are approaching the courts of Heaven, prepared to defend our petition for God to act out His will in a certain way. We sometimes use scripture as in Isaiah chapter 1 which says: *"Come now let us reason together, says the LORD."*

While pleading for others before God in prayer, tell Him how we believe He would be glorified as He pours out His mercy on them. This takes boldness and steadfastness with a clean heart to bring answers from Heaven.

We need more servants of God that when they kneel in prayer can reach Heaven.

"Confess your faults one to another,
and pray one for another,
that ye may be healed.
The effectual fervent prayer of a righteous man availeth much."

— James 5:16

Day 323

20/20 Vision

Key Scripture: **John 9:1-7; 35-38**

Difficult circumstances often prevent us from seeing clearly. We can misinterpret God's plan and fail to understand what He is doing. Questions enter our minds like: "Are you there, Lord? Do you see what is happening to my family? Why don't you do something? How long must I wait for an answer?"

Our problem is we all need God to give us spiritual eyes before we can see correctly.

In today's key scripture, Jesus gave sight to a blind man who had been blind from birth. God used his affliction to display His glory. The man was given "eyes to see" and then believed in Jesus.

The same happens to us as we accept Christ—we are given spiritual eyes to read and understand God's Word, and see the Holy Spirit working in us. He gives us spiritual understanding, so our faith is strengthened. He also gives us wisdom to follow His perfect plan for our lives.

Lord, may we always have the 20/20 vision to see Your direction for our lives.

"Open thou mine eyes,
that I may behold wondrous things out of thy law."
— Psalm 119:18

Love, the Factor that Drives Fear from Our Relationships

Key Scripture: **1 John 4:18**

Ever heard the words "I hate you"? These words said in a relationship is often a sign that one peson is trying to control the other. The prime factor beneath that control is "fear." This destroys relationships and disables lives whenever one is insecure and thinks about what others think of them.

It is an interesting dilemma when we want the close intimacy, but we are scared to death of it. If insecurity destroys relationships, what builds lasting relationships? The answer is "LOVE."

In our key scripture, we see that love expels all fear. Love takes the focus off our fear and puts our focus on loving others.

The moment we realize how much God loves us we can find the power to focus our love on others. Once this happens, you know you never have to feel as though you need to impress others because you realize how much God loves you. Your identity and self-worth are not caught up in what others might think of you.

When you are secure in your relationship with Christ, you are no longer pressured by everyone else's expectations. God's love frees you to love others fearlessly.

"If a man say, I love God, and hates his brother, he is a liar:
for he that loveth not his brother whom he hath seen,
how can he love God whom he hath not seen?"

— 1 John 4:20

Day 325

What Happens when a Christian Dies with Unconfessed Sin?

Key Scripture: 1 John 5:10

Sin separates us from a holy and sinless God; however, we can have a grateful heart because our sins can be forgiven and forgotten. (Psalm 32:5;130:3-4; Hebrews 10:17).

Before answering the above question, I pray we can understand that there are two main types of confession and forgiveness. One is when an unbeliever comes to faith in Christ, and the other when they confess sins committed after they become a believer.

First, let us look at someone who is not a believer. They have to face Jesus Christ for the penalty of their sins, and that is spiritual death leading to hell. When we come to Christ and confess our sins, we are forgiven of our sins, past, present, and future. Our destiny is now heaven, not hell. (Romans 8:1-2; Hebrews 10:14).

Secondly, we look at the situation regarding our title question when one sins who is spiritually alive. As a part of God's family on earth, this one is separated from God the Father in terms of daily fellowship, but is not separated from going to Heaven because the penalty of our sins has already been paid. Whenever we confess these sins our sin is forgiven by God and our daily fellowship is restored. (1 John 1:5; 2:2).

This is the kind of forgiveness the Lord's disciples were to practice: *"forgive us our debts, as we have forgiven our debtors."* (Matthew 6:12, 14-15). It includes forgiving others. God cannot forgive us when we are not willing to forgive one another. (Mark 11:25; Luke 6:37). If we fail to forgive one another, we will miss being rewarded when we get to Heaven. (Matthew 18:35).

The answer to our question is that we will still go to Heaven, but to receive our rewards, confession along with forgiveness is essential. Therefore, although a Christian has unconfessed sin in their life and it affects their relationship with God; they are still a child of God and their destiny is Heaven.

"But if we walk in the light, as He is in the light,
we have fellowship one with another,
and the blood of Jesus Christ His Son cleanseth us from all sin."

— 1 John 1:7

Give Yourself Fully to God

Key Scripture: **Romans 22:1-2**

As Christians, we no longer have to bring sacrifices to God. Instead, He asks us to place ourselves on the altar, meaning we are to live a life of sacrifice, presenting ourselves as a gift unto God. Christianity is not just giving an hour or two each week attending church services or working on a project in the church. Our lives are to be set apart and consecrated to God.

We can and should be motivated to die to self and give ourselves fully unto God because of the gospel. The gospel proves God's love for us and the relationship in Christ is the working of His desire for us to experience the eternal love, joy, delight, and satisfaction that He, the Son, and the Spirit have experienced.

As our key scripture says, we are not to be conformed to this world. We must fight against this because the world's values are totally the opposite of Gods.

Our scripture also says that our minds are to be transformed and renewed. God tells us this because we are to understand what the will of the Lord is for our lives. The Holy Spirit of God works in our lives to accomplish this by changing us inside and out. The outward appearance is manifested by our relationships with other godly Christians.

We also have a desire to hear His Word and apply it to our daily walk. From the inside He changes our hearts, meaning our will, wants, and desires. We will always want God's will for our lives. This is the way God protects us from the world and helps us to live as a Holy sacrifice unto God: our reasonable service.

If He is not Lord of all; He is not Lord at all.

"No man can serve two masters;
for either he will hate the one, and love the other,
or else he will hold to the one, and despise the other.
Ye cannot serve God and mammon."

— Matthew 6:24

Is Beating Yourself Up Necessary?

Key Scripture: **Romans 8:1-2**

Why do Christians punish themselves, if God doesn't? We do this because we feel guilty and think He is angry with us for having done something wrong. We must understand as the key scripture reading says, we are in Christ when we put our faith in Him. So, now God no longer condemns us. In Christ we are completely forgiven, accepted, loved, and secure.

Sometimes, we feel we need to protect ourselves from Him, but this is not true. Jesus was punished in our place. (1 John 4:18-19). God wants us to turn back to Him whenever we sin and experience His grace. (2 Chronicles 30:9).

When we feel ashamed and beaten up, positive thoughts should come into our minds, not shameful guilt. We can be confident as we approach God to receive His mercy and grace. (Hebrews 4:16). Grace means that He no longer condemns or punishes us for our mistakes and failures, because Christ took our punishment.

God shows us this grace freely, so we need to give ourselves grace without the guilt and shame we place upon ourselves. We simply need to agree with the grace God has given us and live knowing God is always there no matter what.

Grasp these truths and place a smile of God's love on your face. Hold your head high and never feel defeated again.

"Being confident of this very thing,
that He which hath begun a good work in you
will perform it until the day of Jesus Christ."

— Philippians 1:6

Day 328

Lord, Put Someone Across My Path

Key Scripture: **Genesis 24**

Have you ever asked God to bring someone your way so that you might be a witness for Him? I personally can say it works as a testament that our God is faithful. This is an expecting prayer that God delights in answering.

In the past, I always prayed this each morning before going to work. I worked in an office and my door was always open. It seemed like I had a big sign outside my door that said I was a lonely-hearts-club counselor. People stopped daily asking advice on many different problems and concerns. I was able to be an encouragement to then, and for that I am grateful.

Remember the story in Genesis 24 when Abraham was old and asked for help to find his son Isaac a wife? He told his chief servant just what to do and sent him off. The servant stopped at a town and prayed that things would go as his master had asked. Before he finished praying, Rebekah came out with her water jar. Things worked as Abraham said, and God answered their prayers.

God puts people in our paths to be an encouragement as well as a witness. However, sometimes we need to change our prayer to: "Lord, send someone across my path to encourage me." The possibilities are endless and exciting, just stay willing to be used of God for His glory.

Four things to remember:

1. Pray.

2. Watch for an answer and be ready.

3. Discern that it is from God.

4. Thank God for the answer.

"To every thing there is a season,
and a time to every purpose under the heaven."

— Ecclesiastes 3:1

Day 329

Is Your Light Going Out?

Key Scripture: **Matthew 5:14-16**

As the scripture says, Christians are to let their light shine. Why does our light go dim in this dark world? The answer could be that we let the busy lifestyle and distractions of everyday life affect our Christian living.

We attend church, sing God's praises, read His Word, and pray for God's will to be present in our daily walk. Then, Satan steps in and interferes with just one of these things because the brighter our light shines, the harder he attaks. With Satan's interference, suddenly keeping God's will becomes less important and our light dims. Satan likes that, because the brighter our light shines the more of a threat we are to him.

1 Peter 5:8-9 tells us we are to resist him and be steadfast in the faith. We are not to neglect our profession or our homes and responsibilities, but we need to purpose in our heart to intention-ally stay focused on spending time with the Lord daily in His Word, praying, and following the path He has laid out for us.

There is an acronym that can help us to be mindful to keep Satan's tactics apart from our walk with Jesus Christ. BUSY: Buried Under Satan's Yoke.

In 1 Peter we are to resist in faith. James 4:7 says; *"Resist the devil and he will flee from you."* So, recapping as to what causes our light to go dim, the answer is Satan. We have the ability in Christ to resist him and we also have God's power to stand in faith to follow Him.

Lord, help us to stay focused, and accom-plish your will for our lives daily. Help us not to get bogged down in our busy life and help us to arrange our priorities to keep our light shining bright for you.

"The spirit of man is the candle of the LORD,
searching all the inward parts of the belly."

— Proverbs 20:27

Day 330

Never Confuse Meekness with Weakness

Key Scripture: **Matthew 5:5**

If you want to make choices to become whole and healthy again, you have to learn to be meek. Many benefits of meekness are mentioned in the Bible: the meek shall be satisfied (Psalm 22:26), God will guide them (Psalm 25:9), they will become wise (Proverbs 11:2), and they will be filled with fresh joy (Isaiah 29:13).

Meekness is often confused with weakness. The truth is they are very far apart in meaning. In fact, the Greek word for meekness literally means "strength under control."

The Bible teaches that meekness is a key factor in stress reduction in our lives. Meekness is: "Letting go and letting God." It is surrendering, submitting, and agreeing to what God wants to do in our life; letting God be God. The Bible celebrates meekness, viewing it this way: last is first, giving is receiving, dying is living, and losing is finding.

When you see someone teary-eyed about something, don't assume they are a weak person. Very likely they are one who may be surrendering a situation to God, and their heart is filled with thanksgiving to God as He takes control of their burdens. Tears are a language God understands. Meekness is not weakness.

"But the meek shall inherit the earth;
and shall delight themselves in the abundance of peace."

— Psalm 37:11

Day 331

Losing God's Glory — Ichabod)

Key Scripture: **1 Samuel 4:12-22**

Thinking about losing God's glory causes me to wonder why and how this could happen. Please be aware, the glory of God would never leave you, but on the other hand you could leave God's glory.

God never changes. His love and intentions are always the same. The problem is, we are inconsistent and have difficulty keeping God's plan. The word Ichabod means "glory has departed."

In the key scripture, Eli and his sons acted in a way that led to the loss of God's glory. They took God's offerings and sacrifices and made them their own. Take a glance at Samson. He was commanded to never have a razor touch his head, and indulged this to Delilah, who he had no business being with. The results cost him his life eventually.

The lesson here: when we take what belongs to God and use it for another purpose, we set ourselves up for the loss of His glory.

Next, the sons of Eli cheated and robbed the people of their dignity. When we rob God's people of the dignity and honor that was purchased by Christ, we are headed for destruction and loss of glory.

Next they defiled God's temple. Bringing this home, our bodies are His temple, and we are instructed to not defile it. In doing so, we must remember that we have been bought with a very high price, the blood of Jesus. (John 17:22.)

These issues are a few and affect the spirit, soul, and the body and have to be dealt with properly. Failure will cause the glory to escape and we would be left with nothing.

Does your situation seem hopeless with no feeling of being able to climb out? Before you write the name Ichabod upon yourself, take this burden to the Lord and let Him restore His glory in your life.

"For whosoever is born of God overcometh the world: and this is the victory that overcometh the world, even our faith."

— 1 John 5:4

Day 332

Should Christians Faithfully Attend Church?

Key Scripture: **Psalm 42:1-2; Psalm 100:2**

Many people would say it is not necessary for a Christian to attend church. I think attending church isn't what makes one a Christian. I do believe, however, that if you are a true child of God you will attend church faithfully. I understand there might be cases when some are not able to attend, but if you are physically able and stay out of church, you definitely have a sin problem.

Christianity is not a willpower religion. It is a supernatural work of God by which you are born again so that you want God more than anything. If this is not true in your life, I would even go so far to say that you are probably not a Christian.

The miracle of the new birth takes hearts that are in love with the world and transforms those hearts so they are in love with Jesus Christ. Our life, our wants, and desires are changed. In order to grow, God encourages that we are not to forsake assembling ourselves together.

Remember the story of Hanna in 1 Samuel? She spent years praying for a child. God finally gave her Samuel, who grew up in the house of God. Spending time in God's presence gave Samuel the opportunity to hear from God.

Samuel became a prophet and he was the one who anointed David as king. The same David who wrote: *"I was glad when they said unto me, Let us go into the house of the LORD."* (Psalm 122:1).

The seeds sown now in going to church will reap a harvest greater than we may ever know in our lives and the lives of our family and friends.

"For where two or three are gathered together in my name, there am I in the midst of them."

— Matthew 18:20

Day 333

Showing Thankfulness By Counting Your Blessings

Key Scripture: **Luke 17:15-19**

'Tis the season when we all should express thankfulness. Are we really thankful or just being thankful for the good things we are benefiting from?

We need to appreciate God's blessings upon us. Being truly thankful requires looking beyond our blessings to the One who blesses. We need to fill our hearts with gratitude to Christ, and not just for what He has given us.

Are you appreciating those blessings we can touch or see, creating an attitude of "thankfulness," even when things are difficult? What about those who are jobless, homeless, have wayward children, have a marriage torn apart, or physical health problems? Maybe counting our blessings is what we should do this year by being thankful.

Think about the Pilgrims. They went through extreme hardship, but still believed they were blessed. They chose to celebrate and thank God even through their hardships.

In verse 19 of our key passage, we see the leper, who had many problems to face in his life. Still, he could be thankful because he heard Jesus give him the greatest blessing: *"Arise go thy way, thy faith hath made thee whole."*

Reading this story made me realize what Jesus has done in my life. I'm not feeling negative for what I do not have, because I know He is not finished with me yet. My prayer today is that my faith will always help me have an attitude of true gratefulness in my heart like the Pilgrims and the leper, who was the only one of ten healed to express his gratitude to Jesus.

I hope and pray that we all can understand more what true "thankfulness" is, and learn to not only thank God for our blessings, but also thank Him for being the One who blesses.

Count your Blessings first, then thank the One who does the blessing.

"In every thing give thanks:
for this is the will of God in Christ Jesus concerning you."

— 1 Thessalonians 5:18

Day 334

Home is Where the Heart is

Key Scripture: **Proverbs 14:1; John 14:4**

Where do you feel your heart is? Asking this question to others you will surely get many different answers. I would say I have two homes, one on earth that's a place where the love of my life rests her heart and head, and the other would be my eternal dwelling with my Heavenly Father.

As Christians, we must not invest our lives in things that rust, but in things that last. Where your treasure is, there your heart lies also. Your heart shows what interests you most. What you spend your time and energy praying for shows what means the most in your life here on earth.

In reality, this earth is only a temporary home and Heaven is my real resting place. Because of that, I spend as much time as I can, seeking to do the Lord's will in all I do.

This phrase "home is where the heart is" means that home is a place where we feel the deepest affection. Our earthly home could be anywhere, but at times this place will leave us with a feeling of loneliness. The opposite happens with our Heavenly home. This place is a permanent relationship with Jesus Christ that connects us to our eternal residence. (Ephesians 2:19).

Our earthly home is stricken with heartaches and struggles, but we have to remind ourselves that this is not our permanent dwelling. Seek the wisdom of God and allow Him to protect us from Satan so we can then confidently say our homes are built upon the Rock foundation, which is Jesus Christ. (Matthew 7:25).

Lord, in our homes, our families, in our circle of influence, help us to seek wisdom to build a home pleasing in your sight.

"Set your affection on things above,
not on things on the earth."

— Colossians 3:2

Day 335

Seeking a Relationship, Not Rules

Key Scripture: **Isaiah 29:13; Mark 10**

I have tried many times to figure out the rules of friendship. I have come up short each time because friendship has more to do with heart-liking, deep-caring, and loving others than figuring out rules.

The same is true when it comes to building a relationship with Christ. It's very easy to turn Christianity into a set of rules, instead of building a relationship. Christ just wants our hearts.

Remember the rich young ruler? He was one who saw rules instead of a relationship with Christ. Rule-following can significantly hinder us in having a real, personal relationship with Christ. Christ loved the rich young ruler enough to tell him the truth about the rules and offered him a way out. Christ asked him to make a decision to seek a relationship with Him.

The young man asked what he must do to inherit eternal life. Christ told him of the Commandments and he answered that he had kept them since he was young. (Mark 10:17-20). His actions and questions showed he wasn't looking for a relationship, but how to get something he wanted. He wanted to know the rules so he could follow them rather than having a personal relationship with Christ.

We can sometimes approach Christ the same way in our lives, wanting to get what we want with our selfish motives. Christ felt genuine love for the young man and told the rich young ruler he needed to sell all he had and give to the poor, thus placing treasures in Heaven.

Christ told him the truth and offered him a relationship, but he responded to Christ's love by walking away sad because he wanted to be identified as a rich young ruler. This meant he did not have a close relationship with Christ. The young man only saw what he would be losing, not what he would be gaining.

Relationships are rewarding and rules are not. We can be accepted for who we are without having rules to follow. Lord, grant us the ability to build our relationship with You out of love and respect. "Thank you for being our Lord."

"But without faith it is impossible to please Him:
for he that cometh to God must believe that He is,
and that He is a rewarder of them that diligently seek Him."

— Hebrews 11:6

Day 336

Can Christ be Seen in Me?

Key Scripture: **Matthew 5:16**

When we accept Christ as Savior, we are dressed in His robe and He covers our sins. If we are covered by Christ's righteousness, shouldn't we then act like we are born of Christ? Shouldn't others be able to see Him in us?

Our lives ought to be living testimonies of Christ's goodness. (Romans 12:1). Therefore, we are members of the kingdom of God and our walk and conversation should match up with our membership.

People should be able to look at us and see the work of Christ living and working in us. They should be able to determine Christ is indeed in us. We need to be reminded that we represent Christ at church, home, and in the workplace through our actions as well as our conversation.

Being what you say you are goes a long way, and will certainly draw others to Christ. At least living this way will allow you to witness to others, because the lifestyle honors Christ.

When our behavior matches that of Christ's, we exhibit the fruit of the Spirit. (Galatians 5:22). Others will see Christ in you and will be drawn to glorify our Father in Heaven.

"Be ye therefore followers of God, as dear children."

— Ephesians 5:1

Day 337

Doing the Right Thing—God's Thing

Key Scripture: 1 Peter 2:21-23

Many times when we get into a situation that requires life's decisions, we look in all the wrong places for answers and don't consider whether it's God's decision instead of our selfish desires. To know and do what is right in all situations, we must seek God's favor.

Doing the wrong thing can produce unjust results, and the suffering could be great. However, when our conscience (heart and mind) is on God, He promises us favor (grace) if we endure. He further encourages us to make certain we remain faithful in seeking right decisions. (1 Peter 2:20a).

Seeking answers from wrong places is sin. God calls His children to answer sin with righteousness. In spite of our circumstances, we must answer wrong with stability, trust, perseverance, and faith. We are called to do the right thing even when others give advice which is wrong. (1 Peter 2:20b).

Doing "what is right" means following God's standards without regard to outside intervention in every circumstance. This call is without exception and is meant for us to implement in every situation in life.

When we suffer injustice, or any adverse situation, we must remember to stand for what is right and seek God's answers because His Word says, Jesus is our example. (1 Peter 2:21-23)

"And who is he that will harm you, if ye be followers of that which is good?
But and if ye suffer for righteousness' sake,
happy are ye and be not afraid of their terror, neither be troubled;
But sanctify the Lord God in your hearts:
and be ready always to give an answer to every man
that asketh you a reason of the hope that is in you with meekness and fear."

— 1Peter 3:13-14 &17

Day 338

Communication is Essential

Key Scripture: **Psalm 27:14; James 1:19**

In a relationship, lack of communication is usually the factor causing people to drift apart. People are not mind readers. Family, friends, and coworkers may all know you very well, but they won't get it right all the time unless you communicate your needs and desires to them.

God desires communication through a relationship with His children, and asks each of us to make our requests known to Him. This is called "abiding" and scripture says that if you will abide in Him, He will abide in you and whatever you wish will be done for you.

In James 1:19, God says we are to listen. God gave us two ears and one mouth, so we are to listen twice as much as we speak. God communicates to us through His Word, wise counsel, and messages from Godly men.

God also says we are to be slow to speak. Allowing the Spirit to lead us into all truth, gives us a chance for God to communicate to us so that what we say is what He wants us to say.

The last thing God says in this verse is to be slow to anger. This may be difficult for some, but it is possible if we are seeking to do what is right in the sight of God. If we are not clear or misunderstand what someone says, we should definitely allow time for the Spirit to lead our thoughts and actions before speaking. God is constantly calling us to view others through His eyes.

As Christians, communication is important in our daily life in, around others, and even moreso with Jesus Christ. Staying close to God (abiding), reading His Word, praying, and walking in His Spirit are essential for our relationship to communicate with Christ.

God intends for us to walk in His ways. He communicated with others and with His Father. Following in His steps in all we do surely will increase our communication skills.

"Draw nigh to God, and He will draw nigh to you.
Cleanse your hands, ye sinners;
and purify your hearts,
ye double minded."

— James 4:8

Day 339

God's Love Is Constant

Key Scripture: **Romans 8:38-39**

Let's think about the key verses today as we go about our busy day. Grasp hold of these words as a child of God. This is a promise of God's constant love today, no matter what comes your way. Nothing you will face or ever go through will separate you from God's love.

We go through so many tests, trials, and setbacks in our lives that it seems like we expect to face them day after day. But God wants you to rest in His unconditional love today. As a Christian, it's important that we trust in God's Word, freely given to reveal to us Christ's love and strength to face challenges this and every day ahead.

You are never alone and most importantly know that in the midst of trials and troubles, God's love forever is yours. Remember this today.

Understand that there is no power above you or beneath that can ever separate you from this constant love of Christ.

So, as you go about your busy day, let your heart rejoice knowing that you are loved by our Heavenly Father. If you are experiencing heartbreak now because of someone or something you are facing, never let these take you from the fact that God is always there and you are never alone or abandoned.

Remember, God's love is constant and cannot be separated by anyone or anything here on earth. God's love is unchanging, even in our weakness and our mistakes. Don't let guilt, shame, or the feeling of unworthiness rise above God's unconditional love in Christ for you.

"Have not I commanded thee? Be strong and of a good courage;
be not afraid, neither be thou dismayed:
for the LORD thy God is with thee whithersoever thou goest."

— Joshua 1:9

Day 340

Continuing God's Call

Key Scripture: **Psalm 84:3-4**

Every Christian has a calling from God. This call can remain constant or it can change. You may hear it as a child or it may come later in life. Trust me, we all have a mission from God for our life.

The calling of God is much different. The word calling means "a profession or occupation." Another definition is: "a strong urge toward a particular way of life or career." The Lord calls ordinary people to be used in His service. (Mark: 46-50). In these verses, God called Bartimaeus, and he never hesitated although he had obstacles that would hinder many.

Sometimes, doubt causes us to question our call, doubt our ability, and listen to others instead of God. All these interfere with our minds staying focused, and we misidentify what our first calling is.

Our highest calling is not what we usually think it is. It's not a job or title we earn, it is simply to respond to Jesus and go to Him like Bartimaeus. We're called to come close. When we do, Jesus draws us near and calls us His brothers and sisters. (Matthew 12:50). He erases the division of our relationship with God (John 15:15).

While our faith leads us into a relationship with Christ, our first and highest calling is to be near Jesus. When this happens, then everything else falls into place—the next step of our call, where our call will lead us, and when to go or stay.

"For many are called, but few are chosen."
— Matthew 22:14

Day 341

God Helps Those Who Help Themselves

Key Scripture: **Isaiah 25:4; Romans 5:6**

This is a popular saying and is often quoted, but it is not in the Bible. Ben Franklin made this phrase popular in 1757, but it originated with a man named Algernon Sydney in 1698.

The real problem with the idea of "God helps those who help themselves" is that we become our first source of help and strength, and God becomes second. God is the One who moves within our hearts and He is the One who can move mountains in our lives.

The truth isn't that God helps those who help themselves, but God helps those who realize they can't help themselves. The problem with this statement includes the fact that we cannot save ourselves, only God can.

To believe this statement, we must realize that our power will fail us but God will not. Trusting in this statement shows the sin of pride, which motivates the belief that we can do everything by our own abilities. But, God is opposed to the proud but gave grace to the humble. (James 4:6).

God knows our struggles, understands our weakness and has provided a remedy. All the help we need, for every aspect of our life, is found at God's throne of grace. Our lives are not about self-help, which look inward within our own strengths; our lives are about God-help, by looking upward.

So, in summation of this statement, we now know this is a false statement and it is not found in the Bible. We need to ask God's help to reveal to us any way we hold to this false statement, so we can repent and turn our trust into God's will for our lives.

We can come out on top by placing our strength, trust, and faith in God's ability to help us as He did for Abraham, David, Joseph, and Jacob.

"But seek ye first the kingdom of God,
and His righteousness;
and all these things shall be added unto you."

— Matthew 6:33

Day 342

Ashamed of God?

Key Scripture: **Romans 1:16**

This post will be close and personal for it will involve my true testimony. As a young boy of 16, I was a new child of God and not grounded in the scriptures, the new faith, and the battle of flesh and the Spirit.

All I knew was that Christ had saved me and I was a new creation. I wanted to share this new life, so I started reading my Bible and sharing my faith. Friends and family started mocking and avoiding me in some cases.

I was now a Jesus freak, holy Joe, and a Bible thumper. I started hiding from my new faith, reading my Bible by flashlight under the covers in my bed. One night I came to Romans 1:16. This verse sank in and I determined in my heart to never be ashamed of God again.

The word "ashamed" means "disgraced" or "personally humiliated," one that has been let down or has misplaced his confidence. So for Paul to say he was not ashamed meant he would never misplace his confidence in the gospel. (Romans10:11 & Isaiah 28:16).

To live unashamed of the gospel means we proclaim it, but it also means we apply it to our lives and show we believe it. We show we are ashamed if we allow sin in our lives and let it go unchecked. (Matthew 3:8).

When we walk in the counsel of the ungodly, we are ashamed. (Psalm 1:1). To live unashamed of the gospel means we allow it to dominate our lives to demonstrate to everyone we come in contact with to see that we are indeed a Christian in thoughts and deeds.

"For whoever shall be ashamed of me and my words,
of him shall the Son of Man be ashamed,
when He shall come in His own glory,
and in His Father's, and of the holy angels."

— Luke 9:26

Day 343

Leave it All at the Altar

Key Scripture: **Isaiah 41:9-10**

Leave everything in God's hands and eventually you'll see God's hands in everything. I have seen truths like this work over and over in my own life such as relationship issues, children's struggles, challenges, career transitions, health issues, and financial judgments.

A very wise person said, "I'm good at leaving things in God's hands, but I struggle to not take it back into my own hands." I have learned through the years to trust the hands of the One whose handiwork declares His glory.

Isaiah 62:6 shows us by God's attributes, we are to have faith which unfold by leaving every-

thing in His hands and by beholding His hands in all things. The joy of leaving everything in God's hands is SEEING God's hands in everything. By faith, leave everything and everyone in the Lord's hands and begin to look for his hand at work through everything and everyone.

Remember, we are God's children. We are fearfully and wonderfully made; He cares about all we do. He wants each of us to trust His Almighty hand to guide us through every situation. His hands are big enough to hold anything that will lighten our load.

"I will praise thee; for I am fearfully and wonderfully made:
marvellous are thy works;
and that my soul knoweth right well."

— Psalm 139:14

Under the Law and Under Grace

Key Scripture: **Romans 2:13; Romans 3:31; Romans 7:12**

Is the Old Testament given way to the New Testament? Does the law give way to grace? These are questions that as a Christian should be addressed and understood.

Did you know that Paul quoted the Old Testament scriptures 250 times throughout his writings? Surely God thought the Old Testament was necessary; He inspired Paul to use it often.

In studying the scriptures we must not use our interpretation, but allow the Bible to interpret itself.

We certainly know that sin is still present in the world and in our own lives. If we think differently, we are calling God a liar. (1 John 1:10). In Romans 6:15; Paul clarifies sin is still present and the law is not abolished.

Grace is God's unmerited favor. In fact, we did nothing to gain it. It comes through the love that He gave freely by the sacrifice of His Son. Please take time to read chapter 6 in its entirety; it explains how the law of God and grace work hand in hand to help us learn God's way in life. The law also teaches us how to love one another and how to live a righteous life by the grace of God. They compliment one another. The grace of God helps us continue our walk with Him.

"In whom we have redemption through His blood,
the forgiveness of sins, according to the riches of His grace."
— Ephesians 1:7

Day 345

Vain Glory (Self)

Key Scripture: **Proverbs 26:6-7; 1 Corinthians 10:31**

Vain glory, selfish ambition, and self-exaltation are all traits that have to do with "SELF," with no mention of God. Many people have tunnel vision in regard to their success, passions, and being the all-powerful number one.

Not only are they deceived, but their family and friends suffer greatly. Scripture says much about vain pursuits, (Proverbs 25:27). "For men to seek their own glory is not glory." If your goal in ministry or employment is self-glory and self-exaltation, or driven by self-ambition instead of love for the glory of God, you are considered a fool in the sight of God.

For a Christian, success is the faithful fulfillment of God's will. Jesus' work was successful because He humbled Himself before His Father and carried out His will submissively; nothing about self, all in glory and humility in the service for others.

It would do us all good to examine the vocation we are pursuing in order to evaluate if this is for self-glory or the glory of God. The temptation for vain glory can be subtle and we have to guard against the desire to seek self-gratification and the praise of others.

We need to put aside the worldly striving and ambition and humbly seek God's glory in everything we do.

"Fullfil ye my joy, that ye be likeminded, having the same love,
being of one accord, of one mind.
Let nothing be done through strife or vainglory;
but in lowliness of mind let each esteem others better than themselves.
Look not every man on his own things,
but every man also on the things of others."

— Philippines 2:2-4

Day 346

Peace Through Injustice

Key Scripture: **Psalm 9:9**

Psalm 35:5; *"Let them be as chaff before the wind: and let the angel of the LORD chase them."* Do we wish the whole world would think this way; leaving everything in God's hands? God is always on His throne, and He is always sovereign. (Proverbs 22:8). The Lord hates injustice and will eventually shine His light of truth on every corrupt situation. In the meantime God has placed us here in His hands to stand against injustice. (Micah 6:8).

How are we supposed to react to injustice when it strikes our life? 1 Peter 2:21 says Christ suffered for us and leaves us an example. Christ's example of suffering serves here to encourage believers undergoing persecution and abuse from those inflicting injustice. Christ himself never returned insults to those accusing Him; instead He surrendered Himself completely to the Righteous Judge, His Heavenly Father. The ungodly may go unpunished for a season, but our responsibility is to understand vengeance belongs to God. In 1 Peter 5:2; Peter relates the Shepherd as the Overseer; he keeps the flock together. Our trust is placed in the hands of the Overseer to bring us to justice, not we ourselves. Christ is the ultimate example and we must follow in His footsteps. Stand up and point out those who are guilty of injustice, but turn it over to Him. As the Shepherd sought to find the one sheep that strayed away, He will seek to keep you in the fold, patiently allowing Him to be our Judge in all situations.

How are you handling injustice in your own life? Do the right thing; follow His example.

*"But ye, brethren,
be not weary in well doing."*

— 2 Thessalonians 3:13

Day 347

Remember, God's Got Your Back

Key Scripture: **Joshua 1:5**

Throughout our lives, we feel abandoned, alone, and no confidence to go forward. As a child of God, we should realize this is not true at all; as in the life of Joshua, who is now the successor to Moses. He had been an assistant and now has the burden to lead the children of Israel into the Promised Land. The Bible does not give details on Joshua's emotions during this time, but it does say in numerous instances God encouraged him to be strong and courageous. God wanted him to know that "He had his back."

Knowing we have someone there automatically gives us courage and confidence by eliminating the doubts and fears and lifts our assurance to press on. Remember the verse: *"I will be with you as I was with Moses; I will not fail you or abandon you."*

"I've Got Your Back." History does show that Joshua took leaping steps of faith and served as a powerful, humble leader, trusting God's Word and His ability to walk with him.

Maybe God is asking you to take a leap into a deeper faith, or to serve beyond what you think you are capable. Calm your fears, trust His Word, because God has said, "He's Got Your Back."

"For ye shall not go out with haste,
nor go by flight: for the LORD will go before you;
and the God of Israel will be your rereward."

— Isaiah 52:12

Day 348

Every Christian is Called to be a Bridge Builder

Key Scripture: **2 Corinthians 5:18-19**

Being a bridge means following Jesus' lead and actually laying down our politics, our prejudices, our passions, our perfect lives, and planned-out futures, and anything on behalf of others.

Jesus invites each of us to get involved in the ministry of reconciliation.

Jesus was the ultimate bridge. He not only built bridges between people, He became the bridge Himself. Building bridges requires sacrifice, meaning taking the time to listen to others who think differently than we do. Isaac Newton once said, "We build too many walls and not enough bridges."

We are too busy building our lives, seeking our own passions for self and not for God, never looking at the needs for others. In reality, it is much easier to turn our heads from the needs of others and focus on ourselves and stay in our comfort zone. We need to repent of this life style and take our goals off self and set our affections on the needs of others. Reconciling others to Jesus Christ is needed now more than ever before.

Quote from LaTasha Morrison; "God didn't draw us through the process of reconciliation for our own sake. He reconciled us so we could bring reconciliation to others in His name..."

Every church, every Christian should determine in their heart to make an effort of outreach to follow Jesus' lead and build bridges for His glory.

"The LORD GOD which gathereth the outcast of Israel saith,
Yet will I gather others to Him,
beside those that are gathered unto Him."

— Isaiah 56:8

Day 349

Interceding for Others by Building Bridges

Scripture: I Timothy 2:1-2

In our circle of friends or believers in Christ we can look just outside that circle and see all around us, people of all walks of life needing what God has given us. Where there is no burden the people perish. We see the fields are white unto harvest, and God commands us to go into the highways and byways to reach them. It takes a commitment, it takes work, and a willingness to "Build those Bridges."

Because Jesus has done the work of intercession and still intercedes for us with the Father, along with the Holy Spirit, He helps us to unburden ourselves, and intercede for others. Jesus Christ and the Holy Spirit have built bridges to God that we may cross over, so that we, too, can build bridges to reach others. We have an incredible privilege of building a span from Heaven to earth, and bring those we are interceding for to God. Never stop praying for those you are burdened for; let the Father know by name those who you are burdened for.

Faithfully pray for them, and be willing to be used of God and go where He leads. Let's remember that Jesus built that bridge for each of us, and with the Spirits' help, we must begin to intercede for others, so their paths may intersect with the path of God and they will walk with Him forever.

Maybe you are thinking of someone right now that needs Jesus and you have stopped praying for them. Please allow yourself to help build that bridge and reach that one for Christ.

"Let your light so Shine before men,
that they may see your good works,
and glorify your Father which is in heaven."

— Matthew 5:16

Day 350

Always Faith, Especially in Hardship

Key Scripture: **Ephesians 2:8-9**

As we go through our daily lives, we all experience difficult situations. Many times we go through pain or suffering, and surprisingly these situations find a way into our lives by forgetting that God has told us we will experience hardships.

When we go through these times, whether they be financial troubles, painful relationships, failing health issues, or depression, it is hard for us to realize that God is still working in us. This is because as humans our belief is based on what we see and not faith.

2 Corinthians 5:7, says it can be difficult to trust God during uncertain times, but as believers we know that His ways are not our ways, and He will ultimately work all things for good. (Isaiah 55:8-9; Romans 8:28). We are given the gift of faith from Him and we are taught to use this valuable fruit of the Spirit. However, in difficult or confusing times we are quick to worry rather than exercise our faith.

The grace of God has given us this gift of faith, not by merit, but as a result of the goodness of God. We should all appreciate this gift with humility, knowing that we have been given something we could never achieve on our own. Having faith in difficult times gives us peace in God's presence.

Being unfaithful in circumstances causes our hearts to be hardened with pride, which causes us to grow distant in our relationship with Christ. We can rest in God by keeping our faith in His infinite Grace.

In the end, it is not up to us how things are resolved in our lives, but it is our job to have faith in God, no matter the price.

"For as the heavens are higher than the earth,
so are my ways higher than your ways,
and my thoughts than your thoughts."

— Isaiah 55:9

Day 351

Freedom, A Powerful Force

Key Scripture: **2 Corinthians 3:17**

"Now the Lord is that Spirit: and where the Spirit of the Lord is, there is liberty."

The simple truth of our freedom in Christ is largely taken for granted. Our sin and bondage often feels like an overpowering web that entangles us. Satan wants to rob us of our joyous life by keeping us confused about the freedom and righteousness bought through the precious blood of Jesus Christ.

I am reminded of the song "My Chains Are Broken". This song helps us to see perfectly clear the deep understanding of the freedom handed to us as children of God.

In Romans 8:1-4; scripture says we are no longer condemned to live under the bondage of sin; we are freed to live under the new law of the Spirit. Remember, *"where the Spirit of the Lord is, there is liberty."*

We are no longer enslaved to this world. Our past no longer has bondage on us. Our future before us is one of peace, joy, and freedom in the Spirit. God has plans for our lives that far surpass simply overcoming sin. Jesus died to give us abundant life bought by the freedom gained through the love of Christ.

"But now being made free from sin,
and become servants to God,
you have your fruit unto holiness,
and the end everlasting life."

Romans 6:22

Day 352

Do Your Friends Steal Your Joy or Lift Your Spirit?

Key Scripture: **John 14:6**

We all experience friendships in our life, some short term, some lifelong, and some we wish to forget. Proverbs 17:17 says, *"A friend loveth at all times…"* unfortunately not all friendships are created equal. They leave a positive or negative impact on our lives. Therefore, we need to examine our friendships.

A bad friendship is like a rotten apple; it can cause a lot of damage, emotionally, mentally, and physically. Because some are easily led, those that seem they never can say no, a bad friend can influence them to do things they shouldn't. Bad friends are selfish and always get their way. They always seek in the friendship to benefit themselves. If you are in a bad friendship, it's time to get out. Be compassionate and try to understand what made the person the way they are.

A true friend is loving; not with a selfish type of love, but with the kind that puts other's needs first. A true friend is trustworthy. A true friend is loving, not selfish (1 Corinthians 13:4-7). A true friend will not lead you astray (Proverbs 1:10-14).

In John 15:13-15 we find what a true friend is. Jesus Christ is a perfect friend. His life is a testimony of what a true friend is like. You never should stay in a bad friendship, but we can always have that perfect friendship with the One that will never let you down, mistreat you, and listens to give answers at the right time they are needed.

Guard against those that steal your joy, and forever seek friends that build up your spirit.

"The thief cometh not but for to steal,
and to kill, and to destroy;
I am come that they might have life,
and that they might have it more abundantly."

— John 10:10

Day 353

Sin and Judgment

Key Scripture: **Matthew 7:1-4**

This scripture shows us that we have a desire to condemn others without examining our own hearts before the Lord. We are showing our prideful spirit by looking at the flaws of others without searching our own wrong doings.

Others may say you are the perfect person, but we are not measured by others; we are measured by God. When we judge one another, anger and unfaithful desires build in our hearts. This affects us spiritually and harms relationships. We must learn to live by placing our faith in Jesus Christ and living in Him rather than judgment.

Whenever we get our own hearts right before God, we will be able to help others in love and not judgment. Living by faith we see God takes care of everything and we are not to worry about the sins of others, but focus on how to deal with our own.

Confronting our sins by means of repentance and asking forgiveness, brings us to a closer relationship with Christ and helps us to abide in His Word. We have been crucified with Christ, so therefore instead of rushing to judgment, be quick to help one another and show one another the true hope in Jesus Christ.

Lord, I want to be in the center of your will. Open my eyes to the sin I allow in my life, and give me the strength to turn from it. Give me more faith so that I may glorify you in all that I do; make my decisions your decisions that you may be exalted and lifted up.

"Judge not, and ye shall not be judged:
condemn not, and ye shall not be condemned:
forgive and ye shall be forgiven."

— Luke 6:37

Finding God's Road for Me

Key Scripture: **Matthew 16:24-26**

Years ago when I gave my life to Jesus Christ, I was not fully aware how this new life was to be. I tried within myself to guide my steps, follow what I thought was the best path for me.

I wanted Christ to help, sure enough, but I wanted to control each situation. I gratefully invited Christ to co-pilot my journey. I wanted Him to help me do things that I could not, expecting Him to guide me through the difficult areas of this journey.

This is the wrong outlook, because in the scripture, God said if we come to Him we must allow Him to lead. As a new believer, it was scary to give someone else control; however, facing the facts now, I know that His heart is only what's best for me.

Fear kept me from giving up my control to Christ; fear of just what He would do with my life or where He might lead. I was focused on "me" and not on Him. Surrender is never easy as a new believer, but as our faith and trust grows, it should come first and foremost in our lives.

Committing to the road Christ has for us does not have anything to do with the good or bad life thrown our way. Nor does it have anything to do with circumstances, my feelings, my weaknesses or strengths, my friends, or church experiences. It has everything to do with believing that God is who He says He is and placing my total faith and trust in the all good and infinitely wise God who is the Lord and Master of my life.

Lord, I pray that myself and others would commit to the road less traveled as your perfect will for our lives today and every day ahead.

"In all thy ways acknowledge Him,
and He shall direct thy paths."

— Proverbs 3:6

Our Heavenly Father Knows All

Key Scripture: **John 2:23-25**

What this scripture says, is that Jesus knows what is in every heart. His ability to know every heart perfectly leads to the unsettling truth that some have beliefs that do not obtain true fellowship with Jesus and eternal life. Many who say they know Him are actually living a lie.

Jesus knows about all people, and no one is excluded from His knowledge. He knows everything about everybody. Read John 6:64.

God is all-knowing and though we think we are hiding personal implications; truth is, there are no secrets in our lives. We can hide things from others on this earth, but not from Jesus. The person who matters most knows most.

You are fully known by Jesus Christ. After the resurrection, Jesus asked Peter three times, *"Do you love me?"* Peter answered, *"Yes, Lord; you know that I love you."* The second answer was the same as the first. The third answer was: *"Lord,*

you know everything; you know that I love you." Peter knew that Jesus saw his heart.

Christ knows what is best in our lives and desires us to follow and always be truthful in everything, from salvation to our thoughts and intents. The sooner we realize that Christ knows far better than we do, exactly what is best for us, our lives will be much easier.

Sometimes we assume we know what's best and other times we disregard seeking anything from Him. Yet, Christ wants us to go to Him with our needs. (Matthew 7:7). He is ready to show His strength through our weakness. He is prepared to provide our every need, if we will ask. (Philippians 4:13)

Let's purpose in our hearts to never again run from Christ; never think we can hide from God, and always seek what is best as He provides.

"The eyes of the LORD are in every place,
beholding the evil and the good."

— Proverbs 15:3

I Need a Second Chance

Key Scripture: **1 John 1:9**

God tells us He is a God of second chances. I am humbly thankful that God does give us second chances;. In the key scripture, we see, *"that He is faithful and just to forgive us of our sins."* The verse continues; *"He will cleanse us from all unrighteousness."* We can be freed from past failures and move forward for God.

Many examples are noted in the scriptures, each showing us the faithfulness of God handing out "second chances." Elijah said he'd had enough and asked God to take his life. He was brought out of his depression and used mightily by God.

Peter denied the Lord three times but got another chance and was used greatly by God.

In 1 Chronicles 21, David, who was not perfect, failed God over and over. David had all the people in the nation numbered and let greed step in, even though God and the leaders told him not to do this. God forgave him and allowed him to prove himself. As we know, David was a mighty king that led his people and was used by God.

Second chances are certainly ordained by God and sound easy. How many times have we had circumstances arise and we have the chance to give others a second chance? Someone has wronged you and now it's personal and you feel justified to hold a grudge. We have all done wrong and grieved the Lord, yet He continues to give second chances because He desires us to have a relationship with Him.

I know I do not deserve a second chance, but that is part of God's glory. He does not hold grudges nor does He withhold His love. He chooses not to remember our wrong-doing and gives us a second chance to start over.

Who do you need to offer a second chance?

Norman Vincent Peale said: "No matter what mistakes you have made, no matter how you've messed up, you can still make a new beginning."

"Remember ye not the former things,
neither consider the things of old."

— Isaiah 43:18

Day 357

Is Being Carnal the New Norm?

Key Scripture: 1 Corinthians 3:3

Have churches become more and more liberal since you've been a Christian? I have been a child of God for 54 years, and I have seen many changes in churches and personally, I know God is still the same unchanging God.

In 1 Corinthians 3:3 we see a definition, as we see that Paul describes the Corinthian Christians as carnal, meaning they "walk as men." Carnality is mere human nature and its manifestations are without the influence of the Holy Spirit. As a Christian, the Spirit has become one with your spirit, and God's design is for us to walk by His Spirit.

To the contrary, a carnal Christian is one who lives a normal life without the Spirit's leading. Carnality is an expression of humanity without God. This is where many of the false doctrines and beliefs creep into churches.

Here, the church at Corinth dealt with sexual immorality as well as following whomever they desired. Some followed Paul and others Peter or Apollos. In many churches today we see nothing other than human efforts, rather than Spirit-led services. This is called "fleshly Christianity." Here, services are geared to excite the flesh and have nothing to do with honoring God.

The only way to escape carnality is to walk in the Spirit. When our human nature is under the control of the Spirit, the proper type of lifestyle is the result. This is what scripture calls a Spirit-led life.

Lord, help us to guard our hearts and minds to always allow the Holy Spirit to direct our lives personally, and to take a stand in our churches to do the same.

"For to be carnally minded is death;
but to be spiritually minded is life and peace."

— Romans 8:6

Day 358

Double-Minded Person?

Key Scripture: James 1:6-8

These words show up twice in the scriptures, and both times occur in the book of James. What does it mean to be double-minded? James writes that a double-minded person is *"like a wave in the sea, blown and tossed by the wind."*

A double-minded person is restless in their thoughts, actions, and behavior; one torn with inner conflict who never totally gives their confidence to God and His gracious promises.

Double-mindedness comes from doubt. Doubt about yourself, your career, your relationships, even to the point of doubting God and His ability to help in difficult circumstances. Doubt causes instability and instability is detrimental to having faith and hope in God. In Matthew 6:24; God says, *"We cannot serve two masters, either we hate the one and love the other…"*

Doubters are double-minded people. In James 1:8; scripture says such a person is unsta-ble. An unstable person is one that sways one way and then another. They have no defined direction, and they never seem to get anywhere. A double-minded person has very little or no faith at all. They cannot be certain about things and doubt is filtered into the equation.

If we struggle with double-mindedness, we should study and memorize the scriptures, for God's Word produces faith. (Romans 10:17) We should pray for faith. God freely gives what is good to those who ask. (Luke 11:9-12). Also it is good to ask God to increase our faith. (Luke 17:5; Mark 9:24).

Give yourself to singleness of mind, by faith, trust and wisdom. If God says to do something, do it; if He says to be something, be it. By faith, stay focused.

"But without faith it is impossible to please Him: for he that cometh to God must believe that He is, and that He is a rewarder of them that diligently seek Him."

— Hebrews 11:6

Day 359

Our Hearts are a Battleground for Love and Hate

Scripture: 1 Corinthians 13:4-5

"Charity suffereth long, and is kind; charity envieth not; charity vaunteth not itself, is not puffed up. Doth not behave itself unseemly, seeketh not her own, is not easily provoked, thinketh no evil;"

1 John 3:15; *"Whosoever hateth his brother is a murderer: and ye know that no murderer hath eternal life abiding in him."*

We watch the news and see that people of authority often downplay wickedness in order to accommodate their personal need to make themselves look good. But, as Christians we do the same thing—we grade ourselves on the basis of everyone else's performance. We will do anything to allow the hate in our hearts to not be exposed to make us look better.

God hates wickedness and we tend to downplay it in order to excuse our sin. Forgiveness is the greatest act of love one for another as believers. On the other hand, God's love is demonstrated by Him showing to us that He has forgiven us of our transgressions. And yet we still find it hard to forgive others.

If our sins are forgivable, the sins of others should be too. Unforgiveness is a burden that keeps us chained to our past, incapable of reaching our future. Forgiveness releases our hearts from carrying around resentment and bitterness. The ultimate sacrifice of forgiveness was shown by Jesus Christ on the cross.

Love and hate is a part of life; love covers a multitude of sins. Let the love of God rule in our hearts richly. We reveal what we harbor in our hearts.

"That Christ may dwell in your hearts by faith;
that ye being rooted and grounded in love,
May be able to comprehend with all saints..."

— Ephesians 3:17-18a

Day 360

Short End of the Stick

Key Scripture: **Proverbs 16:9**

Why does it seem that we always get the short end of the stick when it comes to things in life? Even as Christians, we experience these same thoughts. We are faithful church members, kind to others, not judgmental, and trying to walk the path as a Christian, but we see no reward.

Whenever we experience these thoughts and feelings, our eyes are on our own selves and not in God's Word. The beautiful thing about the scriptures is they never get old. Many individuals in the scriptures got the short end of the stick. Think of Joseph, who was sold into Egypt and thrown into prison. Also, Moses, watching flocks in the desert, and Daniel with his entire generation under captivity in Babylon. These were dark times and one could not see much good in their circumstances.

We know how each story ended, and man was exalted by God for His glory. God made a business of turning difficult times around to exalt Himself, most of which was shown to us through the cross of Calvary with our Savior, Jesus Christ.

God is good. He will always do what is right and what is according to His will and His plan.

When we are in the midst of difficulties, trials, and temptations, we feel like we are getting the short end of the stick. Remember, we can always have confidence in God's goodness. Doubting God's goodness leads us to look elsewhere for help in the midst of troubles. Faith in God's goodness leads us to ask "how long." This is a question of faith, knowing God will act and He will set things right in His time. "Stand still and see the salvation of the Lord."

So, we see that we will experience life's difficulties, but God will exalt us in due season if we remain faithful, and stay in His Word.

"But they that wait upon the LORD shall renew their strength;
they shall mount up with wings as eagles;
they shall run, and not be weary,
and they shall walk, and not faint."

— Isaiah 40:31

Day 361

I Am Right!

Key Scripture: Philippians 2:3-5

I like to be right. This is something we all desire. The problem with this attitude is that we want it so badly we are not willing to be wrong.

In most cases it's easy to apologize or ask for forgiveness. It is clear that if this is not easy, then the individual has a spiritual need in their life. James 4:10; *"Humble yourselves in the sight of the Lord, and He shall lift you up."*

The way up is down. In this case, if we are willing to admit we are wrong, then getting resolution and forgiveness comes very naturally and without regret. What about when you come to a time and know you are right without a shadow of doubt? This is the kind of right where you dig your heels in and stand your ground. These situations in our lives require that we seek God's wisdom.

As you allow Him to work, listen to that still, small voice and remember James 4:10. Even though you know you are right, don't let yourself become prideful. Puffed-up pride has no place as an ingredient in a recipe for resolution.

Rallying support for any circumstance is not helpful, and shows that we are not seeking God's assistance in our problems. By humbling ourselves before God we can rest in His promise of Romans 8:28: *"All things work for good."*

The problems of conflict or struggles in our lives can cause us to build up barriers of pride and wanting to always be right. We must practice humility every day and assure that our interpersonal relationship with Jesus Christ flourishes and guides us to let Him receive glory in all struggles we encounter.

Whatever you are facing today, God's Word always has the answer. Read Proverbs 16:18-20. It takes courage to make room for another person's thoughts and feelings.

"Confess your faults one to another,
and pray one for another,
that ye may be healed.
The effectual fervent prayer of a righteous man availeth much."

— James 5:16

Day 362

Straddling the Fence or Sold Out to God?

Key Scripture: **Revelation 3:14-20**

Today I've been thinking about this world and the state of confusion and unrest it is in. What came to mind is the Laodician Church Age. In this key scripture passage there is a lot to wrap your head around.

Speaking on the subject of lukewarm Christians, we most certainly can relate to what was written as truth. Our world is without a doubt filled with lukewarm Christians. Imagine if you will, there is a split-rail fence running down the middle of the road. One side is the world and the other is side where dedicated Christians are standing.

Ask yourself exactly where are you? Whether we admit it or not, most of us are straddling the fence. We want and desire things of the world whenever we want them, but we still stay in touch with our Christian side of things. Philippians 3:13-14:

"Brethren, I count not myself to have apprehended: but this one thing I do, forgetting those things which are behind, and reaching forth unto those things which are before. I press toward the mark for the prize of the high calling of God in Christ

Jesus."

Riding the fence and dabbling in the world is not where a Christian should be at all, because God desires us to be separated from the world and walk circumspectly with Him. 2 Corinthians 5:17:

"Therefore if any man be in Christ, he is a new creature; old things are passed away; behold all things are become new."

It is time that all believers in Jesus Christ repent from the things of this world and stay off the fence. We need to commit to the things and ways of God. Remember Lot's wife? 1 Corinthians 6:20:

"For ye are bought with a price: therefore glorify God in your body, and in your spirit, which are Gods."

Our eternal security was bought by the shedding of our Savior's blood. Stand with God and separate yourself from the things and ways of the world. This pleases our Lord.

"Love not the world, neither the things that are in the world. If any man love the world, the love of the Father is not in him."
— 1 John 2:15

Day 363

Scars of Sin

Key Scripture: 1 John 1:9

Many years ago, I read a story about a young boy who had lost his parents, so his grandparents became his guardians. This story began with the grandparent discussing what to do with their grandson who was constantly getting into trouble at school. The last phone call they received from school was to demand a meeting because the young boy had chased the girls with a live snake.

The grandfather, a wise old Christian, decided to take things in his hands and work on his mischievous grandson. Taking him out to the barn, they discussed his attitude and why he constantly got into trouble. After their talk, the wise old man gave him a hammer and showed him a nail keg. He then pointed to the large closed door and told him that every time he did something wrong, he was to take a nail and drive it into the door, leaving the head exposed about half an inch from the door.

The lad thought it was a game and he quickly had one side of the door full of nails. Then, he started to realize he had done a lot of bad things.

The wise old man called another meeting and explained that each nail represented sin and that God was not pleased with sin. The nailing soon came to a close as the boy realized he was doing bad things.

Then in a few days, the wise old man took the boy to the barn, closed the doors and sat the lad down and showed him a crowbar. He told him that each time he did something good he wanted him to pull out one nail.

Again, the game started and before much longer, all the nails were gone. When this happened, the wise old man called another closed-door meeting. He told the lad he was proud of the change in him and felt that he now understood that doing bad was sin.

He then called attention to the door, which was full of holes that let the sunlight shine through. He explained that the sin represented by the nails can be forgiven and removed, and the holes that are left are the scars which sin leaves behind and are there forever as a result of the sin.

His lesson was: our scars need not control our lives. Instead, let's understand that they are covered, forgiven, and forgotten.

"There is a way which seemeth right unto a man, but the end thereof are the ways of death."

— Proverbs 14:12

Day 364

Satan Wins!

Key Scripture: **1 Peter 5:8**

Yes, Satan wins! We know that the ultimate authority and power is God Himself. The eternal Son of God had to become man, because it was the offspring of the woman who was to crush the serpent's head. (See Genesis 3:15.)

Though God has the ultimate authority, think just how many battles Satan has won. God has a purpose for Satan. Although we have a free will to do and serve whom we please, God surely wants us to serve Him out of our love and respect for what He has done and for who He is. See 1 John 2:14b-15.

Satan wins many battles in our churches. He attacks inside the church when God's work is moving forward. He puts wrong thoughts in its members, such as jealousy, spreading rumors, discontent with leadership, and a rebellious spirit because of the truth which reveals uncleanliness.

Next, Satan attacks our homes by means of separation or divorce, stealing the joy of marriage and destroying lives. Satan is the only winner in this.

Finally, Satan wins in our personal lives when he tempts us to allow sin to control our lives by not staying in God's Word faithfully. We allow things to become more important than attending church faithfully, such as allowing pride to control our thoughts, listening to music that does not bring glory to God, and allowing our minds and thoughts to go the direction of lust, pornography, and self-desires.

So, we can see that Satan does win his share of battles. What can we do to stand against Satan as we move forward? A list for each of us includes: expect evil (1 Peter 4:12), overcome evil with good (Romans 12:21) and resist evil (James 4:7).

God permitted Satan's fall. He had a purpose, but God has the ultimate authority and He wins the war.

Pray faithfully for your church, pray earnestly for your spouse and your home, and pray God protects each of us and leads us in His paths.

"Ye shall walk after the LORD your God, and fear Him,
and keep His commandments, and obey His voice,
and ye shall serve Him, and cleave unto Him."

— Deuteronomy 13:4

Day 365

Casting the First Stone

Key Scripture: **John 8:7**

We all have sinned and come short of the glory of God. Who is without sin? Jesus said He that is without sin, let him cast the first stone.

Who are we to condemn others? Christ himself told the woman accused of adultery in John chapter 8; *"Neither do I condemn thee: go and sin no more."*

Even though we are guilty of accusing, or maybe casting judgment on others, what gives us the right to do so?

The love of God washes away all sin if and when we come before Him with a repentant heart and spirit.

In Psalm 51:2; God says, *"Wash me throughly from mine iniquity, and cleanse me from my sin."* Also then the promise of God is given:1 John 1:9; *"If we confess our sins, He is faithful and just to forgive us our sin, and to cleanse us from all unrighteousness."*

Some think that a small sin should be dealt with differently than one that is large. Truth is, sin is sin; and both come with a penalty of death, unless that sin is confessed and covered under the blood of Jesus Christ. Christ looks at us all the same without respect one for another.

So, as an example, Christ wants us to treat others without condemnation and with respect. Remember as we point our finger or verbally condemn others we are casting stones at them, and before we do so, we must first look at our own heart. Surely no stones will be thrown if we do.

Help me Lord to not be judgmental. Oh Lord, help me to be more like you.

"Judge not, that ye be not judged. For with what judgment ye judge,
ye shall be judged: and with what measure ye mete,
it shall be measured to you again."

— Matthew 7:1-2

Following is Joseph's last post, written on October 6, 2023. This last devotion was written and sent just hours before Joseph's faith became a reality and his hands touched the welcoming hands of God into His eternal home the next day, which no one could have ever imagined!

His Hand is Stretched Out Still

Key Scripture: **Isaiah 9:12, 17, 21; 10:4**

Recently as I read through God's Word through the book of Isaiah, I noticed that God uses the phrase ***"His hand is stretched out still" a number of times.***

Throughout this book, God uses the prophet Isaiah to deliver a message of judgment to His people. He warned them of their many sins, showing their guilt through the key passage by ending each passage with the powerful phrase: *"For all his anger has not turned away, and his hand is stretched out still."*

Those who fail to believe God, trust His promises, and obey His Word will experience His righteous anger. God cannot let sin go unpunished, and His Words of judgment will certainly fall on those who continue in rebellion against Him.

So, my friends, what hope do we have? In Romans 3:23, God tells us that we all have sinned and come short of God's glory. This means the very best we can do to warrant favor with God is not good enough.

Romans 6:23 tells us that our punishment for our sins is death, as does Romans 8:5. I personally thank God each day that Romans 6:23 does not end by telling us our wages for sin is death. The latter part of this verse tells us that our gift of redemption came in the form of God's only Son, who gave Himself to be our propitiation for our sins. By placing our faith through grace in His finished blood and sacrifice, we can experience God's gift of eternal life.

Going back to the title of this message, can we not see the hand of God "is stretched out still"? He is offering anyone who will put their trust and faith in Jesus Christ a way to escape the judgment of the penalty of sin. My prayer is that if you have not done this, today could be the day the chains of bondage will be removed and you can become a part of God's family.

"The Lord is not slack concerning His promise, as some men count slackness; but is longsuffering to us-ward, not willing that any should perish, but that all should come to repentance."

— 2 Peter 3:9

Acknowledgements

The following have contributed to make the publishing of this book possible: Debbie Miller, Rev. & Mrs. Calvin Rice, Paul Horst, Earl Van Horn, Karen & Gilbert Goetz, Sylvia Stewart and Judy and Clyde Griffin and Linda Robinette. We're very grateful to each one of you.

About the Author

Joseph Nathan Griffin was born and raised in Savannah, Georgia, and spent most of his life in that area. He was one of nine children and the father of four children. He had 15 grandchildren and many great-grands.

Joseph studied Bible at Tennessee Temple College in Chattanooga, Tennessee, and later taught at a Christian school.

He was a man of many trades, and in recent years was the owner/operator of Integrity Roofing Company in Georgia. At the time of his death, he was project manager for JCH Homebuilders, LLC.

Joseph was an avid hunter and fisherman. He enjoyed nature and hunting and fishing with his sons.

Through many difficult circumstances in life, including the death of his beloved spouse, God sustained him. Joseph indicated these were "storms" but said knowing the "One" who can calm storms and bring peace encouraged his writing of these daily devotions.

It was his sincere prayer that each message will build faith and trust that regardless of what we face, our God remains faithful and "He who hath begun a good work in you will complete it."